T0331248

Winning The Mental Game on Wall Street

The Psychology and Philosophy of Successful Investing

JOHN MAGEE INVESTMENT SERIES

WINNING THE MENTAL GAME on WALL STREET

The Psychology and Philosophy of Successful Investing

JOHN MAGEE

Edited by W.H.C. Bassetti

CRC Press
Taylor & Francis Group
Boca Raton   London   New York

CRC Press is an imprint of the
Taylor & Francis Group, an **informa** business

CRC Press
Taylor & Francis Group
6000 Broken Sound Parkway NW, Suite 300
Boca Raton, FL 33487-2742

© 2000 by Taylor & Francis Group, LLC
CRC Press is an imprint of Taylor & Francis Group, an Informa business

No claim to original U.S. Government works

ISBN-13: 978-0-910944-17-5 (hbk)

This book contains information obtained from authentic and highly regarded sources. Reasonable efforts have been made to publish reliable data and information, but the author and publisher cannot assume responsibility for the validity of all materials or the consequences of their use. The authors and publishers have attempted to trace the copyright holders of all material reproduced in this publication and apologize to copyright holders if permission to publish in this form has not been obtained. If any copyright material has not been acknowledged please write and let us know so we may rectify in any future reprint.

Except as permitted under U.S. Copyright Law, no part of this book may be reprinted, reproduced, transmitted, or utilized in any form by any electronic, mechanical, or other means, now known or hereafter invented, including photocopying, microfilming, and recording, or in any information storage or retrieval system, without written permission from the publishers.

For permission to photocopy or use material electronically from this work, please access www.copyright.com (http://www.copyright.com/) or contact the Copyright Clearance Center, Inc. (CCC), 222 Rosewood Drive, Danvers, MA 01923, 978-750-8400. CCC is a not-for-profit organization that provides licenses and registration for a variety of users. For organizations that have been granted a photocopy license by the CCC, a separate system of payment has been arranged.

Trademark Notice: Product or corporate names may be trademarks or registered trademarks, and are used only for identification and explanation without intent to infringe.

**Visit the Taylor & Francis Web site at
http://www.taylorandfrancis.com**

**and the CRC Press Web site at
http//www.crcpress.com**

Library of Congress Cataloging-in-Publication Data

Magee, John, 1901–1987
    Winning the mental game on Wall Street : the psychology and philosophy of
successful investing / by John Magee ; edited and revised by W.H.C. Bassetti.
        p. cm. — (John Magee investment series)
    Rev. ed. of: General semantics of Wall Street. 1st ed. 1958.
    Includes index.
    ISBN 0-910944-17-2
    1. Stocks. I. Bassetti, W. H. C. II. Title: General semantics of Wall Street.
III. Title. IV. Series.
HG4661 .M316 2000
332.6—dc21   00-024725
                                                                  CIP

Library of Congress Card Number 00-124725

TABLE OF CONTENTS

Foreword
Preface

Chapter

PREFACE

This has been a particularly hard book to write. I have found it much harder in some ways than my part of *Technical Analysis of Stock Trends*. It has been two years in actual preparation, much longer than that in its preliminary shaping-up.

It is hard because the subject is both so simple and so complicated. It is simple in that there are only a few basic points and these would be almost self-evident to a child if he were not already conditioned to a great many preconceptions. It is complicated because these preconceptions include a great number of the teachings every person receives early in life. Some, perhaps most, of this teaching is factual and useful. But mingled with it are the legacies of all the prescientific theories, the ancient philosophies, and the theologies, that have come down through the ages. And the mixture of custom, ethics, hypothesis, precept, morality, discipline, superstition, and directives includes a good deal that may not jibe with the observed facts today, may even conflict with or contradict itself, and may not be in the best interests of mankind's development as a race nor of a man's individual welfare.

To make things more complicated, these customs and directives are often clothed in the vestments of high authority. They are often presented in highly colored emotional terms, as absolutes not subject to revision or even to re-examination. Finally, as if to add further difficulties, the structure of language itself tends to contribute to misunderstanding and misevaluation unless that structure and its relation to our thinking is well understood.

There have been a good many books written on the subject of general semantics, some of them far more profound than this one. This particular book was built around the problems of a little cosmos that in many ways provides a good working model of the larger society in which we live. Although the stock market represents only a certain part of the life-activity of a certain part of the population, it presents on its limited stage all the familiar human emotions, fears, and hopes, and it involves problems that have their counterparts in other domains of business, in social life, in the family, and in the intrapersonal world in which each of us lives his own private life.

Some of the thoughts expressed in this book are the outcome of my own experiences in the market and elsewhere, but it hardly seems necessary to add, that the background of much of this material rests on the "time-binding" of others: of Alfred Korzybski, of course, and Lillian Lieber, Norbert Wiener, John von Neumann, Karen Horney, and many others.

I am most particularly indebted to Dr. Daniel R. Wheeler, since the book leans heavily on the philosophy and psychology he has taught and practiced for many years. Dr. Wheeler, in his work as a psychiatrist, has applied the principles of general semantics in a practical way to the problems of family and job and of living with one's self that involve the common questions that arise in the lives of most of us.

Dan Wheeler feels that if, after we have eliminated so far as possible the probable physical sources of "un-sanity," that is, if we find no adequate physiogenic cause for maladjustment, we should look at the mind itself, as it has been taught, as it has been shaped and has shaped itself, and discover, if we can, how it is failing to evaluate and deal with the environment successfully. He regards the work of the psychiatrist primarily as that of a teacher engaged in instructing the student not merely in how to solve problems but in showing the sincere student how to understand the workings of his own mind, and how to shape his further education or re-education so as to make possible a more realistic appreciation of the surroundings in which he lives. After such training the student will not have to be told what to do in meeting a particular problem, for he will have developed the ability to do his own thinking and to come up with answers appropriate to the question at hand.

This is not, of course, a book on psychiatry. Nor is it entirely a book on psychology. It is intended primarily as a guide to help the student of the free market to acquire greater confidence and ability in his contacts with that market, though I hope it may hold some interest, too, for workers in other fields.

Of necessity *Winning the Mental Game on Wall Street* touches on a good many different subjects, some of them controversial. I do not make any claim to be an authority on any of these subjects. However, in many fields there is such a high degree of specialization that the inner circle becomes more or less cut off from the rest of the world. Thus in finance, law, politics, religion, sociology, medicine, education, psychiatry, etc., there has come to be a special language used and understood by the initiate. This is probably necessary in order to set up definitions covering the very specialized concepts involved in particular studies. But the lay public is not welcome behind this veil, and there is not much communication between the dedicated practitioners and the citizenry at large.

It is not possible to have a really meaningful discussion with the workers in some of the specialized fields, partly because of the barrier interposed by the cant or technical vocabulary of the various trades, and partly because the professional workers do not have the time to explain, nor has the public the time to listen.

Furthermore, if one attempts to talk seriously about serious things with the learned members of the learned professions, these specialists will usually repeat (in simple easy-to-understand words) the cut-and-dried official version of what "should" be told. This avoids wasting time in fruitless debate with uninformed outsiders, but it also sometimes perpetuates a circularity of thinking that makes basic progress impossible.

As a rule professional men will not engage publicly in any debate that might challenge their own premises and conclusions, except to the extent of defending the status quo of their preconceived dogma. This may be because, living in a more or less self-contained world of thought , they are not anxious or able to explore any very different approach. There is the suspicion that some of these learned men, through no fault or intention of their own, are carrying on their labors within a framework of medieval philosophy, obsolete science, and prehistoric superstition—in short, that they are doing some very fine work considering the tools they are using, but some of these tools may be as dead as the past from which they were received.

Along with all this, there is the group defense system that effectively seals off each esoteric guild through the organized discipline of the group. No member of a professional group is likely to challenge publicly even the most obvious un-sanity in the credo of his craft. He will explain willingly, but always within the limitations of the party line. If you touch him on some highly controversial matter, he will tell you he is "not the spokesman" for the group and would prefer not to become involved.

For this you can hardly blame him. You cannot imagine a lawyer speaking openly on a radio program about certain tenets of the law. You cannot imagine a banker appearing on television to discuss frankly certain realities of investment. You cannot imagine a priest facing up to certain questions in theology except in terms of the precise dogma of his church.

In all fairness it should be admitted that the great majority of sincere, honest, hard-working professional men do subscribe sincerely to the official line of their group. Most of them, in fact, are far too busy carrying out the important duties of their day-by-day work to have much time for "purposeless" research. They are not encouraged to explore scientifically, in the light of modern understanding, the underlying sources of their convictions. And it may be, too, that some of them feel that the end justifies the means. They do not feel a need to probe too deeply into the basic philosophies of their crafts. There is enough hard and useful work to be done at the low level of practical everyday reality. The lawyer must prepare his cases. The banker must deal with practical business problems. The minister must write his sermons, visit the sick, perform marriages, etc. The teacher must conduct classes as outlined in the curriculum.

But since it is possible to ask the really tough questions and not get the kind of answers we need from the men who should know, and since there is not too much communication between the experts in various specialized fields, we are faced with the prospect of going on very much in the way we have always gone on. That is no longer good enough. If we are going to survive as a human race, we must establish a genuine freedom of thought that will make it possible for men in different fields of study to communicate with one another, to re-examine the very foundation stones of their learning; and, if necessary, to change them…and also to maintain an effective two-way communication with the lay public, that also has a stake in life, liberty, and the pursuit of happiness.

In touching on controversial aspects of some highly specialized professions, I do not mean to be presumptuous, and I realize that there are men in these groups who are well familiar with the problem and who are much concerned about it. But if the men who should be challenging the past and the methods of evaluation in their own professions don't, then it may be necessary for members of the lay public to speak out. We are fully aware of the great steps that have been made on the mechanical, administrative, and research levels. But as long as there remains in our learned professions a hard core of pompous archaic nonsense that can lead to hostility, misunderstanding, frustration, and unnecessary human misery, we must say what we have to say and hope that more able men, within the ranks of the initiate, will have the courage to challenge the unsanities that are hurting them and menacing all of us.

John Magee
August 27, 1958

A WORD OF CREDIT

In the writing of a book, or in any important creative effort for that matter, there are forces behind the scenes that are vital to the success of the job. I would like to express here my heartfelt thanks to my wife, Elinor, and my three children, John, Louise, and Abigail, for their patience and forbearance during the difficult months while *Winning the Mental Game on Wall Street* was being written, illustrated, and produced.

Also, I would like to give my thanks to our technical staff for keeping the ball rolling during this period in the matter of maintaining daily stock charts, the Delta Studies, and the like: to Frank Curto, who has worked shoulder-to-shoulder with me for a number of years, and his wife Marcella, Col. Harolde N. Searles, Carleen Searles, Harry A. Oltsch, Lottie G. Oltsch, Dr. I. Morgan Levine, Robert M. Lantry, Henry Larsen, Olen Norris, Sheridan Carey, and John Moriarty; to our production and office staff: Flora La Riviere, Alyce Scholz, Charles Curto, and Katherine Quinlin; and Amy Jones for her help in typing the manuscript.

I want to express my gratitude to Patricia Kelley, my personal secretary, for her encouragement and help in this difficult and sometimes discouraging job. Most especially I want to thank Muriel Brown, who as general manager of my business has handled the many difficult problems of a growing organization in an outstanding manner. Her own knowledge of general semantics, plus her unswerving loyalty, have given me confidence and inspiration without which the job of producing this book could never have been carried through.

Very importantly, I want to extend my thanks to my brother, Beverly Magee, also a student of general semantics, for his great help in reading proofs and offering constructive suggestions as to necessary changes in the text.

FOREWORD

What is the purpose of this book? Its purpose is no less than to set the reader free. Without arguing deep psychology, John Magee believed, and I believe, that we are all captives of our childhoods and the prisoners of our educations—formal and sentimental. This is true to such an extent that we are often blind to realities which might appear obvious to an unbiased alien (the elephant in the living room—or on Wall Street in this case). Unbiased aliens are the only entities we could assume to be unencumbered by the paradigms of earth.

Buried treasure—or buried truth—that is what Magee's book is. Until this edition you needed a treasure map to find a copy of it. The first edition in 1958 fell on deaf ears (or deaf and dumb ears) so in the day to day practice of his business Magee did what comes naturally—ran a very successful investment advisory firm and sold hundreds of thousands of copies of his more famous book, *Technical Analysis of Stock Trends*. The potential original audience probably looked at the title *General Semantics of Wall Street* and passed on by as quickly as possible. After all if you can't define it, why read about it?

And the word *semantics* itself reeks of the inner priesthood of MIT and Harvard and musty rooms where the ghost of William James haunts the living presence of Quine or Wittgenstein. So the book was buried with a very sketchy map as to its location (I have a copy of the first edition somewhere in my attic) and its wisdom was left to age for 40 years.

Now, having reread it I am consumed with regret that I didn't read it for breakfast every morning during my 40 years of investing, speculating, gambling, and managing money in the markets. Come to it now, like an old raccoon with many scars, it is like finding buried wisdom—the codification of all the non-technical things Magee knew about the market, and one of the books which every investor should read, preferably at the beginning of his career. In order to exorcise the semantics demons I have retitled the book *Elephant and Pig on Wall Street,* but I will continue to refer to it here as *General Semantics.*

This book can prepare an investor for the mental game of Wall Street—that is, the inner game the investor's mind plays with itself as he watches Wall Street whir around. It would be unwise to underestimate the importance of mental attitude and preparation to successful investing and trading. Be assured, the winning tennis player who has great conditioning, wonderful technique, great mechanical skills also possesses something the average tennis player does not have—a different mind and attitude. The same thing is true of effective traders. Through the careful study of and application of this book, in conjunction with *The Technical Analysis of Stock Trends,* the average investor can become an effective trader. This is eminently feasible given the thoughtful and mind clearing instruction of *General Semantics.*

Why is it, after all, that investing success on Wall Street follows Basso's Fishing Rule? (Which is that 15% of the fishermen catch 85% of the fish.) It must be that the successful fisherman knows something the others don't or has better equipment—perhaps a different mentality? This is true--of the fisherman and of the tennis player and of the trader. Ipso facto the successful player, fisherman, trader manifests skillful behavior and thinking patterns, and the average player, fisherman, investor manifests unskillful thinking habits and behavior patterns.

In this book Magee lays out a clear path away from unskillful behavior and to a common sense mentality and method virtually assured of success in the long run. Does this statement strike you as rash—or surprising, or even astounding? It should. My students and colleagues have heard me rail a thousand times against the snake oil salesmen who sell can't miss systems and methods and guarantee success—money back if not satisfied. My mailbox is filled with these offers every morning— offers too good to refuse, except that a lifetime in the markets has left me wary and cynical about such claims.

Why would I make it in this case, then? Because in fact, I believe it to be true. True, but not easy. In fact once you have heard my caveats you may consider it easier to buy one of those automatic can't miss systems.

Naturally I am about to tell you that the Magee mentality and method makes money the old fashioned way—you have to earn it. You see the Magee method is reliable and effective—and it requires some maturity of character and it requires some reasonably intelligent application and it requires diligence and attention.

I suspect that those janitors and little old lady schoolteachers who died with large estates in stocks had these characteristics and I suspect that they had found the same secret to the markets that Edwards and Magee found.

A Secret? You always suspected there was a secret didn't you, just like you knew there was a secret to golf. I'm afraid it's a pretty dull secret actually. I believe it was Jack Nicklaus who said "The harder I work the luckier I get." The secret to the market is like that: right mind, right habits, right techniques over the long term will produce good results. And it is always possible to be lucky, because this approach puts you in the way of luck, whereas wrong mind, wrong techniques invite (if not create) bad luck.

Some decades after John Magee wrote this book and *Technical Analysis of Stock Trends,* investors, speculators, traders and gamblers and easy marks continue to repeat the same lamentable self defeating trading mistakes they have made since the beginning of time. Or the beginning of the markets. One has to ask why—and the answer doesn't seem too difficult to grasp—human nature and ignorance. Or, more charitably, lack of education. You can learn to build a bridge in engineering classes, and how to keep books in an accounting class, but classes in investing in the stock market seem mainly to be given at the New York Stock Exchange and to be extremely expensive in both the long and the short run. People who manage businesses and practice professions very competently turn out to be easy marks when they go down to the stock market casino.

SEMANTICS—IS IT DANGEROUS TO YOUR MENTAL HEALTH?

Well, what is semantics, anyway? (It may be the reason that people who should have read Magee's book didn't. Since they are uncertain of the meaning of the word they suspected they wouldn't understand it. After all, when you start talking about the meaning of meaning, who knows what it means?) In order to further confuse the issue let me start with the most complicated description of what it means, with the promise that I will finish with a simple description.

General semantics is concerned with the relationship between language and the external world. In its study it concerns itself with referential, denotative meaning. And it concerns itself with affective connotative meaning. So we look to our world view for the denotation of the word—the thing. Then we look to our mental state to determine the emotional and personal undertones that surround the word like an aura.

To simplify, general semantics studies the ways in which the meanings of words influence human behavior.

For our purposes we can understand *General Semantics* as the study of meanings in language within the context of Wall Street, with the intent of improving our effectiveness in that world. Wall Street of course is a symbol for the financial markets, stocks, bonds, futures, and commodities. So the general semantics of Wall Street studies the ways our understandings of the meanings of words influences our behavior in the specific context of financial markets.

As a specific example, I say that XYZ is a very speculative stock, and you say you don't buy speculative stocks. Who knows if "speculative" has the same meaning to us? Who knows what "speculative" means? I say commodities represent a better investment than stocks and you say I'm crazy. Consider the denotations and connotations of "commodities". Corn, wheat, soybeans. Horrific leverage. The province of big grain companies and speculators. Only a wild-eyed gambler would get involved. Of course, surprisingly Warren Buffet of Berkshire Hathaway, one of the most successful investors of the late 20th Century, in 1998 bought a billion dollars worth of silver. What's that all about? Does Warren Buffet attribute some different meaning in his head to "commodities"?

Not to worry. This book is not about confusing the unwary or twisting anybody's mind into linguistic pretzels. Like Magee himself it is down to earth, as concrete as a clod of earth in Springfield, Massachusetts. The most complicated thing about this book is this foreword which has to have a necessary and sufficient number of difficult abstractions and hard to figure concepts to make it academically respectable. The wise reader should not let this concern him and skip over anything which appears difficult.

THE IMPORTANCE OF THIS BOOK

Usually when we talk about a book we want to know what it's about—what material it contains—what its argument or theme is. About *Technical Analysis of Stock Trends* for example, we can say that is at one level the definitive symbolic analysis of the price language of the markets. Let me break that down into street language. *Technical Analysis of Stock* Trends suggests that the language of the market may be interpreted as imagistic, that is that it communicates with us through patterns, or ideograms, just as Japanese and Chinese kanji language systems do. In one way that book might be looked at as a dictionary of such symbols. So that when we see a rising triangle we may extrapolate various meanings and intents from it, and when we see a trend we may make some assumptions about it which have been productive in the past.

Just as we find ideograms occurring in market charts which we interpret as symbols having meaning, we hear words about the market which are symbols which we give meaning to. The study of these symbols and their meanings, explicit, implicit, denotative and connotative—is what this book is about, and it is also about improving our efficiency in interpreting and reacting to those realities the symbols represent.

So much for what the book is about. In the case of this book the question is different, or there is a more important question in addition. The question is, what happens in this book? The answer is the mind gets reprogrammed.

In sum *General Semantics* is nothing less than a re-education or re-training of the mind. It is a re-education meant to provide the mind with more realistic and accurate eyes and with an analytical engine to deal with real situations in the real world of Wall Street. This involves a radical re-orientation of the mind to fit it to deal skillfully with reality—or the market—or both.

In the most down to earth of manners Magee attempts to point out the human habits of perception and thinking which hinder our skillful functioning on Wall Street (and the world). Although he does not so name them these habits amount to denial; false hope; greed; impatience; refusal to face reality; refusal to recognize the nature of things; the perverse passion for certainty in an uncertain world; the fear of uncertainty; and foolish faith and the hope of easy money which has cursed the buyers of snake oil since bottlers first learned to bottle it, and advertising companies discovered how to market it. And worst of all, the fear of damage to our good self-regard.

And what are the characteristics and habits he attempts to inculcate and foster? They are the plain old engineering virtues which are of use to anyone with a practical problem to study and resolve. He advocates a flexible method to deal with a changeable world and represents the character traits of the mature adjusted individual—patience, attention to detail, careful planning, discipline, poise.

OPEN MIND, OPEN EYES

Sometimes our discussion or criticism of an area (such as Wall Street) opens new doors of perception or understanding (or even of enlightenment) for the student and reader. Incisive comment can illuminate entirely new aspects of a problem and enrich the reader's understanding and appreciation.

The work of Hamilton, Swabacher, Edwards and Magee is like that. It illuminates a puzzling and complex area of social and economic behavior—the financial markets—and gives us analytical tools and frameworks to deal with them. Note I say deal with them, not understand them because: Like the weather and the sea the markets are not to be understood, but dealt with. Beware of anyone who claims to understand them. And anyone who claims to understand them in depth should be asked to show the performance of his accounts prior to and after the Asian Financial Flu crisis of 1997-98. Perhaps George Soros understood what was going on. Or perhaps he just dealt with it using super fine analytical intelligence and millisecond tactics.

Only psychics, astrologers and philosophers (ontological) can understand the markets—and as everyone knows their advice is highly variable and opaque and cannot be relied upon for trading purposes. That doesn't mean you shouldn't keep an eye on them—like they say the guy with the end of the world sign will be right one day and even more important the guy with the TEOTWAWKI sign will be right even sooner—but they really don't know what to do about IBM right now, and judging from the mutual fund trading records neither do the professional advisors.

In the meantime where are we to turn for reliable investment advice? It grieves me to continue being old fashioned but I fear I will have to recommend a return to a frontier American ethos—self reliance.

In developing that self reliance we have an invaluable companion, teacher and guide—John Magee.

ABOUT JOHN MAGEE

If ever there were an example of "making money the old fashioned way" John Magee from the tips of philosophy to the toes of his slide rule was it. And if ever an individual embodied the good old fashioned virtues of the plain common sense engineer, he was it.

At first I called him Mr. Magee, being young and impressionable when I became his student and client in the 1960s. But he soon disabused me of that practice. He was a down to earth, totally practical engineer, all of which I mean as a compliment in the age of the "Star" fund manager or advisor. Early on he, by virtue of his own character, personality and teachers discovered the essential truths about the market and how to prosper in it, and to my knowledge never deviated from it.

If we look for lineages in teachers (as in race horses) we could not find a better background. After the initial advances in the development of the Dow Theory by Charles Dow and William Peter Hamilton the next advances in technical analysis were made by Richard W. Schabacker in his books *Technical Market Analysis* and *Stock Market Theory and Practice*. In the later years of his practice Schabacker was joined by his brother-in-law Robert D. Edwards. In 1942 Edwards took as his partner John Magee and the two reexamined all the work which had been done before and added their contributions to it and published as co-authors the definitive work on qualitative technical analysis, *Technical Analysis of Stock Trends*. Now in its seventh edition it remains the most important book in the field and has influenced generations of traders and analysts. It is the indisputable bible of technical analysis. Or perhaps, considering the fact that imitations now advertise themselves as "the bible" of technical analysis the book should be considered the Torah of technical analysis and John the great law giver.

When Edwards retired Magee established his own investment advisory company in Springfield Massachusetts where he practiced until the 1970s, selling his company to John Magee Inc. and dying in 1987. During this time he wrote a widely respected weekly letter giving his analysis of stocks and the market.

HOW THIS BOOK RELATES TO TECHNICAL ANALYSIS OF STOCK TRENDS

I venture to say that virtually no serious professional works without the technical knowledge of *Technical Analysis of Stock Market Trends*. If they haven't read the book itself they have read some pale knock off, for there are dozens of imitations trumpeting themselves as "the Bible of technical analysis" or some such. Or they have absorbed the technical orientation through osmosis or experience because the work that Edwards and Magee did established a framework for conceptualizing the market as certainly as Newton established a conceptual framework for physics.

This book, if you will, *Winning the Mental Game...* is the missing companion to *Technical Analysis of Stock Trends*. That book exhaustively deconstructs the activity of the stock market and shows us how to decipher its behavior, teaches us the symbolic language of the markets, as it were. The activity which it studies, the facts, are those of which there can be no dispute—price and volume. Soothsayers can predict earnings all they want to, but there is no dispute as to the closing price on the NYSE this afternoon.

General Semantics has a different lesson to teach us. It has to do with the mental, not the technical questions—the mind set, the preconceptions, the false and misleading habits of mind and upbringing which hinder our efficient functioning in the market.

As an example, if we were taught swordsmanship by a great master who taught us the attacks, footwork, and parries we would only have half a skill. For it is necessary that the master teach us also the mental and emotional disciplines necessary to effectively employ the technical skills we have been given with the sword. Musashi's book, *The Book of Five Rings* which was much in vogue when Japan Inc. was considered impregnable is a good example of a book that intends to integrate the mental with the technical. In Magee's case the technical side has been dealt with in *Technical Analysis of Stock Trends* and the mental emotional perceptive—if you will—behavioral, has been dealt with in *General Semantics*.

Rereading *General Semantics* quite a few years later I can prove by my own experience the wisdom and practicality of its philosophy and approach. I speak as a stray sheep who has returned to the fold. I illustrate personally many of Magee's lessons—one of which (not the only one) being that early success can be as big a problem as early failure. Would that I had never wandered. I forget who it was—probably Moses who said "A smart man learns from his mistakes—A wise man learns from the mistakes of others." A great truth indeed and one which the present reader may contemplate at leisure.

MAGEE'S PHILOSOPHY AND METHODOLOGY

Taking the present book along with *Technical Analysis of Stock Trends* we have a pretty complete picture of Magee's philosophy, his systems and his methodology. Reduced to its essence his philosophy could not be more ancient nor more modern—It is as ancient as Basho the Zen master of ancient Japan and as modern as Baba Ram Dass with his "Be here now." Be awake, be alert. Do not be deceived by what others think or by your own out of date knowledge, by your own concepts which reflect some other reality than that of the NYSE or the NASDQ which valued IBM today at X because in the real world X is always changing. Each moment is a new moment. That is the underlying message of *General Semantics* as well as of *Technical Analysis of Stock Trends*.

Let me start from ground zero. Begin by acquiring a background of skepticism and independent thought. Learn to observe what is what and what is truly going on and to distinguish that from what your teachers, parents, ancient sages would have you believe. Believe your own eyes, not your own ears—after you have learned to see. Observe the universe you are interested in. Study its past. Determine correlations. Develop hypotheses. Apply a mature pragmatic scientific method to your conclusions and test the systems and methods you build with these procedures.

Study the alternatives. Then you will come to realize the wisdom of Magee's guiding methodology: Diversified long term trend trading is the most conservative plan to assure over all long term satisfactory results. In short:

1. Identify the trend and trade with it, long or short.
2. Always have your stop loss identified and calculated.
3. Never fail to execute your plan— exercise mature discipline.

Magee's methodology I believe to be, followed wisely, an almost guarantor of success in investing over the long haul. It contains the seeds of most of the successful tenets of modern investing.

ABOUT THIS BOOK

A important note about the editorial practice followed in this second edition of *General Semantics*. Upon rereading *General Semantics* I was struck by both the charm of the original and by its old-fashioned form. I have attempted in this edition to preserve the charm—and the old-fashionedness where that is part of the charm and to smooth the going for the modern reader. Magee loved to talk and in many places I have excised what I considered excess examples or stories not to the point in the interest of the speed desired by the present readers. I have also removed the exercises from the end of each chapter. In an older age one might have hesitated to take such liberties. But in the age of the internet readers will be able to find the complete text of the original at my web site (www.johnmageeta.com) and collate it with my edition and belabor me with protestations (or praise if that should be the case). In certain chapters I have rewritten rather more extensively in order to minimize the density of the prose or the concepts. In every instance I have attempted to preserve as much of the original as is possible in keeping with clarity and efficiency.

About apparent anachronisms and dates and stock names as metaphors. After lengthy consideration I decided that I would leave the dates referred to in the original as they were. I detest Shakespeare modernized. Also there is a point to be made in leaving the original references as they were—a point which Magee emphasized again and again in his work and which I will make here by quoting from his preface to the Fourth Edition of *Technical Analysis of Stock Trends*: "In the several years since the first edition of this work, the stock market goes right on repeating the same old movements in much the same old routine." In order to further this point I have footnoted instances which might seem dated and cited current examples to illustrate this point.

Further to this question the reader will encounter a reference to U.S. Steel in 1956 and wonder what relevance 1956 and U.S. Steel has to the present world and to his or her (cf. following note on gender) mentality. and that is exactly the point. There is no difference between Microsoft in 2000 and U.S. Steel in 1956. Understand we speak here in metaphor, at the level of symbol. The same mentality which dealt skillfully with U.S. Steel in 1956 deals skillfully with Microsoft in 2000. And in terms of high order abstractions and symbols the two issues are identical regardless of business, regardless of time. Readers will fully understand this point upon reflection and upon reading the chapters on maps and updating maps.

ABOUT ANACHRONISM

Certain anachronisms, or what might be considered anachronisms, deserve comment. A slide rule is the logarithmic precursor of the calculator. Examples may be seen in the Smithsonian. "It consists of two logarithmically scaled rules mounted to slide along each other so that multiplication, division etc. may be reduced to the mechanical equivalent of addition or subtraction." (*Webster's II New Riverside Dictionary*)

During Magee's time, reflecting the economy of the time, the Dow Jones Transportations were called the Rails. I have also left this intact because I am of the opinion that the present usefulness of the Dow Theory is questionable and a subject for research. Certainly at that time its efficacy was certain, but we are now living with a much more complex and diversified economy.

Magee, in Chapter 66, inveighs against the tax system. (As Mark Twain said, "Everybody complains about the tax system but no one does anything about it.") Given the evanescent nature of the tax system I have removed specifics as to holding periods treatment of long- and short-term gains while preserving the general argument as I think that the tax system and the politicians deserve all the criticism the experts and the general public can create.

Readers will note the incidence of the names of stocks which are no longer traded. I have deliberately left these names as they were to make a point. Readers will fully understand this point upon reflection and upon reading the chapter on updating maps.

In cases which were plainly incorrect or inaccurate due to developments in the markets which occurred after the original edition I have either excised the inaccuracy or changed the text to reflect the present situation.

ABOUT THE GENDER IN GRAMMAR

Ich bin ein feminist. How could any modern man, son of a beloved woman, husband of an adored woman, and father of a joyful and delightful daughter not be? I am also a traditionalist and purist in matters of usage, grammar, and style. So where does that leave me and my cogenerationalists, enlightened literary (sigh) men (and women) with regards to the use of the masculine pronoun when used in the general sense to apply to the neuter situation?

In the *Dictionary of Modern American Usage,* Garner notes "English has a number of common-sex general words, such as person, anyone, everyone, and no one, but it has no common-sex singular personal pronouns. Instead we have he, she, and it. The traditional approach has been to use the masculine pronouns he and him to cover all persons, male and female alike.... The inadequacy of the English language in this respect becomes apparent in many sentences in which the generic masculine pronoun sits uneasily."

Inadequate or not it is preferable to she/he/it and other bastardizations of the English language. (Is it not interesting that *bastard* in common usage is never used for a woman, even when she is illegitimate?) As for the legitimacy of the usage of the masculine (actually neuter) pronoun in the generic I prefer to lean on Fowler, who says, "There are three makeshifts: first as anybody can see for himself or herself; second as anybody can see for themselves; and third, as anybody can see for himself." No one who can help it chooses the first; it is correct, and is sometimes necessary, but it is so clumsy as to be ridiculous except when explicitness is urgent, and it usually sounds like a bit of pedantic humour. The second is the popular solution; it sets the literary man's teeth on edge, and he exerts himself to give the same meaning in some entirely different way if he is not prepared to risk the third, which is here recommended. It involves the convention (statutory in the interpretation of documents) that where the matter of sex is not conspicuous or important the masculine form shall be allowed to represent a person instead of a man.

Politically correct fanatics may rail, but so are my teeth set on edge, and so I have generally preserved Magee's usage of the masculine for the generic case. This grammatical scourge will pass and be forgotten and weak willed men (by which I intend to indicate men and women) who pander to grammatical terrorists will in the future be seen to be stuck with malformed style and sentences no women will buy. What would Jane Austen have done, after all?

ABOUT GENDER IN INVESTORS

And, as long as we are on the subject of gender we might as well discuss, unscientifically, gender in investors. Within my wide experience as a trading advisor, teacher, and counselor it strikes me that the women investors I have known have possessed certain innate advantages over the men. I know there are women gamblers; I have seen some. But I have never seen in the markets a woman plunger (shooter, pyramider, pie-eyed gambler). And I have known many men who fit this description (and in fact have done some of it myself). I have also noted among my students and clients that, as a group, women seem to have more patience than men, as a group. I refer specifically to the patience that a wise investor must have to allow the markets to do what they are going to do.

These are wholly personal observations. I have made no study of the question and can't speak to the entire class of women investors. But just as I believe that the world would be better off if more women ran countries I expect that the world of finance will benefit from the steadily increasing number of women investors.

CONCLUSION

This book is the missing companion to *Technical Analysis of Stock Trends*. It exhaustively deconstructs the movement of the stock market and shows us how to decipher its behavior, teaches us the symbolic language of the markets, as it were. But there is nothing about it which can be canned or computerized. Thus it is necessary to use it as a handbook, and not a guidebook to instant success without effort. It's the old fashioned way. Moderate work and conscientious effort are required to trade the markets using Magee type analysis.

General Semantics has been too long out of print. It is to the mental side of Wall Street what *Technical Analysis...* is to the systems and analytical side. The effect of this book is to prepare your mind to operate effectively in the financial markets. It is insidiously subtle in its argument and I don't see how the reader can take it seriously and not find his mind deeply affected. I don't see how anyone can read it and not be changed at a very basic level of perception.

W.H.C. Bassetti
November 1998
San Geronimo, California

CHAPTER 1   INTRODUCTION

Wall Street, as we use the term, is a metaphor. It represents a whole series of abstractions that are ultimately rooted in the most personal and intimate aspects of the lives of men. To understand the strange things men do on Wall Street, we must explore the forces that operate on them, and the relationships between them and the abstractions that Wall Street represents.

Wall Street is not really a place, you know. It's not a narrow little lane squashed between the imposing palisades of the great buildings—not the Wall Street I'm thinking about. On that other physical Wall Street there are window washers and typewriter salesmen and exchange students from Lebanon, and pigeons and curbstones and bits of last Monday's *Financial Times* swirling in a dust devil. There are street lights and old chewing gum rooted to the cracked sidewalks; there's a professor from Bowdoin eating peanuts and a small boy from the Bronx going to visit his uncle's office. There are fire sirens around the corner, boat whistles in the distance. Wall Street is a real, substantial piece of the world and like any piece of the world it's filled with complicated and interesting things. But it's not the Wall Street I mean.

Wall Street, as we use the word in talking about the stock market, is an abstraction, a symbol. It's real enough, but it isn't the kind of reality you can go and look at or take pictures or walk around in. It's a metaphor, the first of many we may encounter before we finish our excursions.

The Wall Street we are to consider here exists in the minds of people. The tangible expression of it is not in concrete and steel and plate glass but in reports, charts, analyses, and the proliferated communications of the tape as its messages are displayed in a thousand boardrooms across the country.

Just as we strip the pigeons and the boat whistles and the cracked sidewalk from our picture of the financial world of Wall Street, just as we generalize the activities of the narrow little New York lane to include all the financial interests of everyone who buys the final edition of the paper in his home town, wherever it is, to check the closing prices for the day, so we again simplify and generalize the financial world of Wall Street. We strip off the superficial and incidental goings-on and we generalize its basic activities. In short, we are trying to see what this thing is, what the essence of it is, and what makes it tick.

More especially, we are trying to see what makes us tick. If we really understand what motives press us to the corner newsstand to get the earliest possible glimpse of the closing price on General Motors, it might help us to understand why we so frequently buy stocks that subsequently sell much lower, and sell those issues that skyrocket so handsomely.

You know, it isn't really Wall Street entirely, either, not even the financial kind of Wall Street. It's purchases and sales, predictions and hunches, profits and losses, the chance to pay off the mortgage on the house, the hope of sending Martha to college, and the desire to own a Cadillac or a Rolls Royce.

Nor is that the end of the chain, either. We can carry the abstracting process even further. We can strip away all the symbols of finance and even all the symbols of what money can buy, and then perhaps we may stand in the presence of a very generalized abstraction indeed. This abstraction is not only very general, but at the same time it is very particular and it very specifically concerns you.

I am speaking now of your "self." Not your flesh, blood, teeth, and toenails but the part of you that wishes and hopes and fears—the part of you that you must do right by, or lose your self-regard. When you have abstracted yourself to the level where you can see clearly that the essential objective in paying the mortgage, sending Martha to college, or buying the Cadillac is all of a piece and is concerned with defending and enhancing your self-regard, then you will realize that the roots of the grubby activities of a dirty little lane in New York have their ultimate flowering in the most personal and intimate recesses of the minds of men.

This may explain somewhat why I have related general semantics and Wall Street. To understand the strange and often irrational things that people do to themselves in Wall Street, it is necessary to explore the forces that operate on them, largely from within themselves.

When you have traced these relations and understand them at the levels of high abstraction, you may find when you come down to earth again that some of the puzzling and threatening problems of the market and of life in all its other aspects—do not seem so puzzling or so threatening as they used to.

CHAPTER 2   THE BIG GAME

To the uninitiated, Wall Street and the market might appear to be a big game, a carnival fling where the outcome is predetermined—the sucker (you) loses. It certainly has this character when we buy a con game from an anonymous voice in a boiler room selling us "a sure thing." Wall Street has a gaudy past peopled by famous (and infamous) operators and traders, but today it is a well-regulated arena where trust and honesty are indispensable to conducting business. The normal amount of dishonesty and chicanery exist there, but in the main the business is extremely efficient and run by dedicated professionals. Millions of dollars change hands based on a nod or a hand signal or a terse phone call.

Step right up, ladies and gentlemen . . . everybody plays! everybody wins! You pick your number, name your prize. It's the Big Game. Hurry, hurry, hurry!

EVERYBODY WINS. HURRY, HURRY, HURRY!

The Big Game. How do they rig these rackets? How does the shillaber land three balls right in the buckets and walk off with the kewpie doll, but one of mine always bounces out? There must be a gimmick. Somehow it's always a shill who gets the Indian blanket, and you and I walk off with a tin whistle for a prize.

Well! It's the Big Game, but maybe it's not your game; and until you can make it your game, maybe you'd better save your quarters for the ice cream cones and the hamburgers. You'd never think to look for the gimmicks where they really are hidden, anyway. Oh, there have been some crude jobs. There still are, here and there, and from time to time. But the SEC and the CFTC have cleaned out most of that sort of thing.

There was a time when Jay Gould and Jim Fisk could rig up a sucker game with the Erie and play it over and over again until the poor crooked wheel was falling to pieces. But that was a century ago.

Right now, as this is written, there are some floaters and drifters who are making their pitch just about the way their fathers and grandfathers did before them; only instead of peddling rock oil it's uranium or nuclear power or something else with a modern streamlined look to it—Internet anti-gravity. It all translates to "con."

The low pitch with the con is a minor nuisance, but we would do well to keep away from these sharpers and small confidence men. Specifically: What do you do when your phone rings some evening just after dinner time, and it's a toll call from New York? A very well-spoken voice tells you that it belongs to a Mr. Simpson of the Utopian Investment Company. The Utopian Investment Company has acquired a controlling interest in North Manitoba Resources, Ltd., and while it is expected that as soon as the assay reports are published the stock will be worth from $8 to $10 a share, they are holding a few thousand shares for allotment to men like you, who will in effect constitute a living endorsement of the firm's integrity. Two hundred shares of U.I.C. are being held in your name at the nominal price of $5. Hurry, hurry, hurry! How can you lose?

This operation, which you may have observed first-hand, is, of course, simply a matter of larceny. It's a criminal activity; the promoters have nothing to offer but a bundle of worthless or nearly worthless stock, and they operate from offices known as "boiler rooms," where batteries of phones are manned by expert high-pressure salesmen working from the sucker lists that are the only real assets of the business.

In this sort of operation, which is strictly the back-of-the-fence sneak job, there is no need for any very deep study of general semantics, or of finance. You would think that anyone who had the sense that God gave to a donkey would know enough not to get roped into "investing" $1,000 with a firm he never heard of in a company nobody ever heard of, on the strength of a call from an utter stranger in another state.

And yet . . . people still try to pick which shell the pea is under. And people still draw their life savings from the bank to buy gold bricks . . . or shares of Utopian.

However, we are not concerned mainly with the shoddy, crooked, and cruel games of the financial swindler and the financial charlatan. It is true that Wall Street is, in a sense, the big game. But, leaving out the nasty little thieves who operate on the sly with their cheap con games, the majority of the operation is surprisingly clean, honest, and open.

For in another sense, Wall Street is not the big game at all. It is not a carnival. The business of Wall Street is the business of evaluating and exchanging the securities that represent the country's industrial plant, just as the business of LaSalle Street is the business of evaluating the country's crops. It is an extraordinarily complex business, and in view of this complexity it is extraordinarily well run. The men who work in Wall Street (or La Salle Street), are mostly hard-working, decent people. They operate under elaborate regulatory codes. In addition, they work under the strict rules of their exchanges and associations. Beyond all this, their own ethical standards, on the whole, are as high as those in any other business or profession.

It is the custom between brokers to carry out a contract made and accepted by word or gesture as faithfully as though it had been executed under bond. The majority of brokers will deal with customers on the same basis; and in case of an error or dispute, a broker will normally accept proper responsibility for a mistake and will make right any loss to a customer for which he was responsible.

The work of Wall Street is much like the work in any other commercial business. There are bookkeepers, technicians, executives, salesmen, office personnel—the same kinds of people you might find in a bank, or in a department store.

The business of Wall Street, that is, the exchange of money for securities and vice versa, is one of the most democratic operations we have. It is much more democratic than our politics, where you have to have certain connections if you expect to get anywhere. When you buy 100 shares of General Motors you pay the same price that anybody else will pay, and it won't help you a bit if you went to school with the senior senator from the state of New York.

In Wall Street, to an extraordinary degree, a man can still stand on his own feet and be recognized for what he is himself, without regard to social connections, family background, wealth, or political pull. Here, "a man's a man, for a' that." You can stand on your own feet, and the victory, if you achieve it, is yours. If you fail, you cannot fairly point the accusing finger at the skyline of New York and say, "They have robbed me." For there is no great oval room where the top-hatted, wax-mustachioed tycoons gather to plot your destruction.

It's all right for the Russian press to draw such a picture, and we can perhaps forgive even the local office-holder who sees a chance to stir up laggard votes with a hate campaign. But you can't inject life into the fading Currier and Ives portrait of the villains of Wall Street concocting a network of wash sales, false reports, and watered stock to rob you of your savings. You will have to place the blame for losses, if losses you have, somewhere else.

CHAPTER 3   BLACK MAGIC

One of the delights of magic is being deceived. We expect and want the magician's hand to be quicker than the eye. But we can learn something about perception if we study how the magician fools us. It's the mind he fools, of course, because he knows how to manipulate our perception. But so do we, unconsciously. We can have a conceptual elephant in our front hallway, but we can't see it until we learn to see it. The market is like an elephant in this. The novice studies all the facts, makes an investment, and gets stung. Everyone told him there was something (value) there. He believes there was something (value) there. But most of the time he loses and doesn't understand why. Who fooled him? And why?

There are certain situations where you expect to get fooled and where you might even be disappointed if you weren't. You don't really expect to win the bridge lamp and the overgrown teddy bear at Luna Park; you expect to lose, and you know there are certain ways in which the probabilities of your number coming up can be substantially reduced; but that's all right if you're just out for a good time.

When you go to a magic show you expect to be fooled. A rabbit, two rabbits, a dozen rabbits are taken out of an empty silk hat—the very same kind of silk hat from which Jay Gould produced common stock in the Erie to cover his short sales. However, don't forget that was nearly 100 years ago.

You expect to be fooled. The saying goes, "The hand is quicker than the eye." But don't believe that. It's just an easy way for somebody to explain something he doesn't understand. As a rule, the magician is not fooling your eyes. That isn't the way it works. He doesn't need to fool your eyes if he can fool your mind so that you think you see something that wasn't really there—or perhaps fail to see what was in plain sight all the time.

It's a matter of knowing something about how you perceive things. And it will surprise you when you find out how much that you perceive can be completely false to fact. Things that, when they are pointed out to you, will seem so simple. You'll say, "How could I have overlooked that? Why, it was in plain sight all the time." It's sometimes as if we overlooked an elephant blocking our own front door, and squeezed past the animal without seeing him at all.

If you're like most people your earliest experiences in the market were discouraging. Only a small minority of beginning investors, by luck or by the power of the prevailing trend, make large net profits at the very outset, and they are more to be pitied than congratulated. For them there is likely to be a day of disillusionment more painful even than for those who took their hard knocks at the start. These lucky beginners are somewhat in the position of the young man who was taken to the race track by an older horse-player; made four successive $2.00 bets, all of which paid off. He turned to his friend, all starry-eyed, to ask, "Say, how long has this been going on?"

If you're like most of us, the first market adventure is a small one, carefully planned and studied. One examines the dividend records and the earnings figures for past years as intently as any horse-player scans the form sheets. He weighs "all" the factors and buys the stock that his intelligence and common sense tells him is the logical choice. It can't go down—not very much. It must go up in value.

And what happens? Wouldn't you think that just on the basis of sheer luck if you selected any stock at random, the probabilities alone would give you a profit about half the time? Why do they always have to go down?

Over and over again, the novice goes through his evaluative procedure, selects his stock and buys it, and then a few weeks or a few months later sells out, takes his loss, and prepares to try again.

HOW CAN HE BE WRONG ALL THE TIME?

Who is doing this to him? Who is fooling him? What is the magic, where is the gimmick, how do they do this?

You know, you can go up after the magic show and examine the cards and the boxes and the wand, and you won't find much. The cards are a regular deck, no markings. What happened? How did he do this to me? How did he fool me?

Well, did he really fool me? Or could you say that he just sort of let me fool myself? Yes! The illusion was not in the cards, the boxes, the wand. The illusion was something in my way of looking at these things.

I saw something that was not there. Just as I saw something that was not there when I bought the stock. It seemed to be there. It looked all right. I had good reasons to support my belief. But when the wand was waved, somehow it turned out it wasn't the way I had thought it was at all.

I was fooled. But who fooled me? And how?

CHAPTER 4   THE VILLAIN

The novice (and the experienced) investor looks for a villain to explain the experience that 85 percent of investors in the market encounter. But there is no villain, only you, the investor, paying a high tuition for experience—a tuition that might continue endlessly unless you can rearrange your orientation to reality. Admit the earth is round. While this might sound simple, a little playing with the idea demonstrates how difficult it is to rearrange our mental equipment. It should be simple. It isn't. Yet the same factors that contribute to success in the markets influence the contentment of our lives.

Take down the picture of the capitalist. He doesn't exist, not like the picture. And tell that magician to step down from the stage. You get up there on the stage! If anybody turned girls into rose bushes and made rabbits come out of empty hats, it wasn't the magician. It was you.

It was you who decided after careful study that Fruehauf Trailer was really worth much more than the $35 you paid for it in 1956. When you saw it drop mysteriously to $9 in 1957. You cannot quite fairly blame the magician; after all, it was all your own doing. You examined the evidence. You made the decisions.

Your fault? No, not exactly your fault. Not anybody's fault in the sense of blaming anybody. But unless there was deliberate fraud there must have been some fault—and you were the one who made the decisions.

There must have been some fault because you had arrived at the conclusion that this stock would soon sell for $50 or more, and on that basis you paid $35 for it. Instead of reaching your objective, it collapsed to $9. Your conclusion was mistaken and your prediction was wrong.

Perhaps if you had not been so absolute, so sure of what the outcome would be, you might not have been hurt so badly.

At any rate, if we look at the records of the average market newcomer, the percentage of success is nothing like what you might expect on the basis of any reasonably good evaluation or even on the basis of pure chance. With rare exceptions he loses money with great regularity until he either runs out of capital, gets discouraged, and quits the market (with feelings of great hostility toward Wall Street), or he ultimately discovers that it is possible to do something to correct some of his most flagrant errors and stop the succession of failures.

It sounds like a very easy thing, to change one's way of looking at things so as to see the reality, and not the illusion. It seems so simple. And it is a simple thing, basically. It's as simple as the fact that the earth is round and rotates on its axis. Yet for thousands of years men believed that the earth was flat and the stars moved around the heavens each night (some still do believe that).

This business of stumbling over an elephant in your own front hall and never even seeing the beast is fairly common. Science is filled with cases where men searched for years for something that eventually turned up, in plain sight, right in their own front yard.

It's much harder to learn something simple, basic, and quite new to you than to learn something that seems quite complicated. It's harder for a high school student to understand what is meant by the square root of minus one than to learn French irregular verbs.

Ask somebody to imagine a number system based on dozens instead of tens, and if he's not familiar with number concepts, it will quite throw him.

If you want to see how hard it is for most of us to adapt ourselves to any changes in the concepts we regard as obvious, universal, and eternal, just try, with a few of your friends, to lead the conversation around to some hypothetical change in our customs or habits. How would our lives be affected if all present taxes were abolished and we had only a single tax on land values? What would be the ultimate effects of a graduated tax on children, the first-born in a family being exempt, the second subject to a moderate impost, and each successive addition to the family carrying a higher price tag?

You may be surprised what confusion it can cause, even among reasonably well-educated people, when you suggest the slightest change in the framework of their habitual thinking. Men who will discuss for hours the advisability of continuing or abolishing capital punishment will hardly deign to consider any scheme of preventing homicide by attacking the causes of murder.

When we say, "Don't look at the magician, don't look at the cards or the boxes; look at yourself," that's a very simple, basic suggestion. It sounds so easy. The things you have to look for are so very simple, so simple you'll say, "Yes, yes"—but you'll go right on the way you have gone before. Unless, of course, you realize that these are very serious matters. These are matters that concern much more than making profits in the stock market. The implications here reach into your personal life, your success, your happiness, and by extension they concern matters of law and order, of material prosperity in the community, and of international affairs and world peace.

CHAPTER 5   THE BLIND

Most of us live in a state of unawareness that might be compared to blindness. We accept our cultural and personal context without questioning it, and we accept its predominant opinions and values. As example, the ancient shepherd knew the stars revolve about the earth. He observed it. Third Reich Germans knew that Hitler made the trains run on time and produced national pride and prosperity.

You may remember a short story by H. G. Wells, a story about a man who strayed accidentally into a mountain-walled valley in South America. The inhabitants, who had a large and prosperous city, with neat houses and carefully-laid-out walks between them, found their visitor strange, probably psychotic. The visitor, it seems, claimed that he could "see"; that he had some sense that he derived from light by means of which he had powers of understanding he claimed they lacked; for the inhabitants of this town were all what we would call blind. For many generations they had been sightless. They had built their lives around the senses and powers they possessed.

This thing called "seeing" seemed to have no place in their lives. It was quite unnecessary to them, since they had adapted their living to ways that did not require sight. In fact it seemed to them a gross abnormality, and in all kindness and friendship they proposed that one of their great surgeons remove the offending growths the visitor called eyes so that he might become a properly adjusted member of the community.

It's not easy to explain to someone a simple, basic concept like seeing. It's not easy for anyone to accept something foreign to his habit and cultural environment.

Let me propose a test case for you. I want you to imagine that you could visit a shepherd tending his flocks by night in the hills of Israel 2,500 years ago. The simple project I have laid for you is merely to explain to the shepherd that the earth revolves on its axis each day and that the stars remain in relatively fixed positions in the sky.

Mind you, this shepherd has done what you have not done. He has sat on that hillside almost every night for many years. He has sat on the solid rock of the solid mountain on the solid earth, and he has watched, with his own eyes, the stars rising from the eastern horizon, moving across the dome of the sky and sinking to the west.

What language are you going to use to make him understand your crazy theory? Are you going to sketch the earth as a round ball, resting on nothing at all, spinning around in space? Are you going to expect him to accept a dreamer's theory spun out of the imagination, as against the evidence of his eyes? Are you going to win out over "common sense" with your weird story? I would imagine the shepherd would either run for his life or perhaps get his fellow shepherds to help you back to town for a serious heart-to-heart talk with the local medicine man.

Or put yourself in Germany, say around 1938. Go before an audience in any German town and tell them the truth as you might see it: Hitler is a dangerous maniac leading their country on a road that must end in ruin. They were slaves to a cruel and stupid system that is exploiting them and destroying them. If you were not stoned out of the hall at once or taken into custody, you would be told that your comments were unsocial, ungrateful, and downright stupid. Hitler had brought back hope to Germany. There were social improvements, aids to the needy, programs of national development, higher standards of living, self-respect and pride, and a sense of great accomplishment. How could you sell your simple theory to these dedicated people? How could you make them see how cruelly they were being deceived, and that much of the deception was of their own making?

It comes hard to see some things. Better to be blind. Yes, really, better not to see at all than to see what hurts too much.

It's easier, is it not, to say that Fruehauf Trailer went down because of a change in basic demand; unforeseen conditions in the industry. Nothing we could do anything about. Nothing in which our thinking was faulty. Simply another bad break to add to the many bad breaks already on the books. This leaves us feeling not quite so hurt.

But it doesn't help at all in preventing the next disaster.

It may be less painful this one time to be blind than to see clearly. But is it, in the final summing-up, less painful to go through a whole lifetime blind, rather than open one's eyes and face the truth?

It's sometimes hard to face the truth. You will revolt at some of the things you are going to be asked to look at. They will seriously conflict with your "common sense." It may be easier not to look at all, and it certainly will not be easy to look and see that some of the idols you have served so blindly for so long are only hunks of weathered clay. But if you want sight you must learn to see. You must be able to bear the pain of the unfamiliar sunshine.

CHAPTER 6   OUT OF THE DARKNESS

While insects spring fully capable from the head of Athena, men are the products of a capacity to learn and of education and training. Helen Keller was a blank slate in darkness until her teacher communicated with her, awoke her, and educated her. The crucial element is communication.

What do you suppose an unborn baby sees? What do you suppose it thinks? How do you suppose it spends its nine months of leisure time before it accepts the irreversible responsibility of entering the world of men?

I wonder if there can be much of anything going on there that you could call thinking. I wonder whether you could properly consider that an unborn baby had anything that we could really call a mind.

Mankind, as you know, comes into this world rather imperfectly equipped for unaided survival as compared, say, with a baby chick. Fishes, birds, even some of the mammals seem to arrive with certain built-in instincts, not exactly intelligence as we think of it, but rather a substitute for intelligence, a nest-egg of mental determinants to which will later be added the products of education and experience.

With insects there is really no adequate hook on which to hang intelligence at all. It seems to lie in the mechanics and structure of the insect. You can't really educate an insect very much. There is practically no learning ability. There isn't anything to work on. The marvelous engineering and social organization, the hunting and home-building techniques we see in the insect world seem to be built on something that is handed down from generation to generation as part of the central nervous system of the insect, built in from birth, complete. Necessary and sufficient.

Not so with man. You and I needed a good many years of spoon-feeding and cuddling, teaching and punishing, before we were ready to matriculate at nursery school, and a good many years on top of that before we could drive a car, play poker, or take the bar examinations. If you want to see how helpless we really are, and how helpless we would remain without the aid of our senses to bring in knowledge from the world around us, consider Helen Keller's story of her early years, black, silent, empty years, until by what must have seemed a miracle her teacher, Anne Mansfield Sullivan, re-established communication, and into the nascent soul of Helen Keller began to flow the basic data needed to set up what became her fine intelligence.

It never would have happened without communication. Miss Keller undoubtedly had the potential, the capacity to learn. But without contact with reality she would have remained a blank.

CHAPTER 7   THE CAMERA

Like the film in a camera the human child records its experiences. Learning occurs as a result of recording, and with learning comes the knowledge, unarticulated, of how to manipulate the environment. The human eye, like the camera, sees the world and, based on its experience and the encouragement of its environment, determines once and for all some basic facts about existence—which way is up. It also absorbs other opinions that it assumes are truth and therefore incontrovertible.

Blank film. A blind sheet of plastic, showing nothing. Leave it in the camera a month and it will be as blank as it was the first day. The only way a picture can be registered is to expose the film to the outside world in a suitable light.

Doesn't the first knowledge have to come from outside? The first bright light to follow with blue eyes. The first sounds, perhaps mother singing to her child. The first sensations of touch, and of taste and of smell. Perhaps all these things are jumbled up and rather meaningless at first, like a coat-room with not enough hooks. There wouldn't be much place to hang and arrange all these sensations at first.

Isn't it remarkable how soon the baby gets the hang of certain things out in the world? Unless you're very careful he will pick up a number of exceedingly stubborn and inconvenient habits in no time at all; and since he has plenty of time and not nearly so many things to think about as you do, he may outmaneuver you in a number of ways if you don't watch out. Also, he will establish some of the successful maneuvers as habits. He will learn (and this is where he begins to lord it over the built-in mentality of the praying mantis) what is most likely to bring him attention or food or warmth or dry diapers or whatever it is he happens to need. Long before he is a year old he will have a practical working method for manipulating people.

At just what stage are you going to say this child has acquired such characteristics as good judgment, good taste, a sense of decency, a feeling of responsibility? There have been various attempts to fix the precise time at which these qualities could be assumed to have matured, and there has been discussion of these points by legal and ecclesiastical authorities. But isn't it more reasonable to suppose that these qualities develop differently in different children, and that in any case they take shape gradually? And also that there is considerable room for differences of opinion as to whether your child or mine has, for example, good taste. But you will agree that you and I and everybody else we know evolved from something that was quite blind and quite blank at the start, and for the most part whatever we know we have "acquired." We have learned it by observation and experience, it has been taught to us, or we have learned it by combining, abstracting and reasoning from the things we have directly experienced or that we have been taught.

Certainly you and I were not born with an understanding of the English language, or any other language. We didn't know, at birth, how to figure a margin account, or for that matter how to tie our own shoelaces. These things, and a million others, were acquired. All your life you have been taking in communications from outside—not only all the things you see and hear and that you record with other senses as direct experience, but as soon as you could understand words, you were being told about other matters outside your direct experience. As soon as you learned to read, you began to take in even more about matters beyond your personal experience.

In both the learning you received from direct contact and in that which came from teaching, you soon found there were oughts; there were some do's and a great many don'ts. If you pulled the cat's tail, you got scratched. A don't. If you put your hand on the radiator, you were burned. Another don't. If you smiled your best smile at Granny, you got a peppermint. A do. If you threw snowballs into Mrs. McCarthy's window, you were a "dirty little brat." A don't. And so on.

You acquired a value system, in a certain sense you were a value system: The thing that made you really "you" as an individual was this complex structure built up out of your stored-up perceptions. You know that what you learn young sticks by you. That's how we get some of our good thinking habits that help us later in life.

Unfortunately, it's also how we get some very bad thinking habits. If you will think of the good, simple, straight-thinking shepherds and their bafflement at your theory of an orbiting world, you will see that it is going to be rather hard for anyone to change the common-sense views that have met the test of experience and acceptance by others during a whole lifetime. It is particularly hard if the concept in question is so firmly built into one's value system that it seems, as we said before, to be obvious, universal, and eternal. To challenge one of these basic simple concepts means digging up deep roots. Like any deeply rooted organism, like the tree roots you dig up in your garden, they keep growing back. They are hard to kill. In fact, even when your intellect accepts a new view and you have intellectually rooted out the faulty concept, you will find it keeps creeping back. It sometimes takes a long time to kill off the old root structure.

It isn't necessary to get into very abstruse and obscure philosophy to see how often our preconceived ideas run smack into facts that don't fit. When you were in second grade you were taught that the world was round. That there wasn't really any "up" or "down" in space. But this new knowledge clashed with what you had learned about up and down before you ever went to school.

Didn't it come hard to think of the Australians living on the bottom of the earth? Didn't you wonder, when you were quite small, why they didn't fall off? And whether they had to walk on their heads? It wasn't until much later that you could really accept a space without up or down, so that you could see all the peoples of all parts of the world, all oriented to different verticals and horizontals but all experiencing the sensations of walking, climbing, falling, etc. in about the same way. Or do you really accept that even now? For some quite grownup people their own up is much more correctly up than that of citizens in Terra Del Fuego or the Cape of Good Hope.

Going back, for a moment, to the "up" and "down" ideas that we get so early in life, and that become so much a part of our perceptive system that we cannot easily change or dislodge them: This chapter is headed "The Camera." In a sense, you're like a camera in that you continually record sensations from outside, through your senses, and preserve them for later reference.

This is especially true of your sight. Your eye is, in a very real sense, a camera, or, to put it more accurately, a camera is a rather crude working model of a human eye. The diaphragm of the iris controls the amount of light admitted, just as the diaphragm of your camera does. The muscles of the eye focus the image on the retina just as you focus your camera. The convex lens gathers the light from the scene before you to invert it and present it in miniature on the retina exactly as the lens of your camera gathers the light, inverts it, and presents it on the film or plate.

Did we say "invert"? Yes. The image is inverted. Here is one of those disturbing encounters with the "up" and "down" words, for it suggests that we are seeing everything upside down! It is almost as alarming as the thought of those poor Australians walking on their heads and occasionally falling down into lower space.

How can we get around the house or do our work if we see everything inverted? Well, of course, we don't. The image on the retina is inverted, yes. The picture is formed on the retina by the light projected from outside, and it is inverted. But we do not see with the image on the retina. The conscious perception, what we call sight, occurs in the brain. Sever the optic nerve leading to your brain and you may still have an image on the retina, but it is not seen, for you are then blind.

Sight occurs in the brain. The brain lies in darkness, encased in the skull. The perception of light is something that is generated in the dark recesses of your brain. What difference does it make, then, whether the reception is from left to right or right to left; whether up is at the top or at the bottom? The process of learning to see is a matter of relating what impulses come in from the retina with what experience teaches us is out there.

If you think that up (as you see it) is absolutely up—one of the absolute, universal, and eternal truths—you should study experiments in which the messages coming into the eye have been deliberately distorted.

Researchers have staggered around in glasses that reverse the images of right and left eye, or which invert the inverted image on the retina. They staggered around for a day or so, their perception revolting at the now-meaningless and paradoxical messages that come in through their optic nerves. Eventually, though, new patterns of perception are formed, and these students have found that it is possible to learn a new way of seeing things. What makes it all so hard at the start in these cases is the need to unlearn what was so deeply learned before.

At this point I am going to plunge into Wall Street for a moment—just for a moment, in order to make a point. Do you know people who have learned certain things so well that they can see them in only one way? So well that, for them, there could be no other way to see, just as you would find it extremely hard to see at first with reversed or upside-down glasses? Do you know some people who see clearly that a stock that pays a dividend must be a better investment than one that doesn't? Do you know people who believe it is important to know how to buy stocks, but who cannot understand why it is just as important to know how to sell them? Do you know people who feel that the only way to evaluate a stock is to read and understand the annual report? These people have learned to see certain things so naturally that any suggestion that someone else might have a different way of seeing makes no sense to them at all, regardless of argument, evidence, or demonstration. We will come back to this later.

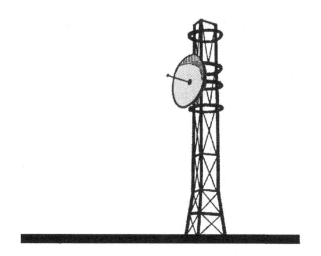

CHAPTER 8   THE PRIMARY RECEPTORS

After a moment we realize there is an "in here" in the brain and an "out there" that is, some sort of reality being perceived by our sense organs and made sense of by our brain. Insects, being hard-wired, are very efficient at what they do, but unlike man they have no capacity to learn and change. Change of ingrained beliefs and habits is not easy for man, but it is possible. The process of change begins with understanding of what goes on "in here."

We have, then, eyes, which are sensitive to light and which transmit to our brains messages that we then translate into the sensation of seeing. Similarly, our ears are sensitive to sound and transmit messages that our brains translate into the sensation of hearing. In like manner, with our other senses we react to incoming stimuli with appropriate sensations.

It is important to understand that our reaction to light or sound or taste is not the same as the light, sound, or taste itself. To use the good analogy of television, what appears on your screen, that is, the picture you look at, is not the same as the waves that are transmitted by the sending studio and picked up by the antenna on your set, for, as you know, these waves cannot be seen at all but must be picked up and translated into a picture. Neither are the waves sent out by the transmitting studio the same as what is being televised.

Nothing is known to us directly except the impulses that come in to our brain through the nerves that transmit stimuli from the outside world to the brain. Whatever else we know must be constructed from the bits of information we receive in this way.

In this, to recapitulate, we are quite different from, let us say, an insect. The insect is a wonderful organism, of course, and marvelously designed to cope with its particular environment. But the pattern is fixed; it is "hard-wired" like the information on a computer circuit. The insect has no capacity to learn anything new, or at any rate its capacity for learning is so slight as to be negligible. For all practical purposes you can't teach an insect anything it does not know already; it does not learn very much by its own experience.

On the other hand, mankind is designed for its particular way of life, which is enormously more complicated than that of an insect. Whereas the insect produces offspring in magnificent profusion to meet the demands of a high mortality, man operates with a lower rate of reproduction and a higher rate of survival. In man we have a problem of survival of the individual to a much greater degree than in the case of the insect. Man is not nearly so specialized; he is able to master many skills, to meet many different kinds of situations, to live under widely varying conditions.

So it is not so important for man to have a single specialized way of living, such as the insect possesses. Man must be able to change himself, to solve new problems, to make himself different according to the needs of the situation. But before you can change your ways, you must change your perceptions, especially those that have become embedded from early childhood in your value system. And before you can do that, you must know something about how these perceptive habits originated, and the mechanisms by which they operate.

Unless you have a reasonably clear understanding of what is going on "in here," you will never be able to interpret clearly what is going on "out there." In short, you will go right on being depressed, angry, lonely, puzzled, and you will continue to make the same mistakes over and over again, not only in the stock market, but in your job and at home.

Which would be too bad, because you are not an insect nor even a donkey. As Alfred Korzybski put it, "We must not behave like animals."

You are a human being, and you have, to a greater degree than any other organism on the earth, a brain that has the ability to build itself, change itself, and solve new problems.

CHAPTER 9   A STARTING POINT

Regardless of our present condition of efficiency or inefficiency we as humans are able to study, understand, and learn. Animals may be faster, see better, be stronger, but only man can learn in the larger sense. That ability gives us a starting point to study how we know what we know.

If the various nerve channels carrying incoming messages to your brain from the outside were severed, you would no way at all to know what was "out there." If these nerves were cut off in your earliest childhood, you would never be able to establish any contact with the outside world. You would never know anything.

If what we call knowledge is one of the ways we are different from the other inhabitants of this earth, then it must be plain that the cables of nerves to our brains are absolutely essential to our humanity. Without them and the messages they carry, we would not just be reduced to the level of the lower animals. We would be infinitely worse off than they are. Animals, at least, do have the receptors, the eyes and ears, to enable them to make contact with and maintain continuous communication with the world around them. That is basic not only for mankind, but for all of animal kingdom.

But, as we have seen, given the primary senses to establish communication with the outside world, man has the capacity to put these impressions to much greater use than any animal. He can't only know what is going on in the world from direct observation, but he can make abstractions. He can deduce and construct from past observation and make predictions and decisions to a much greater degree than animals can. This is not to say that animals cannot abstract and reason, for there is plenty of evidence that they do. The question is more a matter of how much.

We have had a spate of shaggy dog stories like the tale about the hunter who comes across a campsite in a clearing where there is a tent, a small fire, and a man and his dog playing cribbage on a flat-topped rock. The visitor watches the game for a while thoughtfully, finally remarks, "That's a pretty smart dog you've got there, stranger." And the camper replies, "Oh, he ain't so smart. I just beat him three games in a row."

What makes this and all the rest of its ilk funny (and I happen to enjoy them all) is that dogs just don't have that much intelligence. We can love and admire man's best friend, as most of us do. We can take off our hats to his courage, his faithfulness, his ingenuity, his skill. But when all is said and done, the faithful beast goes just so far and no farther. No dog has ever learned to play cribbage, read a book, or extract square roots.

So we start with the primary contacts we have with the world (which we share with the animals); on these, we can build the wonderful network of knowing and thinking to which the animals can never aspire.

H.L. Mencken once enumerated various skills and attributes in which the animals exceeded our own capabilities: the vision of the eagle, the sense of smell of the bloodhound, and the keen hearing, swiftness of foot, brute strength of various other beasts. Apparently it was only in the possession and use of his human mind that man excelled the beasts, and this advantage he is apparently too magnanimous to put to use.

This was something of an exaggeration, of course; the most backward moron is in some respects far ahead of the smartest animal in the use of his mind. But none of us, it is safe to say, is fully using the machinery we as men, and we alone, possess. Here we are—able to read and write and do at least simple computation. We have a vast store of memories and things learned from others. Some of these things have come to us from the past. They represent knowledge written down by our forefathers, long dead. It is only through the miracle of writing and reading that we can avail ourselves of this knowledge.

We will speak of this later. Meanwhile, we are well equipped to study and understand and learn. We can take our present understanding and turn it to advantage by studying how we first learned things. This will help us to find out what kinds of learning are useful and what kinds may be damaging to us. Then we can set to work to correct the damaging factors, to our benefit. This is the starting point for a study of how we know what we know.

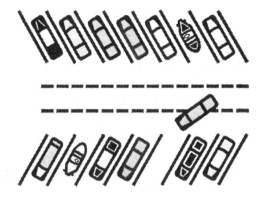

CHAPTER 10   ONE-TO-ONE

Just as cartographers make a map of an area, our minds map the contents of external reality, the "territory." As these maps are interpretations of "out there," disputes over the territory are natural, especially when some people make maps that have no basis in reality. In the best of situations we have a one-to-one correspondence between the territory and the map; we have a verifiable check on the accuracy of the map.

Let us simplify the picture of the world outside and the mind within. Let us assume there is just a single impulse that comes in through the skin or the eye or the ear and registers a stimulus on a nerve. This is not the thing that happens "out there," but something that was caused by something out there.

We have a single impression. Soon we receive another impression. And another. Eventually the mind sets up patterns, it provides hooks for these, and it begins to organize and give meaning to incoming stimuli. Some are tagged as pertaining to seeing, some to hearing, some to tasting, etc.

Eventually these patterns assume a certain order. We are able to recognize certain patterns as similar to ones we have experienced before. We construct something like a picture, so that when a similar series of impulses comes in we can compare the retained picture with the new impressions and say, "This is very much the same," or, "This is quite different."

It's something like a man making a map. He sets down a pencil dot on the paper to represent the position of the big oak tree. Then he makes another pencil dot to represent the farmhouse. Then he marks the position of the windmill, which lies between the big tree and the farmhouse. He does not, of course, think that the marks on the paper are really the farm. It's simply a representation of the farm, symbols to help him know how things on the farm relate to each other. On his map (if it is a good map), there should be a relation between the farm "out there," and the map he is making.

For instance: It may be 150 feet from the farmhouse to the big tree, and this may show on the map as only 3 inches. But if the windmill lies between house and tree, its representation on the map must also lie between the marks representing the house and the tree. In fact, if it is a good map, the distance from house to windmill and from windmill to tree on the farm should be in roughly the same ratio as the distances between these points on the map. In other words, each point on the map should correspond with some point in the territory, and the relation of the various points on the map should be approximately the same as that of the real objects seen.

We do not expect to find anything on the map that does not have some referent actually perceived "out there." This is the way we make maps in our minds, the only way we get to know what is "out there" at all.

It seems childishly simple, yet people make maps in their minds that have no referents in reality at all. They sometimes have the strongest belief that they know something without any supporting evidence in external reality and even in the face of contradictory evidence.

If we have a situation where it's possible to check one item against another, in one-to-one correspondence, there can be no real dispute. If, for instance, there are a certain number of spaces in the parking lot and each space is filled, we do not need to count the number of spaces nor the number of cars to know that the number of spaces equals the number of cars. This is a one-to-one correspondence. Even a person who had never learned to count could tell you whether the number of cars and spaces was equal, whether there were more cars than spaces and vice versa.

There are a great many situations where it is possible to make such a check, cases where we can verify each disputed point on the map against the external reality.

Let us say, for instance, that you claim there are ten houses on the east side of Sylvan Street between Belmont Avenue and Fountain Street, and I maintain that there are twelve. Evidently I have a different map of this territory than you do. Are we going to settle this argument by a knock-down and drag-out fight? Or are we going to go out to Sylvan Street and count the houses? Which way is more likely to settle the argument?

The question here concerns how good our own maps really are—and also whether, in the final analysis, any map is as good an authority as the territory it represents. The picture cannot be more perfect than the thing itself. Therefore, when a question has been raised about the truth, if we can, we go to the territory itself to check the facts. The territory is always better evidence than any map.

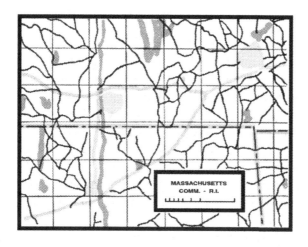

MASSACHUSETTS
COMM. - R.I.

CHAPTER 11   OF MAPS

Maps have different degrees of specificity. A map of the world will not serve to find a picnic spot. Depending on how we plan to use it, we ask the map to have the level of abstraction convenient to us. We also expect any symbol on the map to represent something real in the territory. No map is or will replace the territory itself. As maps represent territories, so our mind makes maps of concrete realities and of concepts and ideas.

In order to understand better how certain things get into our minds, useful as well as harmful things, we are going to use analogies. When we say that our stored-up observations of the world around us, as well as our logical conclusions, our opinions, attitudes, etc. are like maps, we do not, of course, mean that they are actually the same as printed maps. But these mental images are very much like maps in that they are a lasting record that we consult for guidance, and they are (or should be) representations of something else, having a certain relation to external reality.

We use the word *map,* and sometimes *image.* We also use the word *picture* or *photograph* (for a memory is very often so vividly pictorial that we can "see it in our mind's eye"). And we use the word *label* to indicate the names we attach to our mental images, just as we might label maps or photographs or files of information. By using these words we can understand more easily some of the processes by which we understand (and sometimes misunderstand) the world in which we live.

You will agree that a map, unless it is pure make-believe, should be a map of *something*. Whatever you find on the map should have some corresponding feature in the territory it portrays. But the reverse is not true. You certainly won't find a representation on the map of every feature in the territory.

You know this is true of some very simplified maps, such as the ones you will find in the little leatherette pocket atlases you can buy at the dime store. The map of the United States, for instance, shows the Atlantic and Pacific Oceans and the Gulf of Mexico. You can even get an idea of the general shape of the state of Texas. But the little New England states are shown so small that it is hard to see just what shape they really are. On a map like this you'll find at least something recognizable as Lake Michigan. But you won't find Lake Waramaug.

It's true that all the places indicated on the map represent real places in the country in approximately the right place to correspond with the territory, but there is a good deal left out.

Suppose you now get a somewhat larger, somewhat more expensive, atlas. Here you will find maps of separate states, and you will be able to pick out, in Massachusetts, not only Boston, but also Worcester and New Bedford and Springfield. But you will probably not find Essex or North Wilbraham. This kind of map might show some of the principal highways and railroads, and, of course, it would include the larger bodies of water in the state, such as Quabbin Reservoir. All the things shown are features you can visit by taking a trip, and check that they are really there. But you will not find Stackpole's farm, nor the lane that runs down to it from the main road, nor the cow pond, nor the wooded ridge along the north boundary; although all these things, too, are part of the territory and can be verified by going and looking at them. In other words, there is still a good deal left out.

If you want to get a better map, one that represents more features of the territory (that is, more detail), get the U. S. Topographic Survey map for this quadrangle. This will show you the Stackpole farm, the lane running to it, the cow pond, and the hill. It is a much more complete map than the one in the little leatherette atlas. But there is still a lot left out. It will not show you the ell on the house, nor the old well. It does not include the path to the barn. It omits the blackberry patch just north of the barn.

I suppose if you wanted to take the trouble you could survey the Stackpole place and make a map that would show all these things, right down to the rows of blackberry bushes. But it would leave out a lot, still. To get it all (almost) you would have to make a map on a very big scale that would show each separate blackberry bush; and then you would need to sketch each bush so as to show every leaf; and then you would need to magnify every leaf to show its exact markings; and ultimately, if you wanted a complete map you would have to work with a microscope to study the precise structure of the cells in the leaves.

When you arrived at this point you would realize that there was still a lot left out. In fact, if you carried this exploration of the submicroscopic world to its ultimate end, you would find that the reality eventually becomes entirely un-mappable, a cosmos of articles that cannot be described in ordinary material terms and that are not observable in their individual features. The very act of observation would change the reality, and the map at this stage would be in such a constant state of change that from one instant to another it would become obsolete.

It is not possible to map a territory completely. The map always includes less than what is "out there." And actually, as you know, it is not necessary to have all the detail. It all depends upon what your particular need for the map happens to be.

If a child comes to you and asks what the earth looks like, you can get him one of the little ten cent globes, two or three inches in diameter. This will give him a good idea of the shape of the earth and the relative size of the continents and oceans—in other words, a good view of the thing as a whole. There would be no particular point in showing him a topographic map quadrangle, covering an area, say, eight miles wide and ten miles long and including one or two villages, a few roads, farmhouses, schools, hills, brooks, etc., as a representation of what the earth looked like. This would be too particular; it would not necessarily be typical of a large part of the earth, and in any case it would be such a small portion of the earth's surface that it would give the child no help at all in visualizing the planet entire.

On the other hand, if you and your family were looking for a place to picnic, you would get very little help from a three-inch globe of the earth, for there is so much necessarily left out on such a globe that the jungles of Africa, the mountains of the Antarctic, and the deserts of central Asia would all look very much the same. For choosing a picnic spot you would want a map with more detail, very likely the topographic map showing the general area you had in mind. Such a map would help a great deal in locating a pond, a brook, a hillside, or whatever kind of spot your family might consider suitable for picnicking.

You will understand, of course, that we are talking not only of the kind of maps you can get in stores or at the library but the kind of maps you carry in your mind, which (if they are good maps) are also stored-up representations of something "out there." They are also, like the paper maps we first considered, incomplete. There is a lot left out even in the best of them. The question is not whether they are complete, for we know they never are, but whether they are good enough for the purpose, some particular purpose of ours.

For instance: In order to walk from your office to your apartment, if you are lucky enough to live within walking distance, you need some sort of map to guide you. Your feet are not able by themselves to choose which corners you turn and which streets to follow. Something in your brain must have a pattern, something that corresponds to the route you must take, and you must be able to call forth this pattern in order to find your way from office to apartment. Otherwise, even though it might be only a matter of four or five blocks, you would be lost, as indeed some people do become lost if they are suffering from some disease or injury that prevents their "re-calling" the direction.

For most of us the recalling of a previously learned map is so easy that it is done quite unconsciously. We simply walk home. We follow a well-defined and well-understood map that is sufficient for our need. It is not necessarily a very detailed map. You may walk the same route between office and home every day for five years, and still your map would not show you some of the obvious features along the way. You would certainly not know how many houses or buildings you passed in your daily walk. You might never have noticed a grocery store that you passed every day. You would probably never see the four hydrants at all. In this case you would be dealing with a very sketchy map, which is all that is required. There are other situations where a much more elaborate one would be needed. Suppose, for example, you were a policeman on this same beat. It would not be enough merely to know the route from an office to an apartment. You would need to know the location of police telephones, of hydrants, of the principal stores and buildings; and you would probably pick up and store a good deal of other information about the neighborhood, the people that lived in it, and spots where trouble was most likely to break out. In this kind of job you would need considerable detail in your map of the precinct.

But this would still be a matter of relative detail. There would still be a lot left out. No matter how long you walked the beat and no matter how carefully you observed the territory and stored up facts, you would never have complete knowledge of those few city blocks.

The late Irving J. Lee of Northwestern University once invited a group of Evanston police officers to study some of these matters, and for a start suggested that each policeman bring in a box of dirt, on which he would write a complete report. Several of the men faithfully dug a box of dirt, examined it and wrote reports. Lee accepted the reports and then pointed out how far from complete they really were. Did they include the weight, color, granular texture of the dirt? The chemical nature of its various components? Temperature, moisture content, specific gravity, electrical conductivity? This was only a start.

It becomes obvious that no one could possibly write a "complete" report on a box of dirt or on anything else. We have to settle for something less than complete. The expression which mathematicians use is "necessary and sufficient."

What might be necessary and sufficient for one job might not be for another. The measurement of the diameter of a ball bearing may be in tenths of thousandths of an inch. The measurement of a steel girder might have to be exact only to a quarter of an inch. The distance between New York and Bombay can be given with sufficient accuracy for most purposes if it is expressed to the nearest hundred miles. In estimating the value of the country's wheat crop for some purposes it may be necessary and sufficient to express it to the nearest million dollars. But in weighing a letter for airmail overseas necessary and sufficient is to the nearest half ounce.

It may be getting ahead of things a little to raise the question here of what might be considered necessary and sufficient information for trading in stocks. Certainly there are some people who jump into the market with such a glaring insufficiency of knowledge that we can predict with fair accuracy about how long it will take them to lose their capital. It may not be so obvious that there are others, hardly any better off, who collect unnecessary and irrelevant facts the way a pack rat collects bits of colored glass, beer bottle tops, and buttons. Too much information of the wrong sort not only adds nothing to clarifying understanding, it can confuse the issue so hopelessly that it is impossible to see what is going on at all.

This point we will consider in a more specific way later. For now it is important to note that

1. The impressions of things in our minds are not the things themselves. (The map is not the territory.)
2. The map is never as detailed and accurate as the reality it represents.
3. Some maps are more detailed than others, and which map is best for a particular purpose depends on what we are trying to do, that is, it depends on the nature of the job at hand.
4. A map that covers too much ground and is too sketchy in the detail may be inadequate, and a map that is too detailed may be crowded with confusing and superfluous data.

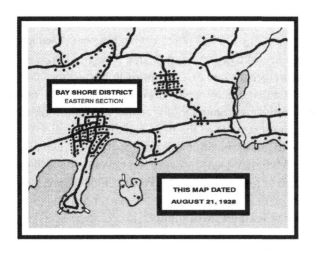

CHAPTER 12   DATING THE MAP

Maps are abstractions based on perceived features of reality. They are useful to us as long as we remember that they are symbolic representations and that they must be referred constantly to the territory "out there" to confirm their validity. A map made in 1650 may have been true and accurate then and be of historical interest now, but if we're trying to find the turnpike to Boston, it's not going to help us much.

If we use the word *map* to cover any diagram, photograph, plan, description, or mental image that represents something else and has a one-for-one correspondence with certain features of the something else, you will understand that this includes not only all the snapshots and blueprints and specification sheets but also all the stored-up impressions in our brains that fill this bill. In fact, although we may speak of maps at times in the sense of printed sheets of paper, more often we will be considering the kind of maps that are not actually printed except as they are impressed on our memory. While we can't pass these around for our friends to examine, we can take them out for our own private examination whenever we

47

want to; and as you know, you carry a vast number of these maps, a really staggering library of them, in your head all the time. You can, without the slightest effort, recall the floor layout of Public School #4, or at least those portions of it that you traversed during your servitude in third grade. You know where the coatroom should be and where to look for the door to the hall, the shortest route to the playground, the location of the washrooms, and how to get to the principal's office. In your own room you can see where Miss McFarland sat, and very likely your map will provide you fair remembrance of just what Miss McFarland looked like. You may also be able to fill in on the map the names of various boys and girls down the rows of seats, or at least a few of them.

You have maps covering your own home, probably in very great detail, and maps of the streets and stores in your neighborhood. All of these maps are constructs of your mind; they are obviously not the places themselves, and they did not come into your mind as direct experience but as nerve impulses from your various sensory receptors. The map (or memory) is something you have built out of the various bits of information from outside, which you can then project into consciousness almost as if you were again viewing the original scene. As a matter of fact, sometimes if you close your eyes and think of past experiences, you can come very close to seeing these things as visual images.

We say "past experiences." If these are memories, based on actual observation, they must be past, for they are obviously not of the present nor of the future. They were seen (or mapped, if you will) previously.

It is a sad thing, and all of us have been disturbed by this discovery, to realize that Public School No. 4 was torn down ten years ago to make room for the larger Consolidated School. That Miss McFarland died year before last. It is a very hard thing to look at that schoolroom in your mind's eye and realize that those children are dead, those familiar faces are gone irrevocably, even though there are some grownup people around town who have the same names. The picture of the schoolroom is a valid map, but it is not a map of the here and now.

A friend of mine showed me a map of the part of the country we live in. It was a valid map made by a competent and observant craftsman who was familiar with the territory. There were a number of recognizable features: the Connecticut River, the Holyoke range of mountains, Springfield, the road from Boston. But on this map there were some rather unfamiliar features. "Indian camp here" is marked at a point that would be, roughly, the center of the town of Palmer. There are references to springs of drinking water, areas marked "good hunting here," a spot inscribed "Josiah Chapin's cabin."

I haven't the slightest doubt that these markings on the map correctly correspond with the territory as observed. I might have a question as to whether some of them are pertinent to me in my particular manner of living, but as to their being an honest record of fact, they ring true. In other words, the map is a good one. But it needs one more detail: In the lower right hand corner the map carries its date: 1650.

This was not a false map. Presumably it was correctly made from accurate observations at the time. Furthermore, it was probably adequate for the purpose for which it was intended, no doubt to guide a traveler across the country and give him the information he needed to find his way and take care of his needs. It might have been an inadequate map, even in 1650, for some other purpose, perhaps for a land survey in connection with a colonial charter or an Indian treaty. As we said, the amount of detail required depends on the job to be done.

Certainly, as a map of the territory today this map is both inaccurate and inadequate. Certain features, such as Chapin's cabin, the Indian camp, and the good hunting country, are no longer correct. Other currently important aspects of the countryside are not to be seen on the old map. There is no turnpike, Westover Field does not appear, nor can we find the line of either the Boston and Albany or the New Haven railroad. But (and note this) the map is not entirely false. The Connecticut River is still correctly represented, and the mountains of the Holyoke range are still in the same relative position. Springfield is still properly indicated.

The important things in studying this map, or any other map, are to know whether the map was a good one in the first place, whether it is adequate for our particular purposes, and what essential changes have occurred since the map was made. In other words, we must date the map. Generally speaking, taking one map against another of approximately equal and similar detail, the map carrying the most recent date will most correctly represent the territory as it exists now.

It should be noted every now and then that there is no identity in the world of reality. Resemblances, yes; similarities, yes. But since we perceive through what we abstract and since we abstract only a very small part of all the facts in any external reality, the identity we sometimes assume is illusion-based merely on the fact that our rather sketchy maps may have shown only certain features we have noted. We must keep in mind that there is always a great deal more that we have overlooked.

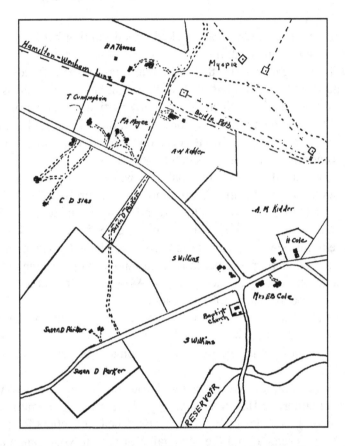

In much of our work we will be dealing with maps that are abstractions based on perceived features of reality. We can deal with these maps and they can be useful to us just so long as we bear in mind that they are symbolic representations, and that we can set up one-to-one correspondences between them and the perceived reality. Whether the reality itself is real is not a question we have to consider in this study.

In this case we are concerned with what we will accept as an external reality, as of 1650 and the present. We know, or should know by now, the limitations of such maps. We know that we cannot properly ascribe to the maps any features not specifically comprehended in them. We cannot assume that we know all about the territory, then or now. We cannot assume that the territory is now what the later map showed it to be. When we are dealing with symbolic representations (and all of our thinking comes into this category), we must recognize the limits that apply and not try to fill in the gaps out of pure fancy.

CHAPTER 13   BRINGING DATA UP-TO-DATE

Maps carry more than objective information. They also carry judgments, sounds, smells. They are multi-dimensional and we acquire them from reading and stories as much as from our own direct experience. A "map" of New Haven Railroad stock bought in 1955 that still valued it at $39 a share would have to be regularly updated with more current price data. We do the same with all our images, updating the data pertinent to our needs.

I have been trying to build, rather carefully, a picture of how all this mapmaking comes about and what it means. No doubt this has made the reading dull, and your own quick mind has leaped ahead of the text. You must already have realized that the map of Room 12 in Public School No. 4 with Miss McFarland sitting up front and smirking at the class, carries also an element of judgment, perhaps, in this case, that Miss McFarland was rather a nasty old witch. Maps can carry more than geographical data.

You may have had a picture of the New Haven Railroad (a map) in your head dated, say, June 1955. The map might include a judgment as to the value of New Haven stock, and this value might carry the price of $39 per share. Be sure you have your mental map dated, and be sure you look at the date! If you recalled this map in, say, December 1957, many features of the railroad would look the same. But be sure you look at the date, for the value you placed on New Haven stock is still to be seen at $39 per share unless you have updated the map. The June 1955 map is not now correct in this feature, for in December 1957 the price should read $5. If you want this part of your map to have a close correspondence with its territory (in this case the price of the stock), you will have to revise the map continuously to adjust to every fluctuation.

It's true that we do have to adjust, revise, and correct maps to bring them up to date. But this does not mean that we have to tear up the old maps entirely. All that is necessary is to change the features that are pertinent to our needs when there have been significant changes in those features.

The constructs we have been calling maps include rather more than lines and surfaces and visual elements. They can include things we hear. We can recall the tune of a song, just as though we had a musical score (a map) of the song written out somewhere in our head. Our maps can also include, at least to some degree, odors and tastes and touch sensations, for these things too can be somewhat remembered and re-experienced.

For the most part the maps we have been speaking of so far could be referred to as descriptions, for whether they outline a school yard, a familiar street, a favorite tune, or the odor of hyacinths and brown earth in early spring, they are descriptive of something we perceive as "out there" or as having been out there once upon a time.

All the data from which these maps were made came in through the senses, the original data. They were all based originally on experiences or contacts with the world "out there," but not necessarily on our own personal experience with the particular place or thing or tune or odor, and not necessarily "here and now." Some of your knowledge has come to you by word of mouth from someone else—and some you have learned by reading it in a book.

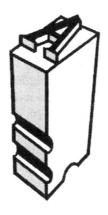

CHAPTER 14   THE 26 LEAD SOLDIERS

**When man succeeded in inventing writing and subsequently print-
ing, with its 26 lead soldiers (the letters of the alphabet), he gave
humans the ability to communicate a map of a map, the remembered
experience of a picture or story. With printing "time binding," the
transmission of knowledge and experience across generations,
becomes possible.**

I am not sure how much study has been made of the response of animals
to experience once removed, by which I mean a picture instead of a real
landscape, a recording instead of a voice, a stimulation of a taste bud artificially instead of by a certain quality in the food, etc. I am reasonably
sure that the recorded voice of the master would be recognized by a dog,
and recorded commands would be obeyed, and no doubt animals can be
presented with visual scenes that their eyes will accept as valid, that
which they would recognize.

If we call the descriptive construct built from direct experience an abstraction, then the descriptive construct we (or animals) get from a picture or a recorded voice is an abstraction of an abstraction, a map of a map.

But the ability of animals to abstract is limited. The very smartest animal cannot abstract as far as the stupidest man. Mankind has developed a very wonderful device that is, perhaps, the characteristic that most distinguishes him from the rest of the animal kingdom. Whereas the animal can abstract, that is, it can see and hear and use its other senses and store these abstractions and recall them for later use (the dog can remember the way to the store, it can recognize its master, it can identify the mailman) it has no great powers of communication with other animals. So far as; these descriptive abstractions are concerned, you can say it has virtually no power to communicate them to another. Also, it has no way of setting down these abstractions in symbolic form so that the knowledge, perhaps forgotten, can later be re-stored in the mind.

The wonderful device that man has invented is language in its broadest sense. Through language, the use of symbols, it is possible to transmit descriptive maps from one mind to another. By talking, one man is able to convey to another the details of how to get to Westfield, or what the facade of the Natural History Museum looks like. By making certain sounds, he can send out data that another man can hear and translate into pictures in his mind, which can be good and useful descriptive maps of a territory.

When you come to think of it, this is a miracle. It is much more of a miracle than television, for language is a process of transmitting pictures, floor plans, diagrams without any visual aids, through the medium of sound alone, without any man-made mechanical equipment whatever— and it has been going on for thousands of years!

Not only that. It is not only possible to invent sound signals for talking, it is possible to invent visual signals for writing. Symbols that can be drawn on paper or scratched in clay can be worked out so as to have a correspondence either with the sounds of talking or with the objects represented, such as a hammer, a house, or a dog. This further extension of language makes it possible for man to communicate not only here and now but also not here and not now. A spoken word, a whisper, a shout can only be heard so far, a few feet or a few hundred feet at the most. Its dying echoes fade away in fractions of a second. The voice must be immediate and proximate, unless it is relayed by some device such as telephone or radio. But the invention of a written language opens up an enormously larger world. Man can not only talk to a man here, he can write a letter to a man a thousand miles away, and the thoughts in his head will be unfolded and disclosed to that distant communicant when the messenger delivers a scroll of paper or the inscribed brick of clay.

More than that: By means of the map system we call language, man can leap forward across the centuries and communicate with his own great-great-great-great-grandchildren, or backward to share the thoughts of his great-great-great-great-grandfather. No animal can do that. Man can, to express it inelegantly, pick his great-grandfather's brains. With the written language the recorded experience of every man becomes the heritage of all mankind.

Do you realize how big a heritage this is? It is the secret of how and why you are a member of the dominant race of creatures on this earth. For the written language is the transmission belt for "time binding." Without language whatever knowledge an individual might grasp would endure only as long as he himself lived. While he might be able to pass on by word of mouth some of this knowledge to his offspring, such knowledge was bound to be limited in extent; and over the years it would tend to become twisted, garbled.

Even where such knowledge was passed on orally without distortion or loss, it would be likely to become ritualized and lose its meaning in monotonous, sterile repetition. But when it is written down, it stays there, exactly as it was set forth by the author. The material can be accumulated. There is no need for memorization or repetition. And there is no limit to the amount of material that can be preserved.

Written knowledge does not stop with the passing on by rote of a fixed body of information. Successive generations add their contributions, building on the experience of their forebears and using the material gathered by previous generations. With the invention of printing the 26 lead soldiers of the alphabet opened the whole world of books so that all who would might read.

This points the way to at least the possibility of a much broader freedom of thought, for since the scholars are no longer chained to the necessary job of memorizing and passing on a body of ancient lore, there is time to digest older material at leisure, to reexamine the evidence in the external world, to compare the maps as described in writings, with the here and now of observed facts in the external world.

Under these conditions, knowledge no longer remains the dread esoteric property of the temple priests and magicians, but becomes the common property of everybody. Also, it becomes enormously more flexible, enormously more adaptable, and enormously more useful.

Written language makes it possible for us to take advantage of the wisdom of dead men, to have communication with thinkers in each period of history, and yet it leaves us free to accept, adapt, or reject any material depending on whether it appears to fit our present needs.

CHAPTER 15   MAPS OF MAPS

When we abstract from a picture or a story, we are making a map of a map. Inherent in the ability of the original map to communicate is the common agreement of humans to label classes of objects, such as "dogs." Depending on the level of detail we want, we can employ higher-order abstractions—going from "dog" to "animal."

We do the same thing with "securities," which in lower order and more detail become "stocks" and "bonds" and then the "S&P 500," the "Dow Jones," and finally "Fruehauf Trailer."

When we read a story about a young prospector riding his burro up the dusty canyon, we have a picture in our minds. We can see the gray cliffs rising sheer on the left. We can see the clear mountain stream swirling and tumbling over its rocky bed to our right. We can hear the splash of the water; our throats are parched from the alkali dust, and we become thirsty.

We have probably stirred into this picture all sorts of bits of abstracted information: the sights and sounds of western canyons as we have learned to know them from the westerns in movies and television, from other stories we have read, and (who knows?) perhaps from our own memories of visits to these western areas.

But we are experiencing, too, the particular topography of the particular canyon our author was describing. He had abstracted a canyon. He had set down some details of this abstraction symbolically (by writing words on paper), and now his words suggest to us the bits of information we have stored away in our own mind.

We recall our own mental images. We see a canyon; we hear the water in the brook; we may even react to the picture by feeling thirsty. It may be a very realistic scene that lies before us in our mind's eye.

In this case we're abstracting not from external reality, but from another abstraction, the story we are reading. It's like abstracting from a picture except that we're dealing with verbal symbols instead of pictorial representations. And, of course, since our own memories are not the same as those of the author of the story, the mental image of the canyon that you may create in your mind may be quite different in a great number of details from the canyon envisaged by the author. In fact, since each reader is free to make up his own picture, there may be as many different perceptions of that canyon in the story as there are readers.

If we call our perception of external reality a map, then we could properly call our perception of the situation and the surroundings in a story we read a map of a map. It is one step further away from the external reality. You realize, of course, that it is only because we can make these maps of maps that we are able to pass on to others, as we do verbally in a short story or a novel, some part of what we have abstracted ourselves.

When we have observed a number of similar features in several different objects, we usually attach a verbal label that means to us "anything that has these common features." It is only by using some of these label-names that a writer can write understandably at all. For while we may not know his particular canyon, we do have some idea of what a canyon should be like.

There may be many somewhat different things under one label. We know very well that the Third National Bank Building is not the Whitney Building, but they both have a certain number of floors with wide corridors and offices along them; they both have elevators and mail chutes, etc., so we call them by the same name, "office buildings," along with other structures of this general type. When we speak of office buildings to someone else, we expect that he also will have a generalized picture of a structure with these features. But it is very important to realize that the label "office building" does not describe or designate any particular office building. It could refer to any office building whatever, anywhere, at any time. Therefore, when we say office building, we cannot expect that our friend will have a very precise idea of just how a certain building looks. We would have to specify the details at a lower level of abstraction. We would have to describe the building, name how many floors it had, what color it was, and many other features; and, to make ourselves perfectly plain, we might want to include the street address.

If we talk and think mainly in high-order abstractions (generalities), we may be unable to communicate just what we mean. People who refer to bull markets and bear markets, or to Republicans, or to "eggheads," are using words that are so "wide" that they can mean many different things to different people. It's no wonder we can't agree on the facts of a case if we talk only about high-order generalities.

Of course, the most serious danger is that we ourselves will fail to discriminate. We often act on a generality like "dogs are friendly," and get bitten because we looked only at the label "dogs: friendly" and not at the atypical beast that charged out of the house at us.

Dogs are friendly as a rule and as a broad generality, but this doesn't mean that we can project that idea to cover each and every dog. In reality it is always a particular, individual dog that we have to deal with. It is also true that we have to deal with a particular individual woman, not women as a class, and we have to buy or sell a particular stock, not stocks in general.

You will realize that we build our mental files in stages or levels of abstraction. First, we observe Bozo and Zorro as individuals. Then we classify them as dogs. At this stage we have a broader picture of the common characteristics of the class "dog," but the word dog leaves out some of the particular details. The label points to the similarities between Bozo and Zorro, but not to the differences.

If we recognize that there are some similarities among all dogs and all goats and all lions, we can group these creatures together under a high-order label "quadrupeds." We have now included more territory, but again we have lost some detail. If we move up from quadrupeds to mammals, the label is of a higher order yet, and includes whales, platypuses, and your sister-in-law. If I say, "Bring me a mammal," you would be able to fill the bill by bringing me a whale, a cow, a giraffe, or any other creature you include under this label. You would not be able to tell the difference between one and another, nor to know which one I really wanted, just from the label alone.

This is one of the drawbacks of using groups in studying stocks. It may be useful to know what the rails are doing as a class, but you must ultimately deal with a particular stock, and the term rail leaves out all the differences (many of which are important) between, say, Canadian Pacific and Union Pacific.

You can carry the abstracting and labeling process higher and higher to any level you want. If mammals doesn't cover enough ground, you can set up the very large category of animals. And so on. In the market this would be like lumping bonds, warrants, stocks, debentures, etc., all under "securities." It covers a lot of ground all right, but it doesn't give you much specific information.

What we're talking about here is like using your camera. The close-up view shows a great deal of detail. When you stand back to get in more of the group, you lose some of the details. If you stand way back, so as to include the entire 2nd Battalion of the State Guard, you will hardly be able to pick out Jim Stowell at all because you can't see the details of individual men. They will all look very much alike.

CHAPTER 16   THE PIGEONHOLES

The use of labels and symbols and abstractions can lead to unnecessary conflict. A fight over two maps—Joe says Al's house has three chimneys and Sam says it has two—can be settled with fists or by taking a ride to Al's and counting chimneys, by checking the territory.

To repeat: the name you call something is not the thing itself. What volumes of police records involving assault and battery might be avoided if citizens fully realized that! Whether the name is shouted across the bar room or silently projected from the mind, the obvious fact remains, that the name is not the thing. Obvious, like an elephant in your front hall . . . but like many elephants of one sort or another, frequently overlooked.

No doubt there are some of your acquaintances who think of you as "wise and noble friend." Others may regard you as "an odd fish, but a fairly intelligent sort." There may well be a few who look on you as "a stupid fool." It's a fair conclusion that you are not *all* of these things, at least that they do not fully and accurately describe you. For if maps (any maps) conflict with one another, they cannot all be correct; and if a map conflicts with the territory, if it does not correspond with the facts, then it, not the territory, must be in error.

Of course, it is quite possible that these various opinions of you may be correct from various points of view and with respect to certain activities. You might be quite wise in your law practice, for example, but quite stupid when it came to buying stocks. Or you might have appeared quite smart on one occasion, but quite stupid on another. This would be a matter of dating the maps, in which case there would be no conflict.

Since the words we use to ticket things are only symbols, short-hand labels, several people might use different words to indicate similar objects. In New York we speak of "the elevator"; in London, it's "the lift." We use different labels. In other countries other labels are used; we have different languages. Right in our own country, there are sectional idioms. Men in various trades and professions have technical terms that have a special meaning to them in a particular line of work. Sometimes men from different crafts encounter misunderstandings that arise on account of the different use of words.

Even in ordinary conversation labels can get us into trouble. In the 1940s it was a tribute to a man's integrity to say that he was "absolutely square." In current teen-age talk to refer to someone as absolutely square would amount to a declaration of social ostracism.

Since the map, name, symbol, whatever we use to represent reality, cannot directly change the physical character of what is being represented but merely stands for it, we should keep in mind always the superiority of the thing itself whenever there is a conflict. Thus, we can put Robinson's contract in the folder marked Contracts-Smith, but this does not change the contents of the Robinson contract. We could call all cows pigs and if everyone understood that "pig" meant a large brown and black creature with horns that mooed and gave milk, there would be no real conflict. All that is necessary is to know (that is, understand) what we are talking about. This applies whether we are talking to someone else or to our own self.

When we set up symbolic maps, whether verbal or otherwise, that conflict with each other or that do not correspond with the facts in a territory or that do not correspond with any demonstrable territory, and where we act on the basis of such maps as if we were dealing with a real and valid map of something or somewhere, then we are headed for serious confusion. In a great many cases it's possible to get rid of the confusion very easily. It's really wonderful how many arguments and misunderstandings could be settled quickly and painlessly if we only took the obvious step. Sometimes one wonders how people can possibly go on being confused or hostile when the answer is so simple and so ready at hand.

All that's necessary is to go and have a look at the territory. Joe says Al's house has three brick chimneys. Sam says it only has two brick chimneys. Before it's necessary to call the police or the hospital, why not all go out together and count the number of brick chimneys on the house? If Joe's map and Sam's map of this situation don't agree, examine the territory.

There cannot be any conflict "out there." It may be that Joe and Sam both had reasons for defending their maps. They had seen the house, or looked at a picture of it, or someone had told them about it. Perhaps Joe had seen it, but he may not have observed the chimneys carefully, or may be confusing it with another house he saw last week. Perhaps he did see and count correctly, but one of the chimneys has been torn down (this, by the way, would be a matter of dating—his map is obsolete). Perhaps he misunderstood what house was meant and has recalled another house entirely (wrong map). Or there may be two Al's, and Joe is thinking of Al Brown's house while Sam is thinking about Al Thompson's house (they are not referring to the same territory).

Regardless of what maps they have, if Joe and Sam go out together and count how many brick chimneys Al Thompson's house has now, they are not likely to continue their dispute. Their maps will be in agreement.

Unfortunately, in too many cases men continue to argue a point far into the night and perhaps come to blows over it without taking the one easy, direct, and conclusive step of taking a look at the territory.

CHAPTER 17   THE LABELS

The confusion of high-order labels ("office papers") and low order labels ("Jones Corporation Contract") can result in ordering "Bessie" and getting "the cow" Bossie. This might appear to be more of a social problem than an investment problem, but when we are invested in Fruehauf Trailer, but tracking the Dow Jones group the results can give us some distress. A wide-angle camera shot gets all the members of the class, but not much detail on any one person.

As we have seen, you're not very likely to get badly confused when it's possible to verify a simple fact by counting or checking the territory by observation. People can get into plenty of trouble by not taking these simple precautions. Unfortunately, it's not possible in all cases to make such a simple checkup. One of the big causes of misunderstanding is the use of a high-order label as if it were a low-order label.

By low-order we mean something very specific. For example, Bessie (referring to a single, particular cow). Or James Edward MacPhee, Jr., who lives at 24 Sheridan Avenue. These are references to particular, definite things, just as is "The Jones Corporation contract No. A-15-62-X, dated March 5, 1958."

There are all sorts of high-order abstractions for which we have verbal labels. The word "cow" is one of these. It doesn't tell us anything about the particular markings, conformation, or disposition of Bessie; in fact, the word leaves out all differences among cows, so that if I asked you to bring me a cow, you could bring any one of millions of various sizes, colors, and shapes, and each one would accurately come under the label cow. What this means is that "cow" doesn't describe in very much detail. About all it does is to differentiate between the world of cows and all other animals and things.

In the same way "James Edward MacPhee, Jr. who lives at 24 Sheridan Avenue" points out a particular man (except, of course, in unlikely circumstance that there might be another James Edward MacPhee, Jr., living at 24 Sheridan Avenue). But the word man leaves it wide open to include every adult male member of the human race. If I am looking for a man, my search will be very easy. Any man whatever is equally good, because the word man covers any one of them. This will not, I grant, help you very much in locating your brother-in-law at the railway station, or in picking out a good operator for an overhead crane, or in capturing the person who held up the Second National Bank last night. We have put everything you could call "man" into one of the pigeonholes. So far as the label on the pigeonhole is concerned, they are all the same.

Where we really get into trouble is where we forget that the high-order abstraction is only a label designating a whole group of pigeonholes, into which we are putting several, perhaps many, different kinds of things. If we fail to specify which particular cow is going to be delivered, even though we have in mind Bessie, we may find that we have purchased Bossie, who is just as much of a cow as Bessie but not nearly the milk producer. If we confuse one man with another man—well, half the literature of the world, from Jacob and Esau on, owes its plots to this particular kind of confusion.

If you have ever worked in an office you know that it may be quite a job to locate the Jones Corporation contract No. A-15-62-X if you have to go through the entire file labeled Contracts. If we do not tell our secretary very carefully just which contract we want, and describe it very precisely in "low-order" terms so that it couldn't possibly be any other one, she is very likely to send the wrong one entirely and we may lose a valuable client.

That sounds simple enough. You can't say "send a cow" and expect the cow you get to be exactly like Bessie. You can't employ (or marry) any "man" and expect him to come out exactly like some other man you knew somewhere once (or possibly dreamed up out of your imagination). And you can't reach into the file marked Contracts, send off the first paper you grab, and expect that it will be the one document you need in the Jones Corporation matter.

It's so simple to keep things straight, in their proper places. Yet people confuse them, and then seem quite surprised when the results are unsatisfactory. They confuse big, wide, general, high-order words, with precise, narrow, specific low-order words. The confusion may be tragic.

If you think that the things I'm struggling to set down clearly and plainly are trivial, consider the price the world has paid for prejudice and racial and religious persecution. None of the murders, pogroms, lynchings, and campaigns of extermination resulting from these projected hates could have occurred were it not for the confusion of levels of abstraction. You know how often the projecting of labels as if they were detailed descriptions has resulted in expensive errors in the market. When, for instance, an investor projects images of "safety," "stability," etc. to securities that he labels "bonds" and associates with conservative investment policy, he may find himself loaded with highly speculative bonds that are quite different from what he had expected.

If we project a name and treat it as if it were a description of reality, we should make sure that we know just how far the name describes that reality and in what detail. We should not ascribe more detail to the reality than is covered by the definition. Wherever possible we should check the reality to see whether the facts are what the definition says or implies. Most of us fail repeatedly to do this. We fail to look at the thing at all, even when it is so easy to do so, and fall victim to a misconception resulting from regarding the name as if it were, in fact, the thing.

If men took these simple steps there would not be so many bankruptcies, nor so many fist fights, nor so many distressing pages of history detailing the persecutions, massacres, and extermination of men and women and children.

Perhaps a thought has come to you, as it has to many of us at various times: If men have turned against categories of men whom they regard as different from themselves and inferior and intolerable, could we not solve the problem by moving to a higher abstraction? Couldn't we quite properly say, "All of these groups, including ourselves, are 'men.' Let us forget our differences." This is the great plea of many humanitarian movements: "Forget your differences! Recognize that we are all 'men'! Let us be tolerant, and kindly, and cooperative in view of our common humanity!"

This is plausible when you first hear it. It is greatly to be desired that all men can live in one world in peace and friendship. By putting all men into one pigeonhole we have wiped out the differences and settled all problems. Unfortunately, it is not a very practical answer, any more than it is a good answer in stock trading to forget the differences and pretend that all stocks are the same and identical with an average.

It doesn't work to dump everybody in the same bin and put the same label on it. It wouldn't make your filing any easier if you put all the files in one big box labeled Office Papers. The label is all right, but like all labels it leaves out details. These particular labels are very high-order ones. They leave out so much it isn't possible to see the facts at all. Putting a label like Office Papers on all the memos, contracts, bills, letters, checks, etc., leaves out the details by which we can tell them apart.

It's the old story of the camera. Get far enough back to include the entire cadet regiment, and you can't tell which fellow is which. They all look alike. But that doesn't make them all alike. And it doesn't make humanity all alike to put it all in one bin. We don't even get very good results by putting the label Christian on a category of our population. Changing the map doesn't change the territory, and this business of labeling does not resolve the differences between Baptists, and Roman Catholics, and Episcopalians.

It's my feeling that the best hope of understanding reality, whether it is the stock market, the religious community, or the races of mankind, is to move closer to reality, not to retreat further and further into higher and higher-order labels. "James Edward MacPhee, Jr. who lives at 24 Sheridan Avenue" we can go and talk to. We can take pictures of him, we can get to know him and his children and his neighbors, and we can make a pretty good and pretty detailed and pretty useful map of him, one that will tell us a lot about what he's like, how he lives, what he thinks, what sort of guy he is. If we describe him just as a Bostonian, the detailed picture fades. He merges with all the other Bostonians in that pigeonhole. If we say he's a citizen of Massachusetts, that gives us a larger and vaguer picture. If we classify him as an American, it becomes vaguer yet. And if we ultimately lump him in with all humanity under the index man, he loses all detail and has no distinguishing characteristics at all. If we did this, we would have gained a fine broad map, but we would have lost most of the reality.

I have seen how far astray investors can go when they begin to attribute details to individual stocks on the basis of characteristics they assign to the averages. Just as you should go and take a look at a particular man if you want to know something about that man, so you should go and take a look at a particular stock if you want to know how that stock is acting. We cannot obliterate differences between stocks (or between people) just by putting generalized labels on them. We cannot make them all the same (except verbally).

You will find the same kind of problem in religion; in the economic clashes between various individuals and groups; and, in smaller scale but of no less importance, within family and social groups.

Someone might object at this point, "Are you trying to understand the stock market, or save the world?" Perhaps the best answer to that would be to point out that we all need all the understanding we can get in every department of life. If understanding the forces that operate in the market helps us to understand ourselves and to see more clearly the sources of family strife, racial and religious tension, and world conflict, this would be a net gain. If understanding the forces that operate in human affairs and the principles that govern them helps us in our investment program, that also would be a net gain. We are interested in personal survival and progress, but we also have a very real stake in world peace and better human relations. It seems to me that helping to save the world is part of everybody's job, and worth whatever thought and effort he puts into it.

CHAPTER 18   NOT QUITE THE SAME

No thing is the same as any other thing—except in a theoretical world. In the actual world it is virtually impossible to find two things the same, marble, flower, ball bearing, whatever. In fact, important-ly, the thing itself in this moment is not the same thing it was an instant ago. Without entering into theoretical physics, Fruehauf Trailer the stock is different today from what it was yesterday.

We have played a game at our house, a game about things. It all started with one of the routine outbreaks of sibling hostility between Johnny, Louisy, and Abigail. The particular bones of contention in the case at hand were three yellow pencils, one of which belonged to each of the children. Through some chance the three were put into the same drawer in the kitchen table, at which they ate, played, and fought their battles. Johnny claimed that Louisy had his pencil. Louisy loudly denied this, and said that, anyway, they were "all the same."

Eventually the issue came up before a sort of drumhead family coun-cil. Obviously, the root of the contention was whether or not the pencils were all the same. It took only a few moments to show that one of the pencils had been sharpened down a little shorter than the other two; and that one of them had been chewed a little, just back of the eraser. There could be no question about the fact that the pencils were not the same. I ventured the opinion that no thing was the same as any other thing.

Two same-looking marbles were produced. A little study showed that the interior convolutions of color were quite different. Two flowers were produced from an African violet plant on the kitchen window sill. It took a rather close examination to discover that the petals of one were definitely longer than those of the other, and that the color was a shade different. Two coffee beans appeared much the same, but after study everyone admitted that there were slight differences that could be observed under the magnifying glass.

Wherever we looked, we could not find two things the same. To point up the moral or point of the study as applied to the human race, I offered the thought that there had never been a child exactly like Johnny Magee, nor one like Louisy, nor one like Abigail before, not in the whole history of the human race.

I did not press the further idea that none of these children was the same at any two times. Not the same last year as this year. Not the same yesterday as today. Not the same a hundredth of a second ago as now. But it is a fact, and perfectly obvious when you come to think of it, that nothing is the same as something else, and nothing is identical with itself from one measurable moment to the next.

Whereas the ancient philosophers took it for granted as an obvious truth that A is A, a good many people recognize today that what may be valid in the purely abstract, purely symbolic field of mathematics is not necessarily true in the world of real things. As a matter of fact, one of the great minds of our century, Albert Einstein, commented on this very point. In effect, what he said was that insofar as a statement was valid in a theoretical, abstract, mathematical sense, it was not true in a down-to-earth, specific, and real sense; and that insofar as it was true at the low order of observed reality, it was not valid in the strict and absolute sense of a mathematical formula.

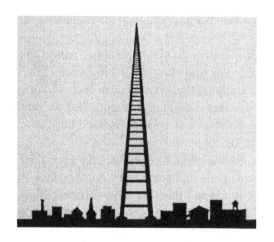

CHAPTER 19   UP AND DOWN THE LADDER

Fortunately we are not constricted to high order maps or low order maps. We can use the level of detail that suits our purpose—and we should.

This brings us to a question that must have already formed itself in your mind. Is it "better" to look at things specifically, close up, as they are in the external world of reality, or is it "better" to see the broad outlines of classes and categories in their entirety. We know that the close-up view shows more detail, and we know that the broad panorama covers a greater scope, but in the first case, we lose perspective; in the second, we lose detail.

There is no rule that we must look only at close-ups, or exclusively at panoramas. Since we have the means for seeing things from many points of view, why not use all of them? There are times when it is most useful to have a detailed map of a small piece of territory, as when we are looking for a good picnic site. There are other times when we need a view of the entire country, as when we are planning a system of continental highways. The important thing is to know exactly what kind of a map or word or other symbol we are using, and not to attribute to it meanings that it does not have.

For example, it is a very good way to study nature to take a particular animal, say a raccoon, and study its habits, its growth, its way of living. By a close-up study of this sort you can learn firsthand the facts as they are in reality for this individual raccoon. But we could make some serious errors if we attributed all of the observed facts about this raccoon to raccoons in general.

On the other hand, we might have collected a good deal of knowledge about many raccoons, facts that seem to be more or less characteristic of the entire breed. It is a good thing to have a broad, higher abstraction. However, we could make serious errors, too, if we regarded this panorama of raccoons as a close-up and expected every raccoon to look and act like the generalized raccoon in every respect.

If you studied only one raccoon, you would not know very much about the life of raccoons collectively. If you had abstracted only the common factors in the raccoon tribe, you would not know the special features of this particular raccoon. You need both maps, and you need to know which is which.

There is a place for speaking of men in the broad sense, and a place for speaking of Harold W. Ericson in the specific sense. It is very important to know whether you are speaking of the class or the individual.

We can go up and down the scale of abstractions, using a symbol or map as broad or as detailed as we need for our purpose in the case at hand. We will not have any confusion so long as we keep clearly in mind just what we are talking about or thinking about, and so long as we realize that we are using symbols, words, maps, that are not the things they represent.

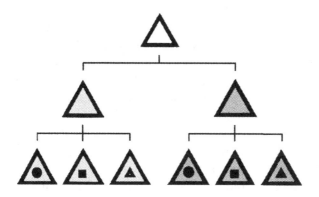

CHAPTER 20   SIMILARITIES—AND DIFFERENCES

The closer up we examine territories, the more we see differences. The further back (or the higher the level), the more we emphasize similarities, as in a group picture we see the similarities of the people rather than their individual differences. A quarrel about General Motors will soon resolve itself into talking about GM the company and GM the stock, two are different things. To confuse the two because of labels can result in a bad investment. In fact, a company can be doing fine (or appear to be) while its stock is heading south.

Some pages back we noted that the broad panoramic view of the student regiment showed all the cadets looking very alike. As a matter of fact, as we know, they were all wearing similar uniforms, were about the same age, and for the most part shared the same interests. There were, in other words, a good many genuine similarities. That is why it is so important to keep in mind at all times, that this is a broad picture, not a very detailed one. It would be very easy to confuse Cadet Sanderson with Cadet Jamison; they look so very much alike in the picture. But we know that

Cadet Sanderson is very different from Cadet Jamison. Jamison has dark hair, a rather long nose, and flat ears. Sanderson is blond, has a snub nose, and his ears stick out. None of these differences can be seen in the group picture. The broad picture, the higher abstraction, calls attention to similarities but does not show differences. Large-size cabinet photographs of Jamison and Sanderson, on the other hand, would show clearly the differences, but they would not point up the similarities.

It is this way with maps, too, as you know. A map of a considerable area of countryside will show the general shape of the terrain. It will not, however, show the special features of a particular spot and the differences between one spot and another.

The same thing is true of words. Like photographs, like maps, they can describe single things, in which case the various descriptions will emphasize the differences: "this six-inch yellow 2-B El Dorado pencil" and "that eight-inch, green 4-H Dixon pencil." Or they can refer, at a higher level of abstraction, to "pencils," in which case they call attention to the similarities of these two objects.

Where things are so much alike that one is substantially as good as another for our purpose, there is no need to be too specific. "Gimme a cigarette" means any cigarette in the package. They are all very similar, and for all practical purposes they are equivalent. So long as we understand that they are not really identical, it's more convenient to consider them all alike.

It all depends on whether the differences are important or not. Very often they are not. If you were to buy 100 shares of Reynolds Tobacco stock, it would make no particular difference to you whether you received certificate number A-4637-WR or number A-385i-XB. On the other hand it would make a great deal of difference whether you received a certificate for 100 shares of Reynolds Tobacco or 100 shares of Reynolds Metals. There is a verbal similarity here that could result in a faulty identification. Most of the mistakes in the world, the funny ones and the sad ones, come about because of confusion of one thing with another.

These confusions are not very likely to occur at the levels of direct observation of reality or at the level of low abstraction, since here the maps (or the words) are usually very detailed and specific. The confusions happen at the higher levels of abstraction. It is at these levels that we begin to move back, away from the close reality, and we lose detail. Rather different things begin to look more alike. If we go far enough, very different things will look the same, and we will have the feeling they are identical. In other words, we can very easily mistake something for something else because of the similarities.

That is what happens when you rush up to a familiar figure on Main Street and slap him on the back and greet him, "Hi, Charlie. I didn't know you were back in town," only to slink away in embarrassment when the supposed friend turns around, and is clearly not Charlie at all but a total stranger. You had, of course, noticed, perhaps quite unconsciously, some features of this stranger that you linked with Charlie, perhaps the suit he wore, or the way he walked. You identified the figure walking down Main Street with Charlie. You disregarded all differences and acted impulsively on the similarities, so you confused an utter stranger with Charlie, and your own confusion was the most distressing of all. If, instead of using the sketchy, loosely drawn map of Charlie, you had moved down to lower, more particular, levels and had observed the figure on Main Street more closely, comparing it with more detailed maps of Charlie's appearance from your memory, you would not have been tricked by the similarities into establishing a false identity.

It is the same in every department of life, and the confusions result from the same kind of error. The Captain orders the private to have his horse shod. Some minutes later an echoing report tells the sad story; the private had confused two similar-sounding words. A sleepy nurse reaches for the tall brown medicine bottle and kills a patient with the caustic contents of another tall brown bottle that looked very similar.

Words can often lead to faulty identifications. If you tell me your nephew is a conductor I may think of him as presiding over the Boston Symphony, though as a matter of fact he's collecting tickets on the Boston and Maine. In this case, you will note, the words do not even refer to the same class of thing. There is a similarity that leads to confusion, but it is merely a verbal similarity with no basis whatever in fact. In other words, there is no similarity in external reality that relates closely the occupation of musical director with collecting train tickets.

You may have had some heated arguments with friends about the merits of General Motors. You may feel that GM is weak, has broken support, and is headed for much lower levels.

Your friends may insist that GM has increased its production, is bringing out new and greatly improved models, and is developing a line of light-weight locomotives that will revolutionize rail travel. Here is a confusion, and a confusion at the verbal level. The term General Motors is a name, a map, a symbol. It is not a thing. We must not confuse names with things. Actually, General Motors can and does refer to more than one reality. The reality of the stock market is an equity, an undivided beneficial interest in the earnings and book value of the company. This reality is itself an abstraction, not a tangible thing. The reality of the high production and the new products does concern tangible things.

When you and your friends engage in an argument about the showing of the stock as compared with the physical features of the company or with its activities, you are comparing two quite dissimilar entities—so dissimilar that it's hard to see how anybody could confuse them. The stock and the operations of the company are, to be sure, related in some ways, but they are not the same.

What *is* the same is the term General Motors, used to refer to both the activities of the company and the performance of the stock of the company. The similarity (which some people treat as if it were identity) exists only in the words. If, as in math, things equal to the same thing are equal to each other, then General Motors the stock is the same as General Motors the corporation. But what is valid as mathematical theory is a matter of symbolic relations; mathematics is not necessarily true by analogy in the world of things. By jumping to the faulty conclusion that the stock is the company, we have again confused abstraction with reality, one level of abstraction with another. In short, we have made a mistake.

You will understand that there are many, many kinds of errors that result from identifying things on the basis of seen, heard, touched, smelled, or tasted similarities. I might, for instance, take a quick glance at my watch, note the time as 3:20, and go back to my work for another half hour. If the hands had actually stood at 4:15, which would have a very similar appearance, I might miss a 4:30 appointment entirely. This confusion would not be verbal, for the similarity is not one of words but of visual appearance. But it could be avoided, like all confusions based on similarities, by a closer examination of the territory, in this case the face of the watch.

Perhaps you yourself have made mistakes on the basis of similarities that are entirely non-verbal. For instance, you may have rushed to answer the front door when actually the telephone was ringing. James Thurber in one of his collections of short stories and essays speaks of non-verbal confusion of the basis of similar appearances. In an article titled "The Admiral on a Bicycle" he tells how his near-sightedness has given him a world of wonders, in which a wind-blown swirl of old newspapers takes on the appearance of a little old man in an admiral's uniform pedaling a bicycle down the street. He speaks of a number of other illusions, all based on at least superficial similarities, all of which could be resolved if one were able to have a better look.

Edgar Allen Poe wrote a short story about a man who was startled when he looked up from his reading and saw a great monster crawling down the side of a hillside about a mile away, and approaching the valley at a terrifying rate. It was only by taking off the reading glasses that the monster could be seen as a moderate-sized insect creeping down the window pane a few inches away. In this case the non-verbal mistake was simply a matter of not scaling the map correctly; something small was perceived as something big. While this particular confusion is not likely to deceive many people, there are many life situations where a small thing is seen out of scale; in fact, we know people who habitually make mountains out of mole hills!

CHAPTER 21   BEYOND THE WORLD
OF THINGS

Some maps are not verifiable or confirmable in the external world. "Red" to you and "red" to me are different qualities, because I am color blind. Red, an adjective, is an aspect of a thing subject to judgment and opinion—just as "pretty woman" is a matter of opinion. We have now entered the world of concepts as opposed to things. Matching our individual maps becomes at best a tenuous activity.

Up to this point we have been considering maps of places, labels of things, words that are symbols of something tangible "out there" that we can point to, or count, or weigh. Even the higher abstractions we have mentioned represent groups or classes of real things. If we say "Bessie," we can take you out in the pasture and show you what we mean by Bessie. You can admire her, listen to her moo, and pat her smooth broad sides. If we say "house," while it does not, to be sure, tell you what particular house or kind of house we have in mind, we can take you out and show you a number of houses of various sorts so that you will know what we mean by the generalized symbol, the word house.

For the very low-order abstraction denoting a single individual thing, place, animal, or event, there is a corresponding reality that can be produced and examined. For all the various stages of high-order abstractions relating to these things, there are realities "out there" that correspond.

But there are other high-order abstractions that refer to a reality that is not tangible and cannot be touched, tasted, or inspected directly by the senses at all. And if there are dozens of ways of becoming confused and deluded in our perception of the solid, tangible things of the world, there are hundreds of traps that lurk in the tenuous upper reaches of the abstractions we are going to investigate now.

It is very easy to mistake the sound of a doorbell for the somewhat similar ring of the phone. Or to confuse this dog with that dog, or to make any of the other faulty identifications we make in everyday life in dealing with such ordinary things as keys and eye-glasses, medicine bottles, and the like. But in all these cases we are referring to something that can be sensed directly "out there," and even the higher-order abstractions, the names we use to call things by, refer to classes of real things.

Animals abstract in this way. Some dogs, for instance, react with enthusiasm and agility to the sight of a running cat, any cat, all cats. Animals respond to calls to food and visual or audible signals that dinner is ready. They can learn to understand and relate the original signals; they can establish chains of abstractions with symbols representing other symbols, very much as a human child might learn that when the clock strikes five we may shortly expect to hear Father's car drive into the garage, and when the car drives in Mother starts to get dinner off the stove.

There used to be great arguments among pseudo-scientific people as to whether animals could think. If by thinking we mean the power to abstract, to generalize classes of things, to recognize symbols that represent and correspond with parts of reality, and to establish chains of abstraction, then of course animals can think and think very well; some of them—well enough to serve their needs and secure their survival.

But there is a vast gulf between the abstractive ability of the smartest dog or horse or chimpanzee and the stupidest man able to live as a member of a human community. The difference between man and animal is not merely the fact that mankind has enormously greater powers of abstraction, covering much greater scope and variety and involving much greater complexity. There are types of abstraction that are not possible at all to the animals. This is because so much of our abstracting is done in language, whether we speak the words or merely think them. The invention of language is man's greatest discovery; his ability to use language intelligently is the great difference that marks him from all other living things on the earth.

When we build a chain of abstraction, we have names to give to the pigeonholes. We can observe the thing, name it (chair), classify it (furniture), put it into a higher order class (household equipment), generalize that class into a still higher order (personal property), etc. We can set up verbal maps to give us much or little detail, to cover a particular thing, or to include various categories. This, an animal cannot do. He cannot do it because he doesn't have the machinery to do it. He lacks the mechanism of language.

We can speculate on whether some animals might be able to develop greater intelligence, reasoning power, etc., if they could communicate in language as we do, but so long as they do not and cannot, this is merely an amusing pastime. The language barrier puts a full stop to the development of the animal.

We have already seen how language sets the pattern for our pigeonholing of information. Using words as symbols we can store up almost unlimited files of information in our minds, ready to be recalled and put to use whenever we need them. If we have learned a little about the nature of language as a system of symbols or maps, and have learned not to confuse words with things or high-order words with low-order words, and not to confuse things that are symbolized by the same word or similar words, then we have the basis for a smoothly operating "thinking machine"—at least as far as the perception and classifying of things and events is concerned.

Up to now, we have carefully skirted a great mountain of verbal maps, since these non-descriptive words bring with them a whole new set of problems and pitfalls. When you say "flower" you are using a symbol that calls up all the kinds of things we call flowers: asters and roses, pansies and petunias, tulips and hyacinths, typical flowers that can be pointed out, touched, and smelled. "Flower" is the name of a class of things. But when you say "red flower," the word red is not the name of a thing or a class of things.

You can't establish communication with someone else about redness as easily as you can about the name of a thing. You can point to something that is red to you, something that reflects certain wave-lengths of light in such a way that you recognize them and call them red. You can establish in your own mind a concept of redness as a fairly high-order (broad) abstraction. You can visualize in your memory various lower orders in this concept of redness that you may call rose, pink, scarlet, vermilion, maroon, or crimson. But you may find it difficult to convey to someone else just what you mean by red or even what you mean by any of the lower-order words that you include in redness. If you have ever tried to explain to a printer over the telephone just how you want him to change the color in the illustrations for a booklet to meet your ideas of how they should look, you will appreciate the difference between explaining what you mean by vermilion (as you see it in your mind's eye), and explaining what you mean by carnation or petunia.

This idea of redness or a certain kind and shade of redness is not too much different from descriptions of things, since there is, after all, a physical referent, certain describable constants that can represent any color or shade in the spectrum. More than a generation ago the language of color was placed on a systematic practical basis for the use of printers, paper manufacturers, commercial artists, etc., by Professor A. H. Munsell. The *Color Atlas* and the *Color Grammar* based on this system were published by the Strathmore Paper Company and the methods of notation were adopted by various printers, ink makers, and some buyers of printing.

However, for the general public this reasonable and highly useful system had no great appeal, and so today we still have our troubles trying to match the beige stockings for our wives, explaining to the painter what we mean by magenta, and wondering what the mail order house will send us when we order stationery of ivory tint.

It's possible, using electric eyes and various filters, to analyze colors quickly, accurately, and uniformly, so that color-matching data can be transmitted and the color reproduced at another point, or so that the data could be stored and the color produced again at a later time. But most of us are tied to the somewhat imperfect color perception of our own eyes, which for this job are not nearly the equal of electronic devices. We still go on talking about baby pink and orchid and powder blue, and go right on bringing home the wrong goods entirely from the department store, as our wives tell us quite frankly and openly.

The fact is that color as we perceive it, is not really a thing like book or hat. It's an aspect of a thing, or rather our particular response to an aspect of a thing. You have no way of knowing whether certain light waves reflected from a thing set up the same sensations and feelings in my mind as they do in yours. For all you know, I may see red quite differently from you. As a matter of fact I do, if you have normal color perception, for I am slightly color blind. I can't show you or explain to you in words or in any other way just how red looks to me, any more than you can communicate your perception of redness to me, but I do know that you're probably more responsive to red, you will notice it more quickly, you will see it more vividly than I do.

Notice that the redness is a matter of my seeing, not a property of the thing. In the dark all cats are black—and all other things, too. Color is not a property of the thing; nor is it even a property of the light that strikes it. It depends on a combination of the thing, the kind of light being reflected from it, and, very importantly, my perceptions. In other words, red is not only a map or a symbol, it is a symbol that is not strictly comparable between one person and another. It has a physical referent in a way and up to a point, but the color as perceived is strictly a personal matter. My red is my own, your red is your own, and they are not necessarily the same. What we are getting at here is that color is a much less tangible, much more tenuous, kind of perception than "wooden table" or "pile of bricks."

I have spent some time on this point, since it is a bridge, so to speak, at the point of departure as we leave the world of things and enter the world of concepts. Instead of calling the flower red, which is what I call the color as I see it, I might have called it a pretty flower. What are you going to do with this one? What is "pretty"? What does pretty look like? Is pretty a thing? There have been a few bloody noses and black eyes on this point: I think she is pretty; you think she is an ugly old bag and say so; the fight is on.

How are you going to measure "pretty"? What are you going to do when there is a difference of opinion? This is not going to be the kind of argument that can be settled by going out and counting the brick chimneys on somebody's house.

We have already said that there can be no conflict in the world of reality. You feel, and I agree with you, that "pretty" does represent something. It is a map that has a corresponding territory. But the reality in this case is not a physical reality in the external world. The only reality at stake is our own opinion. When we say something or someone is pretty, we are not comparing a map to a territory in the sense that we would be if we said, "I know there's a fire hydrant in front of Bill Johnson's house." That statement can be verified by going and having a look, and every reasonable person will abide by the decision.

It is quite different with "pretty." This is a map of a map; the territory we are checking is itself a high-order abstraction in our own minds. You can't produce the evidence. You can't prove your point. All you know is whether Miss America as chosen at Atlantic City measures up to the standards of your own map of what is pretty. That is why "in matters of taste there can be no dispute."

Notice that pretty is an adjective. This is a different territory for each one of us. In general, adjectives do not denote things but refer to some quality or property we attribute to a thing, or, more often than not, to some opinion we may hold about the thing. In spite of all the committees of experienced judges, in spite of all the expert opinions, definitions, and attempts to set up standards, when they are all done at Atlantic City you and I may feel that Miss America doesn't look pretty to us. There is a disagreement.

Since pretty is a "good" word, it is associated with things we like; and since many of us like very much the same sort of things, we may at times agree on what we feel is pretty. But it is most important to keep in mind, always, that it is still an entirely personal matter: What is pretty to me is not necessarily pretty to you.

Consider an adjective you will find bandied about on the front page of your newspaper, in the reports of proceedings in district court, in findings of the post office department, and in pronouncements from the pulpit, the lecture platform, and the governor's office. The word is "obscene." It is an adjective.

You are familiar with the all-too-familiar story of the raid at the Starlight Club, where an obscene performance was being given. Along with this hackneyed news item is another: the clamping down on the ring that has been distributing obscene pictures and magazines throughout the local cigar stores. Ministers exhort us not to visit an obscene play at the local theatre. An obscene book is banned from public sale. And so on.

This happens to be a "bad" word, but in some ways it is the same kind of a word as pretty. At any rate, if you have followed the legal tangles that have built up around the difficulty of establishing a firm definition for obscene, you will realize that this word, too, is not a map of a territory in externality but a map of a map. This is a highly personal map that is not necessarily the same for any two persons—not even approximately.

The difficulty is in writing a firm definition, something that everyone can agree on. This is a wall that lawyers and legislatures have battered their heads against without much result, for in the case of pretty or obscene, it is impossible to write an absolute description that everyone can verify and agree on, since what we are dealing with is not a thing but a concept in someone's head, a map in the mind. We have no way of comparing one man's map in the mind with another's.

The problem is not made any easier by the fact that it almost seems as if we could, if we put our heads to it, write such a definition, since, just as most of us agree as to what is pretty, most of us would agree in certain clear-cut cases, that something was (to us) obscene or not obscene. This is not because we can compare facts and measure, verify, etc., in a scientific way, like counting trees or measuring house lots. The degree of agreement we have is more because of exposure and training in a common culture. It is only an approximate agreement, and it cannot, in dubious cases, be submitted to any hard and fast scientific rules.

Of course, we can change the problem. If we can ask the questions in terms that can be answered by observations and measurements in the external world, then we can avoid the impossible task of comparing mental maps. For instance, as sometimes happens, the judges of a beauty contest may discover that it is going to be impossible to get any sort of agreement on the respective pulchritude of some 70 or 80 damsels. To avoid a deadlock they may resort (possibly in desperation) to setting up standards of prettiness that are not really perceptions of beauty at all but are in fact measurements of external reality. The whole matter becomes simpler all around when it is possible to compare the women point by point with some definite standards on which everyone has agreed in advance. Thus we often see tables of measurements showing the dimensions of "the ideal woman," or those of the Venus de Milo, and the candidates are submitted to a point-by-point comparison with the standard.

This, of course, is a scientific method and can give a positive answer in terms of degree of correlation with the standard. No one is likely to disagree with the findings, and if he does, it is very easy to check back and verify the figures. This way leads to no disputes. When Miss Central Falls is finally selected, we all know that she does, in fact and provably, conform most nearly to the standards of beauty set up in advance by the committee. But whether the selection is going to please you personally or not is another matter. There is no assurance whatever that she will measure up, even approximately, to anybody's mental map of what a pretty girl or a beautiful woman should look like. Until and unless we are able to condition people in such a way that their opinions, tastes, and judgments are precisely the same, we will never quite be able to agree on what is pretty.

It is the same with any other word of opinion or judgment. You have followed the struggles of the bar and the ministry to define obscenity in the sense of an inner awareness of indecency. Probably the most promising efforts, at least the only practical ways open, are to externalize the question and instead of trying to compare mental maps to measure something "out there." If, for example, we agree and pass laws that any photograph of a nude woman is to be considered obscene, that would define something verifiable. This has been tried, as have a great many other definitions of what may not be done, what must be worn or may not be worn, what can or cannot be said, etc. The cop posted at the back of the burlesque house is following some such rules; if this is his regular tour of duty, he knows exactly how much leg and how much body may be exposed, for how long, as well as what words are taboo. These are not definitions of any personal attitude or feeling. They refer to specific items to check "out there"; if the rules are violated, the entire company is packed into the paddy wagon and hauled off to night court. It's as easy as that.

But bear in mind that this is not the essence of the problem, which is trying to measure and compare human perception. It is so easy to assume that what is pretty for you is pretty for me; that what is obscene for you is also obscene to me, that what is good, lazy, contemptible, generous, cruel, honest, ugly, to me will coincide with your feelings in any particular case. Very often we will jump to the conclusion that everyone else feels or should feel the same as we do—a conclusion that will not stand up under study.

By way of example, let me pass along a little story in the next Chapter illustrating how we project our own feelings and assume that something that is really "in here" must be "out there" and observable by everyone.

CHAPTER 22   THE MEANINGS WE ATTACH TO MAPS

In matters of opinion there is no decisive way of deciding which of contrary opinions might be correct. "Brilliant," and "beautiful" are adjectives that are really maps of maps. There is no real territory we can examine to verify that the adjective agrees with an objective reality. We can accept a broad consensus as a standard, but the adjective is still a matter of opinion. And each opinion has its own personal validity though it might diverge from the group opinion. A judgment or opinion may be accurate or false to fact, but in the case of taste it is arguable but not disputable. In order to avoid faulty and unrealistic conclusions, we must always examine the basic premises dispassionately to see in regard to nouns if they reflect reality and in regard to adjectives that they are not totally skewed and eccentric.

I will retell an old story to make a point, a story about the psychiatrist and the new patient: At the very first interview the doctor found it necessary to interrupt the patient's recitation of his symptoms in order to get a little psychological background. He explained that he was making a simple test in which he wanted the patient to describe the situation suggested by several ink blots, which the doctor displayed in a little book.

To the first of these the patient responded that it could be a bedroom; with perhaps a double bed and a man and a woman in it having sexual intercourse.

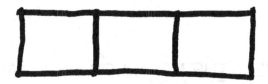

When the doctor showed a second ink blot the patient reckoned that it might be three bedrooms; each containing a double bed with a couple enjoying sexual relations.

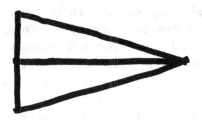

To another ink blot the patient's reaction was puzzlement. However, after some thought he reported that it looked like two bedrooms of peculiar shape, each with a double bed. In one was a couple engaged in rather perverse dalliance; and in the other, two men, carrying on, as the patient put it, "like crazy."

"Well, my friend," said the doctor, "before we go any further into discussing your symptoms, I think I should tell you that you are oversexed. In fact you are obsessed with sex."

"Oh, yeah?" The patient fixed the psychiatrist with a cold and reproachful glare, "and who, may I ask, has been producing all the dirty pictures?"

When we are talking about words that represent an opinion or a judgment, how we feel about something, we can't point to anything "out there," since what we mean isn't out there at all. When we say "dirty picture" or "brave warrior," the "dirty" and the "brave" don't have the same kind of solid reality as "picture" or "warrior." Common nouns name things, but adjectives are symbols that represent values we have come to attach to things, either as a result of experience or, very often, because of what we have been taught. We may have a fairly good idea of what we mean by awkward or brilliant or generous, but these are still maps of maps, and they are several or many steps of abstraction away from external reality. Because of this, although we may concur with other people who have been exposed to the common teaching and preaching of the community on many matters of opinion, when it comes to a really close decision there is no ultimate and decisive way of deciding which opinion is "right."

The point here is that common nouns in general refer to things "out there," while adjectives and adverbs and abstract nouns in general refer to concepts "in here." What one must keep in mind concerning his own understanding and communication with others is that when one uses an adjective or adverb or abstract noun, he is expressing how something seems to himself, not necessarily how it seems to the man next door.

Notice that we use the word "is" or its variants such as "am," "be," and "are," to equate our opinion with some "thing." When we say, "Rover is a brown dog," we are saying that Rover and brown dog are equal and identical. We have already seen that this is not precisely true, since a symbol or map is not the same as the thing it represents. But in this case we are also including an adjective in the identity. Rover is brown *to me*. More than that I cannot really say, since I cannot surely say that he is brown to you; you may not see him exactly the same way I do. If I were to say that Charles Wilson is a handsome man, I should be aware that I am comparing Charles Wilson to my mental map of what is handsome in a man and find that Mr. Wilson fills the bill. He is handsome to me. If somebody else thinks that Charles Wilson has a rather ugly-looking face, that is because Mr. Wilson doesn't match up with his mental map of handsomeness. To him Wilson is ugly, or at least not handsome. I do not know of any way you can challenge his contrary view and prove your own.

The standard method of arriving at some sort of working agreement so that roughly we can know what our neighbor means, of course, is to take the views of a number of people, and accept the consensus as the standard. Thus, where 999 people will agree (that is, will have similar maps of handsomeness) that Charles Wilson is handsome, we will probably accept the idea that a certain appearance such as his, in our culture, may be considered by tacit mutual agreement to be handsome.

This is a sort of extensional bargain, and it is perfectly all right so long as we understand that we are not dealing with an external reality alone but with a judgment or opinion about it. If you think this is a matter of splitting hairs, just consider the types that we consider handsome among men or beautiful among women and then compare them with the typical choices representing these qualities by Eskimos, or Central Africans, or Melanesians! The opinions most people hold are not necessarily the same in other places or other cultures. Nor would they necessarily be the same in other times.

Most importantly, you will realize that these other and contrary opinions have as much validity as your own, but some valid judgments and opinions may be more useful than others in interpreting external reality and in making dependable predictions. As we have said before, a valid judgment or opinion may be true to a degree as it applies to the outside world, or it may be false to fact, or it may have no true-or-false aspect, for instance if it is a matter of taste. The judgment or opinion that can determine your attitude on a matter (and therefore your behavior with respect to that matter) depends on the premises on which you build. Even a very unrealistic attitude may be logically valid, though it may be constructed on premises that contradict observable reality. It may be valid yet false to fact. This we must continually check and be on guard against. We must know where we got our basic premises and we must check and examine them if we want to avoid a faulty or inadequate conclusion.

CHAPTER 23   MAPS WITHOUT TERRITORIES

Usually a map refers in its origin to some real event or real thing, but there are also maps that have no actual territory. For example, "ghost" has no real existence, but the average person upon hearing the word immediately recalls his own map of the word. If asked to verbalize it he would produce a description amazingly similar to that produced by any other randomly selected person. Compared to ghost, some other words have maps of such individual and personal meanings that they can be use to start fights or wars: "sacred," "eternal verities," "true God." By becoming conscious of the wide difference between low-order observations (counting, measuring) and high-order abstractions ("true God"), we can avoid the chaos that results from confusing them.

Because, unlike the animals, mankind has the great tool of language, we are able to make maps and maps of maps, and to abstract not only things and classes of things but also events and classes of events, that is, what people do and real events. Beyond that we make maps of how we feel about these things, such as the ones we have just been discussing. Most of the abstracting is done verbally; our maps are verbal maps, our pigeon-holes have verbal labels.

In all these cases, even opinions, there is at least for our own self a chain of connection to things real. We can trace the word and the meaning we assign to it through a chain of learning and experience that rests ultimately on the solid foundation of events and things that can be demonstrated "in reality."

There are other maps and labels. It is perfectly possible to draw a map that represents no real place at all. We even write stories about events that never happened and never could happen, and we say of the characters in these stories that "any resemblance to any real person, living or dead, is purely coincidental." It is possible through language, to communicate these imaginary things to others so that they will in some degree experience the same adventures, meet the same fictitious characters, and perhaps express very much the same emotions we feel ourselves.

This is all right so long as we understand that we are just playing a game, or at best setting up a map that has some similarity to things and places and events we have known. We might spin a yarn that is thrilling and exciting to our listeners, even though they know it isn't true. We might tell a story that could point up some principle or idea, so that even though it was not precisely a true story, it would help others to solve a problem similar to one in the story. If I tell you a story about a ghost, I think I could make it sufficiently blood-curdling to scare you a little, and perhaps to keep you awake an hour later tonight. Unless you are unusually innocent, you would not expect me to show you the ghost or prove that the story was true. I think we would both understand that the ghost exists only in my mind and that, fortunately, there is no territory "out there" to correspond.

When we speak of ghosts, by the way, my job is a fairly easy one, since you already know a good deal about ghosts. I don't need to tell you what a regulation ghost looks like, because you know very well: tall, white, and shapeless, probably clanking a heavy chain, possibly uttering thin wails from time to time. Not all ghosts are of the regulation type, but there is no need to get into all the specialties.

The interesting thing is that you have in your own mind a map of ghost that is not too different from my own. You have a map that corresponds to no reality yet has a certain one-to-one correspondence with a map in my own head. That is an extraordinary thing when you stop to think about it. I cannot imagine two animals sharing a thought that had no connection with reality. In fact, I don't think such a thing would be possible except through the medium of language.

"Ghost," technically speaking is a common noun. It has the appearance of a word denoting something tangible like book or frog. We must be very careful in dealing with "ghost" that we do not confuse it with something more tangible.

There are other words besides ghost that have no clearly demonstrable referent in externality. Some of these may have a particular meaning to the user, but because they are extremely high-order abstractions, the final terms of long chains of abstracting, it is not always possible to communicate this inner meaning. In fact, by comparison, "ghost" may seem a very solid and precisely defined entity.

How are you going to get together on the precise meaning of sacredness? Just how would you measure disgrace? Terms like these are capable of such broad interpretation that they cease to have much value as means of communication. Whatever value they may have must rest on a purely personal understanding.

A friend of mine once suggested that we could iron out certain differences of view if we could establish a common ground of discussion, agreeing on certain broad principles. (If you recall the case of the camera, you will realize that it is always possible to make different things look the same if we will take a broad enough view and, by moving away from the subjects, get farther from the reality.) In this case my friend suggested that we could agree on certain points and then establish further agreement step by step.

If he had suggested that the agreements we would start with would be the low-order observation of reality, I believe we might actually have made a start. If we had started with looking at, counting, measuring solid, familiar things and then worked up to logical abstractions from these, we might have hoped for a considerable agreement. Instead, he suggested that we agree that we believe in the Great Eternal Verities.

Is this something that can be counted, weighed, pointed at, directly observed? I asked him to define the Great Eternal Verities, and he said that I knew what they were as well as he did. When I pressed the point, he became angry.

I do not want to accuse anyone of treasuring a map that corresponds to no reality whatever. I think it is possible that my friend does have some idea of what he means when he speaks of the Great Eternal Verities. But apparently he cannot reduce his feeling to a lower-order abstraction, not even enough to describe and define what he is talking about. He cannot communicate his map at all.

If you have a map, or a concept, that corresponds to reality, it seems as if you should be able to tell something about the territory referred to. If this were a geographical map, you would surely be able to tell something about the country represented, the various features of it, and their relative location. But here we cannot get beyond "Great Eternal Verities." Wouldn't it seem to you, if you treasured such a map, that it could not fail to be more useful if you could bring this great label down to earth? It might help you if you could determine precisely what you mean by Great Eternal Verities and check how and to what extent they would apply in each specific problem you might encounter in your own affairs.

Please do not misunderstand this. There is a place for high-order abstraction. It is just as important to be able to generalize and proceed by logic and inference from facts to conclusions and from conclusions to principles, as it is to observe down-to-earth reality. But we should not confuse the high-order abstraction with the low-order observation. We certainly should not treat a map like "Great Eternal Verities" as if it were a thing.

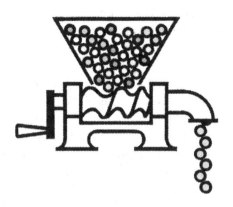

CHAPTER 24   AN EXCEEDINGLY
COMPLEX MACHINE

The human brain is without doubt the most complex and marvelous machine to appear on this earth. It observes and classifies; compares maps, thousands and thousands of events, thoughts, and impressions. By its natural operation it builds for each of us a system of values and a sense of identity or self.

"Values" means the way we give priorities to events and things in our external and internal lives. St. Francis' values are not difficult to imagine, for instance. Economic theory attempts to model our behavior in terms of mechanistic formulas rather than values.

Given the human brain and its extraordinary tool, language, we have a marvelous machine. More marvelous than most of us realize. Some time ago the designer of a rather complex electronic "reasoning machine" explained rather apologetically that he called his creation a "little moron," though the machine was not able even to accomplish the one-thousandth part of the functioning of a human moron. Some of the work that has been done and is being done with electronic computers suggests the ways by which the human mind operates. But no one has even hinted that any such machine is capable of the human characteristics of abstracting and reasoning.

Your brain and mine are stored with thousands and tens of thousands of direct observations, a memory covering all the things you have seen, heard, smelt, tasted or otherwise experienced. You have these low-order maps and then layer after layer of abstraction derived from them, sorting them into categories, sometimes interlocking. Then you have the logical derivatives of these stored impressions, resulting in a further storage of conclusions and inferences, opinions and judgments. You compare maps with maps, maps with new territories. You change maps, change your impression of a reality that has changed or that you have re-examined; if you are using your abstractive machinery intelligently, you change your judgments and your opinions in line with whatever new evidence appears that may require such changes.

Some of the judgments and opinions could be called your values. You may have a very definite scale of values, covering thousands and tens of thousands of items. Every time you buy a newspaper you have to make a value decision about whether the money will be worth more invested in the daily paper or kept for some other purpose. People are continually weighing whether to buy a new television set or a living room table or take the trip to Florida this winter or have a vacation fishing in Maine next summer.

There are all kinds of value decisions. We might have to decide whether to stand the toothache or go and see the dentist. It could be a question of whether to enjoy an evening at home or gain the approval of the PTA committee by attending the meeting. Undoubtedly a murderer must balance the value he places on slaughtering his enemy against the chances of getting caught and punished.

Some values are more highly esteemed than others. Most of us are quite aware of the valuation we place on our homes, our cars, money in the bank. We think of these things as "material" possessions, and if we studied economics in school we have learned to think of these values as inspiring the really important drives in human conduct.

You have possibly plodded through the classic books on economics. You are probably familiar with the concepts of "marginal producers," "law of diminishing returns," "supply and demand," and the like. It is possible to figure out pretty well how commerce and industry will develop, which businesses will prosper, which will fail, and how humanity will fare under the particular system under study.

There is, no doubt, a great deal of truth in economic theory, and it is sometimes useful to isolate a certain system of forces and study it as if there were nothing else in the world. This is the useful (and valid) method we use in studying a mechanism where gears are considered to fit without the slightest backlash and to operate without any friction at all. We learn in physics about the behavior of rigid bodies, though we know perfectly well there are no completely rigid bodies in the real world. We set up fictions; we say that this or that behaves "as if" it were like this diagram. So long as we understand that these fictions are merely means of expressing abstractions, we can use them and with their help arrive at very practical conclusions.

In other words, when we say that for the purpose of studying the relative motion of certain gears, links, levers we will disregard the weight, structural strength, and friction of the parts; we have a right to do this. We will be making a map, as it were, of the mechanism, and as you know, a map is never a thing, and a map never shows everything about what it represents.

In the same way we can talk about economic motives without complicating the problem by talking about some of the uneconomic forces that also operate in human affairs. We can abstract certain points about the economic behavior of man and up to a point the abstraction or map we have drawn will have a certain validity, a certain one-to-one correspondence with the facts "out there." You can show that a hungry man will work hard for a sirloin steak. You can prove that he won't be willing to work quite so hard for a second steak, and that his appetite (and his incentive) will vary inversely with the number of steaks consumed.

You can point up a great many of the true situations in life and business by means of economic theory. But it leaves such a vast amount unexplained! Most of us are conscious of the inadequacy of ordinary economics when we say (though without much conviction) that "Money isn't everything."

Yet (here is one of those elephants practically blocking the front stoop, which we cannot see at all), we are taught to act "as if" money were everything. This "as if" is not quite so valid as some of the others we mentioned before. We say "money isn't everything," but if someone we know happens to prefer skin-diving or water color painting to holding down a good job we feel there must be something wrong with him.

Sometimes, you know, people turn down money. It is not the highest value in our lives. The chances are you would not be willing to set a price in dollars on one of your eyes. You would not want to dicker with a cannibal agent for one of your children of tender age. There are a great many things you would not trade for money, things that, although they are of enormous value to you, you could not even express in terms of money.

Suppose that someone offered you a good price to insult and abuse all your friends. How many dollars would it be worth to lose the respect and goodwill of all these friends? What price to make it worthwhile to be an outcast, hated and avoided? Surely the opinion of others is valuable, yet it comes quite outside the ordinary laws of economics.

You could, you know, have the respect of many people, and also draw a very good income if, say, you were willing to become a spy for some foreign country. For how much would you be willing to sell your self-respect?

How much of a motive is the preservation and enhancement of your "self"—not your body, but the non-material part of you, the part that does the thinking and the feeling and the abstracting and evaluating. There are a good many sociologists and psychologists who believe (as I do myself, and as I think you will if you think it over) that this value is at the very top of the heap. Men will work for money, fight for material gain, plot and struggle to gain the respect of others. But any man will defend his self, as he sees it, with his money, his property, his family, his reputation, and the life of his physical body if necessary.

It is the need for survival of this self, not the physical body, that constitutes the greatest drive that actuates people. This is the highest value we have. You will understand that what makes up survival of the self, what enhances it, and what preserves it, may not be the same for you as for the man across the street. What is being defended and enhanced in each case is the particular set of values held by each individual. These values, as we have seen, are derived from long series of abstractions. We see. We hear. We learn. We abstract certain observations. We generalize and group these, and compare them with other groups from other experience.

We notice similarities, and if we are unusually perceptive we notice the important differences. By logic we arrive at certain conclusions, and these lead to attitudes which express themselves in opinions, judgments, etc. These very high abstractions are our values; collectively, they constitute our value system, and indeed they are the self we have become.

The man across the street may be a pickpocket working out at the race track. It is possible, and even probable, that he may have so directed his abstractive processes that he believes the world is "all crooked" and he is only getting what he is entitled to, and after all he is supporting a wife and two children. He has made it look pretty good. He has to make it look pretty good. If he did not, he would have to face the unpleasant truth about his standing in the community and the real nature of his livelihood.

Your neighbor next door, on the other hand, may be a conscientious and dedicated physician who not only supports a wife and children but also brings new hope to patients who need his expert help. He also makes it look pretty good. And he also has to for the preservation of his self is important to him, too.

From your own point of view, the physician may be noble, and the pickpocket contemptible, but bear in mind that these are simply your own words of judgment, the pigeonholes into which you have thrown these men. You are simply classifying the maps according to your own frame of reference.

We said that these people "have to make it look good." We all know that there is much more, so much more, about anyone than we can abstract in a few contacts or by a few words. ("So much good in the worst of us, so much bad in the best of us. . .") The pickpocket, if we knew more of the facts, might, even according to our own private set of values appear to be actuated by noble motives and we could, no doubt, find more than one contemptible factor in the high-minded medico.

This is not the place to get into a detailed discussion of intra-personal relations. But a man will make his self look good, even if all rational attempts fail, and he has to become the Emperor Napoleon or Jesus Christ to do it.

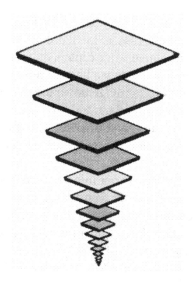

CHAPTER 25   LAYERS OF AWARENESS

Our minds are like archival systems. The most current data are at the top of the stack and the past is stored under all that has occurred since it was originally archived. Contrary to expectation, we can with some effort retrieve data—memories beyond the time we would have thought ourselves conscious. Even by the age of four we have stored numerous impressions, and we have also learned enough to be "socialized." We have learned what is nasty, what is nice, and many survival skills.

But all the while our education and socialization, unless unusual, are moving our minds away from the concrete, the experiential, towards the generalized, the abstract. The whole tendency of culture is to substitute the map for direct experience of the territory. The map is the comforting reassurance, the certainty that the sun moves around the earth, that the earth is flat. So our educators constantly pass on sacred maps to us because their safety and certainty is shaken when a Galileo challenges the Pope.

In most business offices, the active current correspondence will be found in folders or baskets on various desks. Letters that have been answered, with copies of the replies, will go into the regular files. From time to time the contents of some of these files is carried down to the storeroom in transfer cases. Most of the active work centers on today's mail, or at any rate this week's mail. Now and then we have to refer to the file cabinets. Very, very seldom do we have to trudge down to the storeroom.

Yet those old papers are important, too. Perhaps the original charter of the company is in a safe in the storeroom. The transfer files contain important records, contracts, and communications that may have to be used at any time.

It is very much that way with your mind as well. You know this, too, of course. The things that dominate your consciousness are mostly the activities of the day. You think about what you're doing. Sometimes you recall things from a few days ago, or plan for next week, yet really there is a lot going on around you, some of which concerns you, of which you are not particularly aware. If your attention is focused on listening to a phonograph record, you may be entirely oblivious to a hissing radiator. Oblivious in one sense, and yet not entirely oblivious either, for if someone jogs your elbow and asks you if you hear the radiator hissing, you will realize that you have been hearing it, some part of you has been hearing it, all along.

Perhaps you have had the experience of reading the stock tape on a screen. You're particularly interested in some certain stocks. You are checking the prices of these and not watching for any others. In fact, if someone asked you to name several other stocks and their prices you might have some difficulty remembering any in particular. Yet if someone in the room should suddenly inquire, "Has anybody seen any XYZ?", you might startle yourself by popping out with, "I saw 800 shares about ten minutes ago at 43-5/8."

Where did this come from? How did something you never saw break into consciousness on command? It's almost as if our senses were abstracting information all the time, even without our knowledge.

That seems to be about what actually happens. While you're reading the book you're picking up peripheral data on the comings and goings of the family dog, the gradual changes of light with the approach of evening, the sound of automobile horns outside, the neighbor's telephone ringing; all these things are being "watched" in a sense, without any effort on your part, and without your even realizing that they're being watched. You would say, for instance, that the miscellaneous sounds around you were "going in one ear and out the other," but that's not quite true for you may have already discovered, as many of us have, that you can "remember" things not consciously observed if they are later jogged to mind.

There are layers of consciousness, and this is surely not the place to start probing the deep layers of the subconscious. But it is important to keep in mind that down in the transfer files, covered with dust these many years, there may be some vital and important records. If you have a little time and are interested in trying the experiment, you might select a period of your life about which you "remember" very little (say, when you were four or five years old): Take the few little bits of remembered places and people and what you did, and see what else you can connect to them. You may discover a rich and fascinating story buried these many years.

I did this a year or so ago in connection with the time when I was four or five years old. I had only a few sketchy memories of the small Montana town where we lived at that time. I could see the saw mill at Hamilton, the riffles of the Bitter Root River, fast-flowing logs, and shallows over piles of rounded stones. The backwaters with the current swirling in circles and finally running again into the main stream. The quiet pools where black pollywogs wiggled along a yellow-brown bottom. The mill pond and the lumberjacks jumping from log to log, guiding the great trunks to the incline, where they would be hauled up slowly to disappear into the whining, screaming mill. The sawdust burner, like a great silo, smoldering gently through a rounded dome. Winter. Skating on the mill pond. The stakes and signs set out where ice was thin. The cold walk home. And on, and on, and on. The Ravalli Hotel: what it looked like, the arrangement of the dining room, the appearance of the daily menus. Cutting little cardboard sleds out of old menu cards. Main Street. The Marcus Daly Ranch. Walter Gregory's camp, and Dr. Buchan's. The great wall of the Bitter Root Range looming above the valley mile after mile.

How much to recall. I don't know. I've written many pages on just this setting and just this time, always with the feeling that there is so much more to write: not forgotten, not lost, merely stored away in the downstairs transfer files.

If you try it, you will find, too, I'm sure, that there is more in those old files than you realize. You will gradually recall the faces and scenes of many years ago. You will remember the names of friends you played with before you went to kindergarten. You will realize that although you have covered up these old impressions for so long, the perceptions of a young mind are durable; they last a long time.

Just how durable they are you may know if you have a very aged relative. It's a very common experience for old people to "live in the past." My Aunt Esther Putnam couldn't remember whether I had come to visit her yesterday or three weeks ago. As a matter of fact, she often confused me with both my Uncle John and my Uncle Howard. She saw and heard what happened today, but her tired old mind did not abstract very much that was new, and what she did take in was not impressed very deeply.

Ask her about her trips into Mexico with her late husband, though! Pick up a little Mexican bowl, or a piece of raw turquoise, or a set of rattlesnake rattles! Aunt Esther could tell you just where she and Professor Putnam found this bowl, about when it was made, and what tribal patterns it carried. She could give you dates and places and a wealth of detail on her treasures. All these things were abstracted at a time when Aunt Esther's mind was very active and very impressionable. What we learn young, we learn well. It sticks by us.

While we have spoken of recalling times when we were four or five years old and learning fast, you must realize that by the time you were four you had already learned a great deal. You had learned to walk and climb and perhaps scrub your own back and generally make your body do what you wanted it to do. You had learned to use your eyes, to recognize the faces of people important in your life, and to know who was "with" you and who was "agin" you. You had learned about lollypops, and bean shooters, birds' nests, running through the lawn spray, how to play some games, how to fight. You knew colors. You had learned to like some kinds of music. Very importantly, you had learned to speak and understand the wonderful system of communication we call language.

Along with all that, by four we have all acquired the basis for a good many judgments and opinions. At four years of age we knew what was funny and what was naughty, what was nasty and what was nice. Sometimes we learned by direct experience, the "burned finger and hot stove" process by which it is recognized that a certain course of action is likely to lead to certain desirable or undesirable results.

As a matter of fact the child of four is perfectly able to make chains of abstraction on matters that concern him. Suppose, for instance, that a rather tough bully from the third grade, who usually wore a red coat, cut through the yard every afternoon after school. The four-year-old is quite capable of understanding the threat and getting out of the way, taking any toys or rolling stock, when this character looms at the fence. He is very likely to take refuge if any boy wearing a red coat appears suddenly along the fence at about three o'clock. He might even go so far as to pack up his equipment and move indoors a little before school lets out, just to be on the safe side.

We are not going to suggest that he would necessarily shy away from red coats for the rest of his life, or that he would become apprehensive in mid-afternoon after he was grown up. Normally, as he acquired more experience, he would learn that "red coat" and "three o'clock" were not the sources of the danger in themselves. But where an impression has been made, very strongly, on a young mind, and through deliberate teaching and repetition has been etched deeply, where there has been no word of experience or teaching to modify the original impression, the impression will remain unchanged, conscious, unconscious, or deeply subconscious.

Many of the concepts we have called opinions and judgments are taught this way. They are learned, well learned, and never seriously contradicted. They are high-order abstractions, symbols, maps —not things at all. But they are as durable as things, and in fact more durable than most things. These are the words that often relate very closely to our inter-personal and intra-personal relations. "Good," "bad," "sneaky," "generous," and "evasive," are words of this type, associated with social concepts and carrying a very strong aura of approval or disapproval.

One of the most dramatic demonstrations of how early learning sticks with us occurs sometimes in connection with the sense of smell. It is too bad that we do not have any systematic education of the sense of smell; you might almost call it the neglected sense. We have no very satisfactory nomenclature for odors. People usually ignore the odors that surround them, and except for politely sniffing a lilac or syringa once or twice a season, we don't go out of our way consciously to use this means of abstracting from the world of reality.

Smells are generally in disrepute. We think of the stink of chemical labs, of railway station washrooms, of garbage trucks on a hot day. People avoid a room over the kitchen that is exposed to cooking odors. Even perfumes compounded for our delectation are tinged with the pervasive condemnation that we attach to lusts of the flesh. The sense of smell is treated as a poor relation amongst the senses—not only a poor relation, but a somewhat disreputable one, like a drunken cousin. We are not encouraged to train and develop this important sense. You hear a great deal about the "aroma" of coffee, especially the particular brand being touted on your TV or radio. Actually, we sell short our sense of smell, we neglect it; it is given very little attention in our culture.

Yet, even without cultivation, we do have this sense, and even without training it operates to some extent, and ties into the great perceptive machinery of our minds. The aroma of coffee. If you want to bring back the original connotations, try grinding a few coffee beans in a hand grinder (as we do every morning for breakfast). Put your nose down in the little receptacle where lies the fresh-ground coffee. What kind of map does this call for?

Remember, no stimulus can recall anything that was not previously recorded. I have no doubt that the rich odor of the ground coffee would call forth in my children a picture of the East Longmeadow Super Market.

That would be the map related to that stimulus, for them. But for me, and perhaps for you, this olfactory stimulus will recall elaborate maps of other stores, in other places, at other times. It will take me into a narrow store each side of whose sawdust-sprinkled floor is bordered by long ranges of counters. Back of some of these counters are black japanned bins, lettered in gold, containing various sorts of coffee and tea. On the counter in front is a large grinding mill, operated by turning a handle on a big wheel at the side. Mr. Van Heule stands there, cheerful and rotund, ready to grind the pound of coffee and pour it from the metal scoop under the grinder into a paper bag. Nearer the front are boxes of fancy crackers, eighteen-inch cubes open at the top, or perhaps lidded with glass. In a space behind the counter there are barrels of more ordinary crackers; in front of the counter near the door there are several small kegs containing dried prunes and apricots. Opposite and towards the rear is the meat counter, with its scale and pile of weights, and the butcher ready to suggest, "We have some nice pork chops today, Mrs. Magee. Or would you want some halibut?" Overhead, in the gloom of the high ceiling, revolve slowly the enormous fans, like leisurely helicopters. And one knows that, come mid-afternoon, Charlie will be hollering up the back entry, "Grocery boy!" as he lugs the wooden box full of today's provisions.

All this from a whiff of fresh-ground coffee. All this and so much more from a map, and an obsolete map at that.

You would think that in the matter of human relations, including your own self-evaluation, it might be important to reduce high-order judgments wherever possible to something as close as possible to reality.

You might tell me that Sam Goodman is generous. I would know more about him, and would have a better basis for making an intelligent opinion myself, if you told me precisely what he did that led you to this opinion. Where and when was he generous? Just exactly what was the action as you observed it at that time and place?

You might say Dave is dishonest, because he told his wife he mailed the gas bill Monday when actually he didn't mail it until Wednesday. And you might consider Mike dishonest, because he is a professional safe-blower. The word is the same: dishonest. But the situations in reality are nowhere near the same. We have taken two dissimilar events and created an identity that is purely verbal.

We all learned these judgment words and opinion words, and some expressions of approval or disapproval that are not expressed in words, at a very early age. They are drilled into us. They constitute a major part of the value system by which we evaluate the world, the people we meet, and most especially ourselves.

The saddest part is that when it becomes a question of going by the map or checking with the territory; many, possibly most, people will choose the map instead of the territory.

You will probably agree that among the worst offenders (and the word "offenders" is used advisedly) are well-meaning parents, priests (including all ministers and rabbis), teachers, and lawyers. These are the molders of the culture, the custodians of the home, the church, the school, and the state. And they are still, in the main, oriented to a philosophy of high-order abstractions.

As we learn, we are trained to move away from reality toward these higher abstractions. This is all right so long as we also learn that we are making the move. But we are not taught that we are making any move at all. For instance, in defining any object we learn to put it into higher- and higher-order categories. If I ask you what "it" is, you tell me "Bozo." And what is "Bozo"? A "Labrador retriever." A Labrador retriever is a "dog." A "dog" is a "mammal." A "mammal" is an "animal." We are not clearly taught that the "is" that suggests identity at each stage is simply throwing "Bozo," "dog," and "mammal" into bigger boxes, vaguer categories. Is it any wonder that we confuse things on the basis of similarities, when we are not taught to look for the differences? Is it any wonder we cannot see things clearly, when we are taught to look far away from the reality?

If you have a personal problem, like getting a job or paying your bills, you may be able to solve it by studying your own resources. If you cannot, you can take it up with your family, who may be able to advise you or to provide some material help. If no family help is available, you can apply to a city agency (we are moving away from you and your particular, immediate problem, are we not?). If the city agency is not able to help, you can go to the state. This may involve more red tape, some misunderstandings may arise, and you may feel rather regimented (and why not, for you are moving away from the world of your individual problem?). If the state is powerless to aid you, you can write your congressman to see if some federal agency can lend a hand. And if that, too, fails, you can petition the United Nations. If nothing is forthcoming there, you can "lift up your eyes unto the hills."

There is a place for close observation and attention to detail and there is a place for highly abstract generalities. But in the case of getting a job today so you can pay the landlady for the room and buy some new shoes, which is closer to the reality of your problem: to get out and answer the ads and check the employment agencies, or "to lift up your eyes unto the hills"?

We are taught that "mammal" is more important than "Bozo," that "mankind" is more important than "me," that principles are more important than actions. We are taught to move away from the evidence in external reality.

CHAPTER 26   TIME BINDING

The ways of learning for the human animal are more varied than those for the bear or beaver. Not only can we learn from direct experience, we can also learn from direct instruction. We can even learn from long-dead humans, through their recorded writings. Korzybski, the great linguist, has called this "time binding." It is another thing that separates man from the other animals.

There is more than one way to learn. As we have already seen, we can learn from direct experience and observation, that is, by looking at things, touching them, or smelling them, and we can learn by being "taught," either by a teacher or from reading in books.

We can also learn, in a sense, by combining the things we have experienced or observed or read or that we have been taught by others into new ideas, new solutions to problems, and new ways to go about things. We can take the knowledge we have previously abstracted and construct new knowledge through logic, inference, and deduction.

However, at the base of such higher-order abstractions there must be a solid foundation of lower-order information.

This basic information we could classify roughly as that which we have directly experienced or observed, and that which has been communicated to us from others.

In the first category is all the seeing and listening and trial-and-error finding out that must play an enormous part in the learning a child acquires in the first few years. In the second category is all that is passed on by others. The child gets his share of this through commands, punishments, and expressions of approval or disapproval from his parents: "Don't leave your shoes in the living room!" "People won't like you if you go around looking like that!" "You should love your little sister!" The child, indeed, is deluged with "don'ts" from dawn to dark, and in the first two or three years he has had knocked into him a good deal of education, a large part of which is in the form of directives, the things he should or should not do. The child gets something of a course in "How to Make Friends and Influence People," especially how to make friends with and influence parents.

Eventually, the directives that are repeatedly banged into him assume the character of values. He will learn that these are the ways one must live in order to win approval and not to get into trouble. He will acquire a sense of right and a sense of wrong. And he will not only judge others by these values, he will also judge how he will "rate" with other people. Most particularly, he will tend to rate himself, using the same values as a standard.

Along with these value elements, the child is also being taught other things: how to count, the letters of the alphabet, the names of the various flowers and trees and animals, stories, songs, jokes, games, bits of family history, and a thousand and one other things that cannot be directly observed but must be expressed in language, and that are communicated in words from the parents to the child. As the child learns to read, he is able to take in these communications from others without the others being present.

It is just at this point that his humanness breaks off sharply from that of the little beaver or the bear cub. These other creatures learn from direct experience. They are taught and are given directives by their parents (though not in the rich detail possible to mankind with the tool of language). But there is no other animal that ever lived that has been able to accomplish the great miracle of the written language.

With this tool the child can learn from his parents even when they are not in the room. He can read their messages even if they should take a trip a thousand miles away. Not only that, and here is the greatest miracle of all: The child can learn from people who are no longer living. When a smart beaver dies, his mind dies with him. But when a great human thinker dies, his thoughts live on in the pages of his writing, so that a thousand years later a student can have the benefit of that great one's own thinking.

You and I have a pipeline to the past. We do not have to count entirely on the hard experience of trial and error to learn about life. For we have not only the means of communication with our parents, teachers, and others, but we can reach back ten years, a hundred years, five hundred years, and communicate with the philosophers, and teachers, and law-givers of other times.

This is "time binding", as Korzybski calls it. It means that once we have acquired the use of the written language we can literally tap the wisdom of the ages. It is not necessary for each of us personally to perform an experiment that has been made by someone who came before us. To a very great degree we are freed from the need of starting from scratch. It is as if, instead of a young man having to earn his way from the start and painstakingly build up a fund of savings, he was presented at the age of 15 with a key to the world's treasure. In our hands, and in our children's hands lies the key to the stored-up knowledge and experience of the ages. In books and scrolls and papyri, on clay tablets and on the walls of temples and caves, the thoughts of men have been preserved. They are all ours if we can read them.

What this means, of course, is that we are able to start where others left off. If it were necessary for each of us to work out the theory of mathematics from scratch, we would have no mathematics. It is only because we have the record of the step-by-step development of number concepts and mathematical theory over the centuries that we are able in a few years to master mathematics that go far beyond the abilities of the greatest mathematicians in ancient times. We have all this, not only in mathematics, but in every department of human knowledge. It is a wonderful, an unbelievably rich treasure.

And if we are able to start our life work where the greatest minds human history left off, then we should be able to add something to human knowledge. It is not necessary, and it is not expected, that each of us will revolutionize the sciences. But with a whole lifetime to live, and with the wisdom of the past handed to us on a silver platter, doesn't it seem possible that some of us might be able to add one crumb of knowledge, some little contribution, to the mighty mass of humanity's treasure?

This opportunity to add something entirely new is a great challenge. It offers a chance to achieve security, a feeling of success and well-being, in our own lifetime, and a chance to pass on to our children a little increment to the most important part of their inheritance.

This opportunity for time binding is also a way of immortality. The new discovery, the original theorem that you or I or someone else can add to human knowledge, is not just for today. It becomes a part of the body of human knowledge that will remain and be a substantial asset to our children's children.

CHAPTER 27   STOP! LOOK! LISTEN!

The tendency of human experience has been to treat precious knowledge and teachings as sacred or inviolable. To be truly educated and conscious we must constantly examine past knowledge and confirm by our own experience and investigation that it still fits the territory. If not, we find new knowledge and methods or modify the old. In a word, we must bring the maps up to date, regardless of how sacred they appeared to our forebears.

All this about time binding sounds as if we had something wonderful here. And we do—provided that we know exactly what we have and what to do with it.

You will remember that when we were talking about low-order and high-order abstractions there were times when it was good to creep up close and take direct observations from a near reality, and other times when it would be best to stand some distance away and view the territory in an abstract way. Both ways, and all steps in between, are right and may be useful in their place, but it is important to be conscious of the order of abstraction we are using, so as not to become confused.

A similar warning applies to this matter of time binding. It is a wonderful thing to be able to reach into the past and learn from great-grandfather, or Benjamin Franklin, or Euclid, or Confucius, but if we become dazzled by the prospects that open up to us in tapping the wisdom of the ages, we may forget to do any time binding ourselves.

Notice one or two things about time binding. Note that everything that comes down to us in writing is in the form of symbols—words. Symbols are maps, which are supposed to represent a territory in significant respects, but because they are abstractions of higher order, they are not as detailed as the territory. They leave out a good deal. They cannot fully represent what they denote.

Moreover, some of the verbal maps that come down to us from the past may be maps of maps. Where a writer is pursuing a chain of logic or inference, or where he is discussing something that is a matter of judgment or opinion, it is not possible for him to communicate his meaning as precisely as he might describe an animal or a person. It is none too easy for us to communicate matters of judgment and opinion even between our contemporary neighbors who have been educated in a common culture and idiom. In dealing with material that comes from the past and perhaps from another part of the earth, from a greatly different kind of culture, it is more than possible that what the writer means by "rational," or "wicked," or "holy," or "treacherous" may be quite different from what we might mean by the same words today.

This is because we are dealing with a system of symbols that is not necessarily the same as our own in meaning. It is similar to the problem of a translator who finds that it is sometimes impossible to render the meaning of what an author has set down in another language based on different cultural values. It is also because the concepts of what is treacherous or what is rational may be different here and now than they were there and then.

There is another point we must keep in mind before we open our minds indiscriminately to the inherited writings of times gone by: The territories may have changed. As you know, one of the vital pieces of data about a map is when it was made. Of two carefully drawn maps representing a particular area, we must choose the most recent, the one that shows the latest changes in the territory. The 1958 road map of Western Massachusetts is a better guide than the 1940 edition. For one thing, the newer map shows the new turnpike, the new South End Bridge at

Springfield, and a great many other features that do not show on the 1940 edition.

An ancient historian may describe a city located on an island in a great river. Today, the city may be no more than a monument and walls, and the river may have changed its course by several miles. The description is valid, so long as we assign the correct date to it, but it is not as good a map of that part of the world today as a recent map published by the National Geographic Society.

The territories may have changed. We are familiar with the elaborate maps of human conduct presented in the Book of Leviticus: directives and injunctions covering hundreds of aspects of human life, marriage laws, dietary laws, laws relating to property and inheritance, laws relating to hygiene and public health. The importance laid on these laws and directives suggests that at the time they were first set down they were regarded as of great practical importance, vitally related to the very survival of the Jewish people. Today many scholars recognize that the conditions that required some of these laws no longer exist or have changed to the degree that they no longer apply as they were originally stated.

In the heritage of science and philosophy that has come down to us we find a good deal that will not stand up, some because it is inadequate and newer discoveries have made revision necessary, some because the hypotheses on which it was based have been supplanted by newer hypotheses that more nearly fit the observed facts, and some (let us face it) because it was sheer nonsense in the first place and never had much validity at all.

It implies no disrespect to the scholars of years past to suggest that their findings should be brought up-to-date in line with changed conditions, or to include the discoveries of their successors. After all, these pioneer time binders did the hard work of breaking ground into unknown territory. Chemists worked without formulas, without any knowledge of the elements. Astronomers tried to solve the riddles of immeasurable space without the simplest kind of telescope. Mathematicians labored to solve impossible problems, not having the knowledge to prove that what they sought was not to be found. We must take off our hats to these men who, out of a wilderness of ignorance, blasted the first narrow trails of understanding. As we travel the broad highway of modern science and philosophy we should not sneer at the wandering, uncertain courses of these ancient trails, for it was over the paths of alchemy and astrology that the pioneer scientists traveled to discover chemistry and astronomy, and in almost every field of thought the early stages were filled with stumbling and error.

A few hundred or a few thousand years ago time binding was not so easy as it is today. It was not simply that men did not have computers and high-speed presses, excellently printed books, public libraries in every city and town, and all the machinery of setting down and reproducing knowledge that we have at our command today. There was also the fact that without the labor-saving devices we take for granted it was not possible for very many men to spend their lives in study, contemplation, or writing. Leisure to learn was a luxury that very few could enjoy.

Under those conditions, it is hardly surprising that when a great teacher or philosopher appeared, his work was valued as something irreplaceable. Such a leader might not come again for generations. It would be most important to preserve the important work of this man, his sayings, teachings, and discoveries, so far as was possible. In the very ancient days, the wisdom of such a sage would be passed on by word of mouth, father telling son and son, in turn, telling his son.

Consider the danger here of losing the irreplaceable wisdom. Nothing could be added to information; it could only be passed on intact. Any slight alteration might change the original meaning; if a single word were dropped or changed in any way, who could say after a few generations how much had been deleted or distorted?

With such knowledge, a certain rigidity was inevitable. The words became of paramount importance; it was not permitted to suggest any revision. Present conditions could not be surveyed to bring the ancient knowledge into line with current facts. Changes in custom or in the use of language would not justify tampering with irreplaceable wisdom. Thus, in the futile hope of preserving alive the living message of the past, men frequently found themselves worshipping the tattered relic of obsolete science, obsolete ethics, and obsolete law.

We are very much concerned with this, because a good deal of our educational process has been rather heavily tinged with this kind of sterile time binding. In other words, we have an altogether disproportionate and unrealistic respect for the knowledge of the past.

A proper understanding of the real value of what comes down to us from the ages takes account of the errors and losses in transmission and translation. It allows for changes in conditions, and for later knowledge that has made obsolete some of the original findings. It puts to work the great treasure of accumulated knowledge on the practical basis that it will be used where the presumption is strong that it was valid in the first place, and where no later discoveries have nullified it.

We will use as much of the old knowledge as will stand up under examination. Here is the rule for testing: If a theory or proposition from the past is presented to you, see if it is reasonable in the light of other information you have. If it seems valid in theory, put it to the test of practical experience today and see how it works. If it still stands up, use it. If it does not entirely meet today's conditions, see what changes might bring it into line to make it currently valid.

One of the contributions we can make to time binding is this process of re-examination and revision. We will not be honoring ourselves or our ancestors if we merely accept and stupidly apply the directives and opinions of centuries ago without checking the map and making any amendments necessary to bring it up to date.

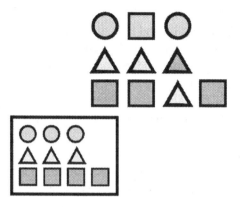

CHAPTER 28   CONTRADICTIONS

The general tendency of human education is to teach us to accept established authority without question. In other words, go by the map rather than the territory. And in fact, if there is a conflict between the map (higher authority) and the territory (current objective observation) we had best go by the map, according to our teachers and elders. Men and women love certainty over reality.

Some time very early in life we have, each of us, run up against the problem of the old-time wisdom versus the immediate evidence of our senses. We find ourselves forced to reconcile what we can see, hear, and touch ourselves with the weighty pronouncements of ancient wisdom. If we are quite young, and have been taught to respect our elders, we are very likely to repudiate what we have learned by direct experience and accept what we read or what we are taught, on the basis that "It would be presumptuous for innocent unlettered little me to disagree with the great philosopher."

Of course, it is quite possible that you will be selling yourself short unnecessarily. We can admit Aristotle's greatness without accepting every piece of nonsense he ever wrote. After all, Aristotle did not have the instruments and formulas that we have to help him today . He did not have so much time binding behind him to make his way easier. In many ways the average high school lad today, equipped and trained as he is, may be expected to have more understanding of some of the great problems of mankind and the universe than Aristotle ever possessed, in much the same way and for much the same reasons that the modern Air Force pilot can muster more strength for his attack than Hannibal and all his elephants.

When you hear or read a statement from an ancient authority, you can honor it. You do not need to scoff at it or repudiate it out of hand. But you have more than the right to verify it in every possible way, for that is your clear duty if you expect to make any practical use of the information. Yet we are not always taught to make these checks and verifications. No. On the contrary, we are often taught not to check or verify. We are taught to accept the ancient authority without question. We are taught to go by the map rather than the territory. We are taught that if there is a discrepancy between the map (higher authority) and the territory (current observation), it is better to accept the map.

You are familiar with the Hans Christian Andersen story of the emperor's new clothes. Briefly, two swindlers had convinced the court and the emperor himself that the new suit they were making for him would be visible only to the pure in heart. Under the fear of disapproval everyone "saw" the fine new clothes. It was not until a little boy asked why the emperor was marching through the streets stark naked that the people admitted the truth. In other words, if the high authority says the emperor is wearing a fine new suit, and the eyes show that he is naked, a good many people will reject the evidence of observation and cling to the pronouncements of the high authority.

Every child is faced with conflicts between what he is told or what he reads and what he actually observes. In civics or social studies he is taught how, in a democracy, the people vote freely and select the best qualified men for public office, abiding loyally by the decision whatever it may be. Perhaps it would be natural for a very young child to accept such statements, for he would have had no opportunity to observe for himself. But it is hard to understand how grown men can continue to cherish this noble fiction and defend it as if it were the actual truth; even while living in a city where the usual choice of candidates includes men of such obvious ignorance and corrupt association that the discrepancy is glaringly apparent. Anyone who has worked in a municipal election in Massachusetts knows that the usual candidate for any public office could not possibly be described as the best fitted by any ordinary standards. Yet we continue to admire the fine, clean, beautiful map and reject the down-to-earth, matter-of-fact reality.

This preference of the map for the territory is so pronounced, so emphatic, that it hardly seems possible anyone could fail to see it in everyday life. Yet it is another of those elephants that so many of us squeeze past, crawl under, and climb over, but cannot see at all.

We consider honesty a virtue. Yet there is a great deal more attention paid to whether someone is honest than to what he did at some time, at some place. We speak of generosity as though it could be separated from particular incidents and events. We talk of purity as if it existed in a vacuum.

We are taught to set principles above specific acts. We are drilled to think in terms of high aspirations to a point where it almost seems that the high-level words are more important than how we live and what we do.

In the stock market, the question is always, "What is the market doing?" not "What is Southern Pacific doing?" or "What is Jones and Laughlin doing?" If a man asks you, "What do you think of the market?" and you answer, "Just what particular stocks are you interested in?" he will very often become quite irritated with you. He doesn't want specific information about something we can check and verify. He wants a big, broad generality.

When we deal with the law we cannot consider the case of a particular man who has complicated life problems and who has become involved in difficulties as a result. No! We cannot look at the man. We have to look at the label, the map. This man is a murderer. Or he is a rapist. Or he is a burglar. Since when do we learn more about human behavior and human suffering and the solution of desperate human problems by staring at a map than we do by searching out the particular details of this one man's experience? Is Burglar A the same as Burglar B? Do we get a clearer picture of what is causing Burglar A to act unsocially by classing him as identical with Burglars B, C, and D? Are we likely to arrive at a more practical solution of modern crime by limiting our study to a discussion of verbal maps crystallized into law books, dated, for the most part, before the invention of the first automobile?

Oh! but this is authority. This is precedent. This is the Wisdom of the Ages.

Very well. Credit the Wisdom of the Ages with some value. But if the Wisdom of the Ages conflicts with the facts of a teen-age gang fight on West Madison Street at 11:15 pm, Saturday, March 29, 1958, which will it be? Will we back the directives on the ancient map? Or will we take a hard look at the facts before our eyes today?

When the Voice of Authority says, "Turn the other cheek," and the hard facts say, "Fight for your life or die," you are faced with a contradiction. Perhaps you should follow the directive of ancient wisdom. Perhaps you should fight for survival. At any rate, it is necessary, when there is a contradiction, to be able to make a choice. And if your choice is already bound through long training and habit to the ancient wisdom regardless of circumstances, then you cannot weigh the evidence impartially.

On the very day that this page is being written there appeared a feature article in the Sunday magazine supplement This Week by a well-known evangelist, entitled "Why I Believe in the Devil." The reasons this person gave for his belief are: (1) The Bible plainly says he exists. (2) I see his work everywhere. (3) Great scholars have recognized his existence.

It seems hardly necessary to ask whether it is necessarily a material fact because the Bible states it. We know that the Bible frequently uses metaphor and very high-order symbolism. We know that the men who set down the words in these books were not equipped to understand the external world as we are today. This is ancient authority, but is it verifiable today? Was it ever intended to have the material meaning this man attributes to the word "devil"? Do we know what we are talking about? And if "great scholars" have recognized the existence of the devil, we must not forget that great scholars have, in their gropings toward better understanding, held to beliefs that are recognized today as absurd. The Apostle Paul, referred to in the article as "one of the greatest Christian scholars who ever lived," lived a long time ago. Have we not learned anything about devils in nearly two thousand years?

Isn't it clear that the writer of this article is confusing a map with a territory? He is projecting an image of a "real" devil (one having material existence in the external world), and speaks as though we were observing something "out there." Isn't it clear that the devil is something that exists in men's minds, a very high-order abstraction representing various unsocial or socially disapproved concepts in our culture? When the evangelist says that he sees the devil's work everywhere, what does this mean, if it does not mean that he sees in the world around him various actions of people that do not fit his maps of proper and decent human conduct?

How can we expect men to think intelligently about their neighbors, their families, and themselves, when they are deliberately taught to think in terms of such high metaphor that there is no way to prove or disprove the assertions except by verbal argument? How can we expect people to cope with international problems of an atomic-age world, or with the economics of today's living, or with the stock market, if they are being harangued to look not at all at the facts but to close their eyes to the world they see before them and set their course on the basis of the mystic writings of pre-scientific sages?

It is all very well to believe in sin providing that we understand that we are here comparing what we see with the map of our own value system. But to embody the cause of sin in a real, tangible, personal devil (and this evangelist is very specific on this point, he is not consciously speaking in symbols)—that is teaching men to value maps more than territories. To value maps more than territories is to move away from reality. And to move away from reality is to move away from sanity.

There is a proper place for high-order abstractions, and if we use the word "devil" in quotes, to represent all that we abhor, that is all right. Just so long as we do not confuse the symbol with the external reality.

As you must know, there are millions of children today who are being taught in school, and millions of adults who are being instructed elsewhere that, among other things, a piece of bread can be and is transformed into a piece of flesh, not as a symbolic or metaphorical representation, but as a matter of substantial fact. People in this modem world and in our own country are being taught that if the evidence of eyes and of taste, yes, and even of laboratory examination were to say "this is bread still;" in the material world of external reality, they must reject the evidence of direct observation and accept the directive of ancient ritual. They are taught that it is better to accept and believe without question, than to re-examine the facts. They are taught to accept the map in preference to the territory, to reject the world and accept the things of the spirit. They are taught that it is more blessed not to have seen and yet believe, than to seek the facts in reality.

Would you say that education on a basis of faith alone, and of conformity with ancient doctrine, was a good preparation to meet the problems of a constantly changing modem world? Do you believe that the way toward a peace and brotherhood that have never been even remotely attained in the past by the philosophies of "believe and do not look" will be best served by these now when the problems of human survival have become enormously more complicated?

It is not necessary to reject the aims of high abstraction in moral and spiritual matters, but when we teach people to confuse and identify the immaterial with the material, we are educating people in un-sanity, whether it is in the teaching about sex in the home or about the devil in church, about market evaluation, or in any other department of life.

Some readers of this book will remember the to-do about vaccination. Here was a new process, intended to protect mankind from the terrible scourge of smallpox, but to some people it appeared to be in contradiction with some of the ancient wisdom, and for many years there was a concerted effort on the part of sincere objectors to prevent the use of vaccination. Similarly, in cities throughout the country, most notably in the city of Northampton, Massachusetts, there has raged a battle between ancient wisdom and modern knowledge in the matter of fluoridation of the water. According to the verbal maps that some people carry, it is contrary to nature, wicked, dangerous to put "rat poison" in the drinking water. This map means so much more than the territory that all the evidence of public records, the opinions of state and federal authorities, the reports of medical and dental societies mean nothing. If we are going to go by the map alone, then no amount of evidence "out there" can affect our opinion.

The world today is faced with a population problem. Where the productive capacities of the earth may be considered to increase roughly on an arithmetical basis, the population tends to increase on a geometric basis. The weight of evidence seems to show that populations will increase to the survival limit. This is a condition that must result in a world of malnutrition, poverty, and all the tensions and hostilities that arise in the minds of desperate men.

But how do we look at the problem of world peace and the prevention of war? Do we examine the evidence impartially? Do we accept the facts as they appear in the light of modem scientific appraisal? Do we face up to the inexorable question, "What are we going to do about the birth rate?" Or do we retreat to the pre-scientific philosophizing of well-meaning theologians who lived centuries before the present crisis even appeared on the horizon? Do we take out the old maps and solemnly publish, as "God's law," the old directives to "increase and multiply"?

This is what we mean by valuing a map (and an old and obsolete map at that) more highly than the thing itself.

This is a book about the market; at least, it is written around the problems of the market. In the market, if you accept the old wisdom as you read it and as it comes down through the mouths of traders and boardroom habitués, you can lose your money. You can be wiped out if you are not willing and able to look fearlessly at the facts and to revise or even to reject the old wisdom if it does not fit the case.

In some other departments of life, if you cling to the map and refuse to look at the territory you can lose much more than your money. You can lose your life, your civilization, and humanity itself.

We have got to stop putting maps before realities, symbols before facts. This does not mean rejecting all the valid thinking that has been handed down to us. We have already pointed out that this knowledge is our greatest heritage. All we have to do is to reexamine the territory, compare the old directives with the present situation, and make doubly and triply sure that the directives still hold. If they do not, we must change them to correspond with present conditions.

I think we could say quite safely that this is exactly what our great thinkers of the past have done. Moses and Hammurabi, Galen, Newton, and Jesus, all presented the accumulated wisdom of their times, reevaluated and restated to meet the current situation. If these sages were with us today, would you expect them now merely to repeat what they said in other places, at other times, under other conditions? Or would you expect them to do what we must do today: take another hard look at the reality and revise our maps to date.

We have spoken of high-order maps, symbols, etc., some of which are so far removed from reality that they seem to have no referents in the external world. A very common example of this sort of symbolism is the word "they" as it is regularly used by those who frequent brokers' boardrooms. "They" are putting the market up on account of the election. "They" are selling out now before the annual report comes out. "They" are buying on balance under cover of the decline. And so on.

Reputable brokers, and the New York Exchange itself, have been sufficiently disturbed by the loose and misleading use of the word "they" to warn associates and employees against it. In some cases, rather severe punishment has been dealt out. By using a broad, high-order word such as "they," it is possible to create a false picture of the secret activities of infinitely wealthy, infinitely smart, and infinitely powerful forces in Wall Street—forces that, it may be assumed by the naive, are able to manipulate the market to their own design.

Strangely enough, the question is seldom asked, "Just who are they?" If it were asked, the ghost might disappear in a wisp of vapor. We have "they" working behind the scenes in politics. We have "they" in matters of public opinion and morals. Many people are vulnerable to a scare technique based on the machinations of a sinister "they."

"They," like any other high-order noun is not the same kind of "they" we use when we refer to "the three children" or "the people next door" or even "Paine, Webber, Jackson & Curtis.[1]" The word sounds and looks the same, but in this connection, "they" is far removed from real people. It is a long shot at something or somebody vaguely suspected, moving in the shadows of the far distance. It must be somebody that is causing us to fail, to be wrong so often, to lose money so steadily. It must be a "they."

If anyone tells you "they" are doing this or that to the market or to a stock, find out exactly who "they" is, when "they" bought this or sold that, at what prices. If your informant cannot produce any evidence, if he cannot point to any territory in external reality, tell him to go to hell (a high-order abstraction). You'd be better off without his advice.

One of the many glittering generalities is planted in our young minds is the belief that government is more honest, more dependable, and more ethical generally than business. Somehow we acquire the idea that the government of the United States is about the most solid, most incorruptible, most thoroughly admirable institution in the world. At the same time many of us become indoctrinated with the idea that private business is actuated only by greed, corruption, and the expedience of the greatest personal gain. This is the book. This is the way we learn it in civics class, by implication if not by direct statement. This is the way statesmen speak about it. This is the way people seem to regard it all.

Government bonds? The safest investment in the world! The pledged word of the United States of America. A question of business ethics? Who to believe: the tax authorities and the investigating commission or the

---

[1] A brokerage house, circa 1950s.

subject businessman himself? What is the word of a grubby profit-seeking businessman against the civil servants of our government?

One does not have to become a traitor to one's country to use his eyes and ears and ordinary intelligence. The securities of government, our own or those of other countries, have been notoriously manipulated, misrepresented, and sometimes repudiated. The bonded pledge of the United States of America was repudiated with respect to the payment in gold of its obligations in the 1930s. The taxability of income from government bonds has been handled evasively, some would say, dishonestly; in other words, the large type does not disclose all that is stated in the very small print. Our government has sold its bonds to the people of this country using every device of propaganda and advertising, on the misleading premise that by putting aside $75 today, one would receive a third more principal at the end of ten years. This is true so far as the number of dollars is concerned, but for a government that more or less supported a program of continuous inflation for many years, it is a misleading statement, some would say deliberately misleading, by which people have been induced to "invest" their savings now in the hope of a return of greater purchasing power in the future, only to discover that the final payment comes short of buying even as much as the original capital. It is hard indeed to believe that these operations have been entirely innocent.

We know that government can and does reconsider its contracts, re-study or re-value former decisions. The pledged word of government is not enforceable in the way the contract of an ordinary business can be enforced. The sovereign people can feel great satisfaction in their collective sovereignty and power. They had better enjoy it, for in many ways they have little sovereignty and little power as individuals.

In Wall Street we have had great frauds, deceptions, and all the sorry history of human frailty and dishonesty, but on balance I wonder if we could not match each fraud and each deception on the part of private business with an equivalent fraud or deception on the part of government. On the whole, I wonder if business wouldn't come out with a somewhat cleaner record over the long pull. A great deal of our private business is conducted on the basis of personal integrity. A verbal agreement to buy or to sell stock or commodities is regarded normally as binding, even though one of the parties may suffer heavily because of it. There is in Wall Street, and in LaSalle Street, mutual respect and a self-respect that enforces the proper execution of agreements and the maintenance of confidence among the many persons concerned. For every case of shady dealing or corruption there are hundreds and thousands of transactions that are handled according to the accepted rules and conventions without question.

In government we find an air of suspicion surrounding every operation, as if everyone were potentially crooked at heart. No matter how many thousands of dollars you may spend with the post office, you cannot get credit for a single postage stamp to complete your mailing. Clerks are spied on, and complicated systems of vouchers and double checks are set up to prevent theft and fraud.

You will find the same suspicion and checking and red tape at City Hall or in the State House. Whatever the government touches it stains with the smudge of petty politics, the suspicion of small thievery, and all of the hostility toward the general public that we associate with customs inspectors, tax collectors, post office clerks, and the like. Certainly private business has no wings and no halo, but in spite of all the check-ups and vouchers, the peep-holes and the civil service codes, somehow we still find an amazing number of relatives on the payroll of public officials. There are still great unexplained gaps in the budget items relating to the new voting machines, the storm sewer installation, and the purchase of police motorcycles and military wrenches and toilet seats.

Aside from the hostility and lack of courtesy manifested by our public servants toward the "sovereign" people, our public servants seem to do quite a lot of stealing, directly and indirectly, from these same sovereign people. Perhaps this stealing (or quasi-stealing, such as the outside employment of firemen supposedly on full-time jobs for the city) is necessary to eke out their artificially low wages, for it is true that government and civil service pay is nominally lower than that in private industry. But why do we act as if the nominal pay was the real pay? Why do we send school children to admire the marble and bronze facade of the post office and not tell them about the slovenly and hostile clerks that grudgingly and inefficiently wait on the line before the one open window? Why do we speak of the indomitable determination that gets the mail through under any and all conditions, when the facts, which we know if we receive any mail, are that the slightest train delay, a snow storm, a holiday, or an epidemic of winter colds can seriously impair the mail service?

Why do we do honor to the mayor, the governor, the congressman, etc. as if they were better or more important than the manager of the local department store or a chemical engineer at one of our factories? No one ever invites a dentist to make a speech before the graduating class. No one ever saw an insurance salesman on the reviewing stand. Just what is it that makes the office of an alderman or a state senator more "honorable" than the job of running a hot dog stand on Main Street? What values and measures of human worth are we using? Who is best serving his fellow man? I am not implying that all hot dog stand operators are leading more significant lives than any senators or aldermen. I am simply raising the question, "What standards are we to use in judging a man?"

We know that there have been some very able and very valuable men who have served in public office intelligently and well. That is not the point. The question is whether the mere fact that a man is elected to public office, or the fact that a certain security is identified as a government-sponsored issue should in and of itself clothe the matter in such raiment of purest white that we cannot fairly judge the merits of the case at all. We are thus regularly presented with faulty, retouched maps, and we are taught to respect the map and not examine the territory.

Why do we set up these pictures of something so fine and so good and so clean that it is not possible? We have made a picture of Our Democracy, a map, if you will. We honor the ideal. We like to think of a cooperative community in which men work together for their own good and for the common good, and will not stoop to robbing their neighbors for personal gain or advancement. We fervently wish our governor were a great statesman. We would like our mayor to be a dedicated and able leader. We want a government that is efficient and capable and honest, one that respects the individual citizen and treats him fairly.

These are all good ideals. They are goals worth seeking. They are maps of what we hope to be true, and what we work to make true. But it does not help matters to act as if the map were *actually* the territory, and to assume that "because we say it's so" makes it so in very fact.

If we want to cope with the problems pressing us so hard, the practical problems of the high cost of government, the corruption of elections, the parking problem, the school crowding problem, the crime problem, and all the rest, then we should first look at the facts, not at the map. If the mayor is a former associate of racing interests, and if his record includes various investigations and perhaps criminal accusations, we should recognize all this, and also recognize that this is not an unusual picture in the matter of governors.

Perhaps we could at least compare the overall realities of government and business. We could ask such down-to-earth questions as, "If I had to place my trust in somebody in a matter of personal importance, which business men of my acquaintance could I go to with confidence?" and "Which of the politicians that I know would I trust?"

You must know that in certain cities and certain states it is necessary for you to have certain connections in order to expect to be successful in politics, or to serve even in a humble capacity on the public payroll. It may be a very definite (though unwritten) requirement that you be of a certain race (or not of a certain race), or that you have certain church affil- iations or certain family connections. Imagine a Jewish mayor of Boston! Just try to picture a Negro governor of Alabama![2]

There may be and no doubt is discrimination in Wall Street, but when you go to the broker and deposit your margin and place an order to "Buy 100 shares of U. S. Steel at the market," or "Sell 5,000 bushels of Chicago May soy beans," you are not asked what your social position is, or whether you are a Roman Catholic or an Orthodox Jew. You may be a man or a woman, well-dressed or shabby, young or old. No one can "put in a word for you" to obtain the advantage of a single eighth. Your money is as good as the next customer's, and no better. It is here in Wall Street, not in City Hall or the State House, that genuine democracy is practiced, and without fanfare or parades.

Isn't it time, then, that we stopped treating maps as if they were "things"? Isn't it time that we look at the facts first and then make our abstractions.

In other words, isn't it time to stop talking nonsense?

---

[2] As of 1998 an unblemished record.

CHAPTER 29   LET'S NOT BE TOO ANTHROPOCENTRIC

High-order abstractions—like "God's grace"—are not measurable, just as a "good company" is not measurable. The only way to deal with the vagueness of these terms is by mutual agreement on their definitions. There is no other way to avoid dispute over terms that have such different maps for different people.

We have studied the relations of various orders of abstraction, and we have seen that there is a place to count and recognize the individual trees (low order), and a place to view and perceive the forest as a collection of trees having some similarities (higher abstraction). The difficulties most of us get into result from confusion of the levels of abstraction, come when we identify "ghost" as a thing, "devil" as a person, etc.

In the living of our own lives, and in spite of much that we are taught, our self is the center and most important factor. We must learn to live with ourselves, and to respect ourselves. We must also learn to live with others. This is a sort of extension of the self: One identifies his neighbor with himself. We have a Golden Rule that concerns our relations to our neighbors and that is basic in many religions.

A few great philosophers are able to extend this concept of common humanity to common life. Such men as Albert Schweitzer have a feeling of neighborliness and brotherhood not only toward all men, but toward all living creatures. It is not specifically important here to consider what it is that shapes Schweitzer's super-humanity, but it is perhaps worth considering why and how it is that most of us attach such overwhelming importance to "mankind." If we are to be tied to a narrow philosophy that sees man as the center of all creation, we are perhaps making much the same kind of error that the ancients made when they took it for granted that the earth was the center of the universe, around which moved, as a matter of course, the sun, the stars, and the remotest galaxies.

It is necessary for us as children to be able to abstract and see our own relation to external reality, to see our self as related to all humanity and humanity as a perceived higher abstraction. If we can then see the broader relation in which man and the animals are all part of the still broader manifestation we call life, we have advanced in our thinking. If we can also see that the trees and ferns and algae are also part of life we have extended our map. And if ultimately we can see that "I" and "humanity," and "animal life" and "all life" and "all creation" are part and parcel of a single universe, then we have attained a very comprehensive view of the cosmos.

It may help us to understand nature if we see it as a variety of workings-out of the laws of probability, of thermodynamics, and of relativity. Then we will not smugly consider that the deer were put on earth to be shot down by hunters, nor the fish created merely for us to murder in their homes. We will have a proper respect for the universe and appraise ourselves with dignity and honesty without any phony overtones of special creation or other delusions of grandeur. What is important is for us to be able to see ourselves in our real relation to the rest of the universe. It is not necessary to grovel as less than the dust, and to engulf ourselves with self-condemnation as miserable sinners. Neither is it necessary, if we have a proper understanding of our place in the scheme of things, to bolster our sagging egos with self-glorification as children of God, created a little lower than the angels, and the like. If we are to achieve sanity we must learn to think sanely, and for this we do not need to don figurative golden crowns and lord them over our less gifted cousins among the lower animals; nor do we need to put on sackcloth and grovel abjectly for being what we are.

The sane man will recognize what he is and how he is related to the rest of nature. He will learn to make of himself the best-fitted organism to deal with the situation in which he finds himself. This is the goal, not only of general semantics, but of all human effort.

CHAPTER 30   SANITY MUST BE ACHIEVED

There is sanity, and there is un-sanity. Un-sanity is what we get as a result of being brainwashed by our culture, our formal and informal education, and the forces of the status quo that are ready to burn every Galileo at the stake to prevent knowledge that threatens their survival. The only way to true sanity—in the market as in life—is to cast off the blinders and see what is.

We speak of the "insane." The term calls up pictures of the great gray building on the hill, beyond the edge of town, where howling maniacs are confined in padded cells. You and I, thank God, are sane, like most of our neighbors.

Are we, indeed?

Name ten of your friends who are sane in the sense that they are reasonably well-fitted to the environment in which they live. Name ten of your friends who are able to realize their full potentialities in life. Name ten of your friends who are free from all neuroses, alcoholism, domestic maladjustment, phobias, sexual aberrations, and personality problems.

137

We take it for granted that everybody is sane unless he has been duly certified as a lunatic and confined in an institution. Oh, if only this were true!

How can we expect people to become adapted to living in the world where they must live when they are taught to not look at it but to accept the directives, maxims, proverbs, laws, morals, scripture and superstition accumulated through the ages? How can we expect people to be sane when they are taught un-sanity and forbidden even to look at or discuss the facts?

Do you question this? Do you feel that we do have free thought and free speech and a free press? Then consider what would happen if you attempted publicly to discuss sexual behavior, or the existence of God, or birth control, or the democratic system, or the criminal law, or any of a number of other subjects charged with emotional content, such as laissez faire capitalism versus Christian Marxism. Especially if your conclusions tended to support the view that would be popularly considered the wrong view.

You can write or speak on any of these subjects so long as you agree with what has already been stated and accepted as true. You may not completely express your contrary views, on pain of social rejection or worse. You may not express them at all unless you are able to pull your punches, softening your arguments to a point where they are relatively innocuous. And so we are taught to think un-sanely. We are forbidden to speak entirely sanely on certain subjects.

We bury some of the real causes of human misery because we are not allowed to talk about them. Then we try to solve the problems in carefully emasculated language, if possible without reference to any basic questions. Why did Chapin kill the two children? Why did Starkweather spread a path of death across Nebraska? Why are the Russians hostile? Why are prices going up? Why is my wife so cold to me? Why does the market go down?

We cannot answer these questions because our lips are sealed. No newspaper would dare print a forthright answer. The only answers we can make are those derived from the kindergarten-type education we have received. But sanity does not come through faulty and inadequate training. Sanity, meaning the full realization of a man's manhood, or a woman's womanhood, is not something we can take for granted. It must be worked for, it must be won back, to some extent, from the forces of restraint, of training, of teaching, and of civilizing.

There is a certain ruthlessness about education for sanity that frightens people who have been coddled behind the walls of aphorism and tradition. If we are going to achieve sanity in the market or any other aspect of life, we must have the guts to break with tradition, to re-examine, and, if necessary, to repudiate the highest authorities.

If we can divest ourselves from the compulsive necessity of following blindly what we have been taught, we can learn to see what is before our eyes and evaluate it accordingly. If what we find checks with what we have learned, we can benefit greatly from the experience of the past, but if the evidence does not support the teaching, we must be able to reject the teaching and accept the evidence.

This is the direction of sanity. This is how we intend to look at the market and at every other aspect of the life around us.

CHAPTER 31   THE THINKING PROCESS

Learn facts, not analytical processes: this is the message of much of our education. Memorize and regurgitate past wisdom and sacred opinion.

Or open your eyes, learn to think, to observe critically, to test all received knowledge and opinion and truth. Then, based on informed and aware observation, abstract conclusions and opinions to arrive at your own map of reality. In the process be carefully aware of levels of abstraction, of real and theoretical territories, of what is verifiable and what assumed, of what is sacred and suspect and of what can be tested by the scientific method and what must be derived by unafraid logical analysis.

There have been a good many magazine articles in the past few years about the relative values of the classical or liberal arts education and the practical or shop-and-laboratory education. I wonder if the subject could not be discussed in a little different way, using somewhat different labels with perhaps somewhat different meanings.

We could speak of the tendency of education to look back at tradition or to look straight ahead at the current situation. The contrast I am thinking of is between the memorizing of dates and speeches and poems and descriptions of battles and the observation of things and events as they are directly perceived now.

I realize, of course, that things and events are not directly perceived, and that we need not only our own past experience as a means of evaluating the present, but also we need the handed-down experience of others. But there is a great difference between the young botanist who memorizes the names of 1,673 varieties and species and genera of plants and the young botanist who spends each afternoon watching the growth and development of a bean plant.

To a good many people education is a matter of how much assorted data you can cram into one brain. Some schools seem to be organized along these lines. "Never mind looking! Just listen!" ("Study the map; throw reality away.") It is this kind of "education" that leads to arguments about why a fishbowl with a fish suspended in the water will not weigh more than the same fishbowl if we remove the fish. (Not true, but it has been seriously debated.) Or why men have more teeth than women. Or why a large iron ball will fall faster than a small one. Or how it is impossible for a man to run faster than a turtle. Or how many angels can stand on the head of a pin.

A good deal of our schooling still consists of memorizing a lot of material that could be looked up, if it were ever needed again, in The World Almanac, or Webster, or Kent, or whatever reference book might be appropriate. Actually, a good deal of the information is not likely to ever be called for. In all my life since leaving eighth grade no one has ever asked me the date of the first Olympiad. I do not believe I need to know the order of succession of the French monarchs, and if it should be necessary for me to produce the dates of the principal battles of the American Civil War I could easily find them at the library, though I cannot imagine just how this crisis could arise.

The radio and television programs in which a wisecracking master of ceremonies exploits a prodigy give the impression that education is a matter of how many novelists of the 18th century you can name, or who was the Democratic candidate for vice-president in the election of 1928.

The training and development of an omniverous memory is not the kind of education that leads to creative imagination, or to an understanding perception of the world around us.

Education, in the sense of understanding life and living and the world we live in, is a much more complicated thing than mastering the atomic weights, the conversion tables, and the lists of irregular verbs. It must involve direct observation, abstraction—perhaps many stages of abstraction—comparisons with past experience, the recognition of similarities and of differences, and the use of whatever material has come from others through teaching and through books.

Of course, in the early stages of childhood one picks up facts from direct observation and learns through signs and gestures, rewards and punishments, that certain things are approved and others disapproved. The child, through language, picks up knowledge from others, not only with regard to things and places but also with regard to opinions, judgments, and values. He accumulates a lot of do's and don'ts and a value system. However, as we have seen, and largely because of the nature of language, he is likely to have only a dim understanding of the process by which he learns, that is, by which he abstracts.

It is most important for the child to learn as soon as possible to recognize which of his thoughts represent something he knows about material reality, which refer to a conclusion or deduction derived from facts, and, in short, how he knows what he knows. If a person were reasonably aware of the process by which some of his most firmly held beliefs, prejudices, and judgments got into his head in the first place, he would be able to give them their proper value. The maxim handed down by an aged great-aunt that "an itching palm means you will find money" is not exactly on the same plane as a report from the weather bureau that the precipitation during the past 24 at Bradley Field was 2.5 inches. It is one thing to hold to the family opinion that Uncle George is scatterbrained and something quite different to consider the fact that Uncle George has held nine different jobs in the past year. The first is a high-order judgment; the second is a report about the facts.

You will notice that the report about the facts may not necessarily be a true one. Uncle George may have held twelve different jobs in the past year or he may have had no job at all, but this is a question that can be settled by reference to the records in the case. The question of whether or not Uncle George is scatterbrained is not referable to any external authority because it is a matter of opinion existing only as a map in someone's head.

In learning to think, sanely and in an orderly way, the most important foundation stone is to become aware of the order of abstraction, to know at all times whether you are considering something close to the object level or at the high altitude of conjecture and opinion. Just as in building a house we do a more substantial job if we start with the foundation, rather than with the roof; the first data, the most basic, is that obtained at very low levels of observation and personal experience. To this we can add the communicated observations and experiences of others, checking them directly, if possible, with the observed facts and otherwise evaluating them according to the dependability of the sources. If the facts we read or that we are taught come from a source that is of questionable authenticity, or if the original fact-finding was a long time ago or under different conditions or in a different place, then we should perhaps discount or modify the information rather than accepting it at face value.

If we have some idea of at least the approximate level of our further abstractions, we can avoid some of the most serious semantic traps. We should know that "maple tree" is a higher abstraction than "this silver maple tree," and we cannot attribute (project or read back, that is) everything that applies to maple trees in general to the particular silver maple growing in our backyard. On the other hand, we should know that "maple tree" is a lower abstraction than "tree," and we should not attribute to all trees the features we find commonly in maple trees.

Most especially, we must avoid confusing very high-order concepts with very low-order concepts. "Generosity" is not the same as "Joe gave fifty cents to a beggar." "Virtue" is not the same as "She has never slept with anyone but her husband." "Success" is not the same as making a million dollars.

If we can build a fund of factual information and then erect on this foundation a series of abstractions generalizing these facts and deducing logically certain common features, we can progress to higher levels where we reach conclusions. From these conclusions we can form opinions and judgments, which in turn will determine our attitudes and through these our behavior in various circumstances.

In the processes of logic and deduction we must generalize and we may quite properly use symbols, metaphor, analogy, or any other device that helps us to construct useful maps to understand what is going on "out there," and what it means to us. So long as the symbols, metaphors, analogies, etc. have a verifiable correspondence to something in external reality, these can be considered useful maps. It is only necessary that we be aware of their nature and that we do not set up the map, the symbol, as superior to the thing it represents.

Just as an architect manipulates small models and makes drawings on paper to represent the buildings he plans to construct, just as the engineer uses formulas and charts to make it easier to see the relation of more complicated things, so we use high abstractions to engineer our own higher thinking.

There are hardly any limits to what we can attempt and how we can use these devices. The rules are few and simple.

1. We can use a high order abstraction to represent some features in lower-order reality. But we must not confuse and identify abstractions at different levels.

2. If we intend to project our abstract thinking to external reality, we must be sure that there is actually a territory in external reality to which our maps will apply. True, there is no reason we cannot construct maps for which we have no corresponding territory. A great deal of philosophical and mathematical speculation has been concerned with purely hypothetical territories. This is all right so long as we do not then try to force the theoretical map onto a real territory. There have been cases, especially in the field of chemistry, physics and pure mathematics, where a theory built around a hypothetical territory has later been applied in a very practical way. These are cases where a territory has actually been discovered such that the previous map does have a verifiable correspondence with the territory. Here we are thinking of the discovery of certain elements by spectroscopic analysis before their discovery in nature, the aberrations of light in gravitational fields, and the theoretical development of the non-Euclidean geometries of Riemann and Lobachevsky and their later applications.

The observations and conclusions must be consistent with themselves. As you know, there are no inconsistencies in external reality. Inconsistencies and contradictions arise from faulty perception. Thus, someone may report that there are four houses on a certain block, and someone else reports that there are six. If we have decided, as the second observer did, to include hen-houses and out-houses, he would be correct, but there is no contradiction in what is actually "out there." The contradiction is simply in how we define it and speak of it. It is necessary in any orderly system of mathematics or scientific analysis to set up definitions in such a way that there are no internal contradictions in the system.

CHAPTER 32   THE VAGUENESS OF THE
HIGH ABSTRACTIONS

High-order abstractions take on the meaning given to them by the user. If you and I are to have a productive discussion on the subject of success, of necessity we have to agree on the definition of this high abstraction before locking horns. "Pencil" we could probably discuss without that necessity.

Let us take a further look at the high-order abstractions. We have compared them with a long shot with a camera, as contrasted with a close-up. Because they are some steps away from observed reality, the details are obscure. In extreme cases the details disappear altogether or become so tenuous that it is hard to assign any precise definition to them, and it is certainly impossible to communicate much meaning about them to someone else.

In religious matters we have such terms as the attainment of "grace." This word, which sounds like a common noun, is not quite so precise as "pencil" or "horse." It is not possible to measure grace, to weigh it, ascertain its length or temperature or electrical conductivity. In the stock market we frequently hear of "good" companies, and "growth" stocks. These are very high-order words, so vague that it is hardly possible to measure or evaluate them. If, for example, someone says that General Motors is a good company, ask him "How good?" What is the measure of "goodness"?

There are hundreds, perhaps thousands, of terms we use as though they represented tangible realities, but that cannot be measured or directly observed because they are of such a very high order, like hope, love, envy, peace, or thoughtlessness. One such word, which we will discuss at some length is success. It is not impossible to define and measure success. It is a high-order abstraction, a map in your own mind, and you may attach whatever definition you wish to it. You could, if you wanted, decide that to you success would mean giving away all your money to the poor. It could mean unseating the president. It might mean integrating a coast-to-coast system of railroads so that people could have the same uninterrupted ride that a hog may enjoy. Success could mean being chosen Queen of the May, or owning a steam yacht, or getting in the movies, or memorizing the five-place logarithm table.

But if you are going to talk about success with someone else, it is important that you and he agree as to what you are talking about, and that you have approximately the same values. Otherwise there will be (at this high level) a contradiction that does not exist in reality.

This matter of making sure you are actually communicating with someone in terms that have about the same meaning to both of you is nearly as important as the matter of checking facts externally in case of a difference of opinion. Both of these precautions will eliminate disputes; between them they can eliminate most of the disputes that are likely to arise.

CHAPTER 33   "TO ME"

When we hear a speaker assert that the Empire State Building is 1,250 feet high we may note that it is an objective statement. But if he begins to speak of evil and good and loyalty—to speak, that is, in high-order abstractions—we know that he is onto maps, opinions, and subjectivity. A test to discriminate the objective from opinion and subjectivity is to add the phrase "to me" (or "to him") to the statement. "This is evil" can then be heard as "This is evil to me."

Several times we have used the expression "to me" with respect to high-order abstractions. You will understand by now that when we are referring to a dog or a table or a copy of yesterday's newspaper, it is possible to point to the thing, to look at it and abstract some of its features, and to arrive at a good agreement with anyone else who may be present as to what sort of thing we are referring to.

I am assuming here that the parties concerned are of ordinary intelligence and equipped with the usual sensory apparatus. You will recall the story of the several blind men who, abstracting by means of the sense of touch, were unable to concur on the nature of an elephant, one man maintaining that it was like a wall (the side), another that it was like a hose (the trunk), another that it was like a rope (the tail). But we are not thinking of people so handicapped.

Most of us can agree on the gross features of ordinary objects. It is when we get into the realm of highly abstracted concepts, many steps removed from the original factual observations, that we get into trouble. This is because, as we have seen, it is not possible to point to or touch the high order abstraction, for it exists, like a mental map, only in the mind. We have no way to compare one such concept directly with another's concept in regard to the same matter. When you speak of your love for Marjorie, how can you tell me how much you love Marjorie? You are dealing with something that is very real to you, but it cannot have the same reality to me, and there is no way you can precisely communicate what your love for Marjorie really is.

Matters of opinion and judgment, most adjectives, and abstract nouns, all partake of the nature of high-order abstractions, and to a great degree they are personal and not communicable. When we say to ourselves, as we leave the house, "This is a beautiful morning," we should, to be strictly accurate, add, "to me." It may be a wretched, stinking day to someone else, perhaps even to your neighbor next door. When I announce, either to myself or to others, "I am a success in life," it is quite important to add the qualifying "to me." After all, one's success must be measured by one's own values. Whatever my standards of success might be, I am sure that there are people who would violently disagree with me.

Even such an apparently factual statement as "This is a difficult situation" is actually a "to me" problem. I might find it very difficult, for instance, to have to explain the operation of the New York Stock Market to a visitor from Japan who had no knowledge of the English language. It might not be a difficult situation at all for someone who spoke Japanese.

An experience that one person will honestly regard as horrible may be perceived by another as merely annoying. It is all a matter of how we think about it, and how we see it. How we see it is very often how we say it. If you are expecting that the extraction of a tooth will be a horrible experience, you may well find it horrible. If you have learned to speak of certain things as nasty, beautiful, or awful, you will probably "see" the nastiness, beauty, or awfulness you are expecting. But it is quite important to keep in mind that the nastiness, beauty, or awfulness, whatever it may be, is not of itself "out there" but is strictly related to your perception; it is not a material attribute of the thing itself, and not necessarily true for any other observer.

It can be dangerous to forget that the higher abstractions we attribute to things are maps and not territories. Your former partner may appear beastly to you, but the beastliness is not something that can be observed and compared and measured factually by anyone interested. The beastliness is actually not something about your former partner at all; it refers to how you feel about him. Your feeling may be entirely justified, or it may be unfair, but it is a matter of how something appears to you and this beastliness is a symbolic representation of your appraisal of the man.

Suppose that you are evaluating not your partner's actions but your own. Suppose that according to your own standards of conduct you have erred very grievously. Then you will feel "guilty." Is this guilt something factual and observable about you? Or is it the expression of your own judgment? You have framed and focused the image of your actions and compared them with the projection of your picture of proper conduct, and you find that you have not measured up. Therefore, you appear guilty to yourself.

It is important to understand the subjective nature of such a concept as guilt, for it is such concepts that people are very likely to project "out there" and regard as if they were facts in external reality instead of opinions or judgments. The amount of damage that has been done through habitual attitudes of self-reproach and self-condemnation is incalculable.

If we can keep our maps separate from our territories, we can avoid confusion that may result in real tragedy. For example, to use the case we have just considered, if we recognize that we have certain standards or values of conduct and that this is a map to guide us, we need have no compunction about revising the map, bringing it up to date, correcting any errors in it, and generally making it more suitable to the function of guiding us in our living. We can then recognize that our conduct in such-and-such a matter on such-and-such a date did not conform to what we ourselves have set as the minimum requirements of proper conduct. It is not necessary for us to pin the label "guilty" on ourselves as a permanent brand; we simply note the failure and plan to "go, and sin no more."

Very often in the market a man will compound his own error or misfortune because he overlooks the fact that his judgments about himself are not matters of fact but matters of opinion. A trader will feel small, or sorry for himself, or guilty. He will hesitate to "make a fool of himself" by admitting his mistakes. He will defend his own wrong tactics rather than change his methods. He will, in short, act as if he were dealing with physical features of himself, instead of with maps and directives concerning his conduct.

If I am a "miserable, stupid fool," that does not make me feel very good about myself, and it does not bode very well for my future. But if I understand that I feel miserable because I have made what I now realize is a stupid and foolish mistake, I can look forward to changing my ways and not getting into that particular kind of trouble again. Also, I can preserve, or at least restore, my own self-regard.

One of the first rules we might observe in reading an editorial or listening to a sermon or political commentary, is to question any statement that may have a "to me" character. When a writer or a speaker tells you the Empire State Building is 1,500 feet high, that is a matter of record it is either verifiably true or provably untrue. But when he speaks of evil and loyalty and discontent and aspirations, he should add the important words "to me"; if he fails to do so (and he will fail to do so), you will do well to add these words yourself. Then you will understand when he is talking about facts and when he is talking about his own personal attitudes.

What you apply to editorial writers, speakers, preachers, etc., you can also apply to yourself. When you express an opinion based on how you feel about something rather than about its measurable, factual features, you might well add those important qualifying words, "to me."

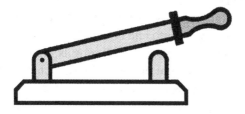

CHAPTER 34   EITHER/OR

**In general our teaching tends to lead us to employ two-valued think-
ing, the logic of dichotomy. A man is either sane or insane, guilty or
not guilty. The market is either bullish or bearish.**

**Either/or is the hallmark of the careless thinking that seeks to
simplify life to black/white perception. Simplistic thinking is a hin-
drance to intelligent analysis. More careful thinking will enable us to
see that when most stocks are bullish some are bearish and act
accordingly.**

There was a song a few years ago titled "It's Gotta Be This or That."
There are in life many situations we could call "two-valued," that is to
say, there are two possibilities, two answers, two ways to act. You can
either get married or stay single. You can then have a child or not have a
child. You can go to work or not go to work. You can flip the switch to
turn the light on, or you do nothing and sit in the dark. In many elections
you can only vote either Democratic or Republican. The patient in the
accident ward will either live or die. And so on.

Two-valued situations seem so common that some scholars have considered them universal. At least, they have acted as if all problems could be

reduced to two-valued situations, like the on and off of an electric switch. A basic assumption in classical (Aristotelian) logic is that A is either B or not B. This is a generalized statement of the two-valued situation.

We are taught to think in a two-valued way. It is either this or that. As though there were two boxes, into one of which every statement, opinion, judgment, must be placed. We say that Jimmy is either good or bad in school. His answer is either right or wrong. He is honest or he is dishonest. When a man is charged with a crime he is expected, no, required, to plead either guilty or not guilty. There is no opportunity given him to explain that perhaps he is a little guilty, but not very guilty. There is no room in an either/or situation for part-way measures. There are two boxes, two categories, and the answer must lie in one or the other. You cannot, for example, run a simple electric switch on "part way."

If a man is picked up by the police because he is "acting strangely," he will be examined to determine his sanity. He will be found either sane or insane. In Wall Street many people recognize only two conditions. It is either a bull market or a bear market.

Now ask yourself whether the world as you actually know it and experience it is built entirely on the either/or plan. Do you love your work completely and absolutely, at all times? Do you hate your job entirely and always? Or does the answer lie somewhere in between? You like your work generally, perhaps, but there are times when you abhor it.

Do you consider yourself absolutely honest? Did you never, on any smallest matter, do or say anything that was not completely truthful? Well, then, would you say that you are entirely and absolutely dishonest, that you have never done or said an honest thing in all your life? Well? Then the answer must lie somewhere in between.

A is not entirely, and absolutely, and always B; neither is it entirely, and absolutely, and always not B.

Have you ever known a time when the market was entirely bullish— or entirely bearish? Not even in the panic years of 1929 to 1932 were all stocks going down in price. Not even in the lush years of the 1954-55 boom[3] were all stocks advancing. How can you say the market is either bullish or bearish when individual stocks can act as differently as they do? (Or have you ever looked to see?)

---

[3]Or 1985-1998.

How? There are ways. We can set up arbitrary standards. We can establish, for instance, certain formal definitions that will establish either guilt or innocence. These, however, are maps; they are abstractions we agree to treat "as if" they represented something in external reality. There is a great body of legal fictions, "as if" situations, by which it is possible to categorize the law and avoid the embarrassment of actually looking at the facts in individual cases.

We can do something like this with problems of sanity. We can set up definitions of what is sane and what is insane, and then measure our subject by comparison with these standards. We can say, then, that according to the method used he is either sane or insane, which merely tells us that he corresponds with the definitions (or maps) we have set up, and that therefore we can put him in one of the two boxes or pigeonholes marked "sane" and "insane."

This, of course, does nothing to clarify the real condition of the person, helps not at all in understanding his problem, and does nothing whatever toward getting him back into useful life again. It overlooks all the particular features of the case and lumps the entire problem into two high abstractions representing the "either/or" dichotomy.

It is much the same in dealing with the market. We can set up definitions of what we decide to call a bull market or a bear market and then place any market in one or the other of these categories according to how it compares with our own definitions. But this covers up all of the significant action of individual stocks and does nothing to make clearer our view of what is really going on. We can make any definition we want, of course, for the map is not the reality, and your map may be quite different from mine, but we each have an equal right to draw our own maps. You may use the Dow theory. I may use the Dow theory with certain variations. Jim may follow the odd lot indexes. And Milhous may work with cycles based on the motions of the planetary bodies. These are all maps and each may provide for categories labeled either "bull market" or "bear market," but since they are far removed from the reality and are, as you must know by now, high-order abstractions, it is hardly any wonder that no two maps (or opinions) of whether "it" is a bull market or a bear market, will agree.

One of the hard things about studying the "either/or" view, and particularly in seeing its very serious dangers, is that it is not wholly wrong.

As we saw in the early paragraphs of this chapter, there are a great many situations in life where things are either this or that. Also, in the very many cases we used as examples (and by the way, we could pick a great many more illustrative cases from everyday life), there are many times when there is no problem in making an either/or choice. When a man comes into court with a bloody nose, swearing at the police officers and threatening at the top of his lungs to "knock the hell out of that Jerry Mullens," there is a strong presumption that he is guilty of being drunk and disorderly as charged. If a man were brought in under suspicion of insanity and soberly claimed that God had ordered him to take possession of the moon with the title of Emperor and Lord above all the angels, one might reasonably concur that the gentleman was sufficiently pixilated to qualify as insane.

If the Dow Jones Industrial average were to drop to a ten-year low on heavy volume, most reasonable observers would be willing to classify the action as a bear market.

Someone might very well ask, "If many life situations can be represented accurately as either/or cases, and if many other situations can be so classified most of the time, why should we bother about this question? Why not use the either/or all the time?" And, of course, that is just what many people do, and what our teaching tends to lead to.

But this overlooks the fact that either/or does not apply entirely even in the extreme cases we have mentioned, and that a tremendous field lies in between that cannot be considered either/or. In fact, if we deny that gray exists and stretch everything to be white or chop it off to be black, as Procrustes adjusted the dimensions of his visitors to the size of his bed, we are again setting our map at a higher value than the territory it represents. We are not looking at the thing, but at the symbol.

When we call for a plea of either guilty or not guilty, we are overlooking any degrees of guilt. When we find a man sane or insane, we have deliberately swept under the carpet all the differences that mark his case as unique. On the one hand, we may have classified a slightly disoriented person as in precisely the same category as a raving maniac. On the other hand, we may have given a clear bill of health to a person who can be suffering from depression, irrational fears, delusions, or other symptoms that may become progressively more acute, and possibly dangerous.

When we classify a market as bullish, we tend to overlook the specific action of particular stocks, and we may fall into the error of projecting this bullishness (which is not a matter of external reality, but of opinion) onto some stock that is by no means bullish and that may collapse even as the market soars to new all-time peaks.

Like all other maps, either/or must be used with full consciousness of its arbitrary nature. We must recognize that it is not a complete picture of nature, as we will see in the following chapters.

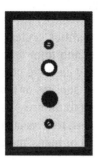

CHAPTER 35   THE DANGEROUS NATURE
OF DICHOTOMY

**Perhaps the greatest danger of dichotomous thinking occurs when we
come to consider success/failure. If you are not a success, in two-valued thinking, you must be a failure. In such highly emotional high-
order maps or abstractions it is valuable to stop and analyze, to
define terms, and to add "to me." I am a success to me. Because I am
. . . happy . . . living in New York . . . have a yacht . . . whatever. He is
a failure to me, because he lives in the woods in a cabin and writes
indecipherable philosophical papers and sends people mail bombs.
Success is getting what you want (which you must define precisely).
What the world calls success is getting what everybody (presumably)
wants. But like other emotional maps, there is a spectrum or contin-
uum hiding behind the dichotomy.**

There is one particular application of the either/or orientation that can be
especially disastrous. Keep in mind that the high abstractions are vague,
and that the higher we go in abstracting, the vaguer become the outlines
of the reality they represent. Also, keep in mind that either/or is a very,

very high abstraction, since it eliminates all but two possibilities in any situation. The particularly dangerous case we have in mind is the success/failure dichotomy. If we are to apply the two-valued system to this, there are only two possible eventualities: a clean-cut and absolute success on the one hand, and an absolute and total failure on the other. Since, if we are operating on this basis, any case we consider must be either B or not B, then a man must be either a success or not a success. Not a success is generally regarded as equivalent to failure. We are taught in our culture, to work for success, to seek success, to expect success. You might almost say that success was the great goal of many men. We are taught to seek it.

Yet we are not taught precisely what this success that we seek really is. That is left open, undefined. Success can be regarded as election to the Colony Club, or possession of two Cadillacs, or the acquisition of an honorary degree from alma mater. It can be the acquisition of money, or of popular approval—almost anything, according to one's own definitions.

There is a further question that certain bears on the problem: How much? How much money to constitute success? A thousand dollars? A hundred thousand? A hundred million? How do we measure the necessary qualifications of success? And if we cannot measure it, that is, if we have not set any measurable standard to define it, how can we tell when we have attained success? For many of us it is vitally important to be a success, for if we are not, we automatically, according to our habit of either/or judgment, fall into that other dreadful category, failure. That would be disaster.

We can get into trouble in at least two ways with this one. Sometimes we do not define the term at all, so that no matter what riches, honors, and rewards come our way, we cannot with certainty say that we have reached our goal, for we have never set a goal in verifiable terms. Sometimes we may set the goal so high that it is quite impossible to reach. And in some cases both of these factors may be operating. For example, In the course of a conversation over luncheon one Saturday noon, my companion mentioned a conference he had attended at which he met an important industrialist, a man reputed to own some $20 million in corporate securities. My friend asked, "Why should this guy have $20 million?" This, of course, was not quite the right way to ask the question. "Why," in this connection, is meaningless, for it hardly permits of any definite answer. Apparently, the question represented not so much a desire to get information as to register a protest at the unfairness of it all.

It was such a broad, high-order question that it overlooked some details. One of these, quite obviously, was that $20 million in securities is not precisely the same as $20 million in cash in the pocket. These millions are, in a certain sense, fictitious, or at least artificial and arbitrary. One can go out in the open market and sell ten shares of Westinghouse, or a thousand shares. But you cannot call up your broker and sell a hundred thousand shares at anything like the present market value. Also, from a tax viewpoint, and from a functional viewpoint, the $20 million invested in business is not actually consumer spending money. It's more or less fixed or frozen in corporate activities, and the accounting of this money is mostly handled as a business not a personal affair. Furthermore, it is not reasonably possible to consider $20 million as pocket money for drinks and dinners, mink coats, sports cars, and the like. Anyone could have such luxuries to meet his most extravagant desires for a small portion of this capital.

I think my friend was using $20 million as a symbol of the success he was vaguely craving—not that the craving itself was vague, but the particular shape of the goal was not clearly drawn. The goal was set too high, far beyond the reasonable needs of anyone, and far beyond even the limits of almost unlimited indulgence. Also, the goal was vaguely stated in that there was no clear understanding of just what this $20 million really consisted of. For a man of 60 to start thinking of success in terms of $20 million, unless he already has several legs on the prize to begin with, is to make sure of failure. For if one is not a success, under a two-valued system of evaluation, one must be the only other choice: a failure. The goal, as stated, is not reasonably possible to attain under the conditions stated.

There is also the possibility that, assuming it might be attained, it might be hard to know just when the precise accumulation of $20 million had been accomplished, for the accounting of $20 million invested is not by any means such a simple bookkeeping problem as counting the currency in a bank vault. When we talk of the value of a large amount of invested capital, we have to consider a number of debatable questions, such as the value to be assigned to patents, to good will, to land and buildings, machinery, etc., and appraisal of various notes, mortgages, accounts receivable. So the goal of $20 million is actually both too high to be realistic and too vague to be determinable. In other words, the man who sets such a goal is predestined to disappointment; he is bound to be a failure.

Sometimes we can solve a problem by re-stating the proposition in different terms, or by changing the words, or modifying the values. If, for example, in this case my friend had looked at his own real needs, he would not have fallen into the trap he did. He would then have realized that what he was complaining about was not the fact that somebody else has $20 million, or even that he did not have $20 million. What he was feeling was that he did not have enough.

If he took a realistic view of this and considered how much was enough, he would surely realize that his immediate and pressing wants did not involve millions of dollars. A new garage. Not more than a thousand dollars. A fur coat and some winter clothes for his wife. Perhaps a new model car. Paint the house. A vacation trip. How much altogether? $5,000, $10,000, perhaps $20,000, but not $20 million. It might be difficult to meet a goal of accumulating $20,000, but at least it would be a definite goal, and at least it would be within the realm of imaginable possibility. Such an objective might be hard to reach, but the project would not be foredoomed to failure from the start.

The reaching for non-existent or vaguely defined or impossible goals is not a trivial matter. It touches the roots of a great deal of the disillusionment and despair of people in every department of life, including, of course, the market.

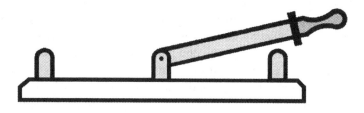

CHAPTER 36   THREE-VALUED ORIENTATIONS

Choices in life can often be evaluated with a three-valued orientation: In the market, we may buy, sell, or remain on the sidelines. Confronted by a lion, we may kill him, make friends with him, or run away. A three-valued system allows us to examine more alternatives, more courses of action, than a dichotomous value system. More flexibility results in better outcomes.

We have seen how people are taught to think in either/or terms about many aspects of life, including some that are much better not regarded in such absolute terms. We have also seen how this habit of thinking can lead to a single-valued system when one side of an either/or situation will lead to self-reproach or public disgrace. But these are not the only ways of evaluating life situations.

There are other systems of evaluation that in many cases offer a great deal more flexibility. There are three-valued systems. For example, let us suppose I am confronted by an immediate and present danger. Let us say this danger is in the form of a lion, escaped from the zoo, which I encounter when I step into a small storage building behind the animal house. Assuming that I do not want to be eaten that day, I must take some definite steps for my protection. If I have a heavy whip in one hand and a pistol in the other, and knew how to use both, I could simply advance on the lion and beat him into submission or kill him. In short, I could attack. *Or* it is conceivable that I might be able to ingratiate the lion, to talk softly to it, to scratch its neck and pat its sides. I could make friends with the lion. And if I were not strong enough to fight the lion to a standstill and not sweet enough to charm the lion, I could run like hell and slam the heavy door behind me. In other words, there are two ways in which I could win a positive victory, and there is one way in which I would not lose.

This is basic. People who go through life tied to a one-valued system of evaluation and those who are limited to a two-valued (either/or) system should consider the possibilities of the third move, or rather, might well consider the advantage of having three moves instead of only one or two. We can lick the gang. We can join the gang. We can keep out of the gang's way. Three courses of action, two positive and one somewhat negative, but in any case we will not get our heads bashed in.

We can consider confronting Russia with overwhelming military power. We can consider a program or conciliation and mutual friendship. Or we can build our defenses and cut ourselves off as far as possible. Not one of these may be a complete or fully effective answer, but together they lay down the patterns along which international strategy must be made. Three basic moves.

Like most of the situations we have been studying, you will find this same structure over and over again in many different life situations. Some men dominate women. Some men seduce women. Others avoid women like poison. In the market, we can buy, we can sell, or we can stay out entirely.

Three basic moves—the move against, the move toward, and the move away—can provide much greater flexibility than we have in one-valued or two-valued systems. But we have already seen how a two-valued system can become a one-valued system when one of the two alternatives is suppressed or forbidden. A somewhat similar limitation often applies to the three-valued system. Most of us have been trained not to be aggressive. We are forbidden, in many cases, to attack. We cannot move against certain persons (parents, teachers, the blind, nuns, the aged).

We cannot move toward a reconciliation in some cases. We are forbidden to have much friendly feeling towards certain persons (alcoholics, Communists, sex perverts). Nor can we move freely away to protect our interests. It is forbidden or at least disapproved to move conspicuously away from certain persons and groups (family, church, native culture, and all of the social and cultural enclaves in which we move.)

We are "forbidden" from acting entirely freely even in the market. We can buy; that has a good sound to it, and enjoys social approval. But we cannot sell, certainly not in the sense of selling freely, selling short, as readily as buying. There is a great deal of suspicion and social disapproval connected with short selling and a good deal of this has penetrated into the value systems of investors, so that they fear to sell and may actually feel guilty in making a short sale. And while it is not specifically forbidden to stay out of the market (the move away), there is such social approval connected with investing that it amounts to a definite pressure to buy "sound" stocks. That is why the man who keeps his money in an old sock or in the savings bank does not enjoy great public approbation or self-esteem.

If we could learn to use three strategies instead of only one or only two, if we could learn to evaluate so that we could be free to act according to the real needs of a situation instead of reacting to the social pressures that have been built into our own value systems, then we would more often be able not to be eaten by the lion, that is to say, not to be hurt.

CHAPTER 37   MULTI-VALUED SYSTEMS

Having been so educated, people tend to find themselves in situations demanding limited choices or alternatives—dichotomies and trichotomies. In reality much of life, and the market, can be viewed as multi-valued. The gambler will win big or go broke. The intelligent observer may diversify his bets, hedge some, and employ a diversity of tactics and strategies.

By this time it must be quite clear to you that there are various ways to solve problems. When we say one-valued, there really are such situations. If you slip on the back steps, you grab for the railing. It is the only rational thing to do. There are plenty of two-valued situations as well, where you have two possible courses, and if one is not socially forbidden or suppressed in your value system, you can take either course. You can accept the banquet invitation, or you can decline. There are three-valued problems: You vote Republican, you vote Democrat, or you stay home.

Of course, in some places an election is not merely a choice between one of two parties or staying home. In France we might find half a dozen or a dozen parties on the ticket. We could have many choices.

People forget they have many choices. People overlook opportunities as big as elephants. Joe, for instance, may feel that, being half-committed, he must do right by Mary and marry her (one-valued). He may forget or overlook or reject the possibility that he could either marry Mary or not (two-valued, either/or). He will not give himself the choice that he could marry Mary, marry Joan, or not marry at all (three-valued). And you could hardly expect a lovesick swain to consider that he might marry Mary or one of ten other girls or not marry at all (multi-valued).

Multi-valued strategy would make it unnecessary for the gambler to go for broke. There may be more to the game than either shooting the works or folding. A man can bet $1, $5, $100, or $1,000; he often has a multi-valued choice. Yet, as you know, many card players consider only two courses: bet the pot, or quit.

It is hard to believe how strong this impulse to limit choice can be. A majority of commodity traders, for instance, seem to prefer to pick out a single delivery in a single commodity, the "one best," as they see it and speculate as heavily as possible on the favorable outcome of that one commitment. They will reject quite violently any suggestion that their funds be distributed in a number of commodities so that they will not suffer total loss if any one or two of their contracts go against them. They do not want a multi-valued situation. They want to reduce everything to either/or, which in the final analysis means rejecting the "bad" alternative and following a single inflexible choice.

Actually, the world we live in is filled with multi-valued situations. The telephone book is a directory with many values. We can call up any of thousands of different numbers. The indicator on an automatic elevator is multi-valued, though you are restricted to the choice of definite whole numbers for the floor you want to reach (you can't ordinarily push a button for the 4-1/3 floor), and you are limited by the number of stories to the building, including perhaps one or two negative integers representing basement and subbasement. Some automatic alarms are designed to provide a multi-valued choice of rising time, with intervals of 15 minutes. With some timers you can set the clock to turn on the radio at 7:00, 7:15 or at 7:30, but not at 7:03 or 7:16.

Stock prices, too, are multi-valued. If a stock is quoted in variations of one-eighth it cannot move up or down less than a full eighth at a time. When we study the geometry of a circle we learn that by inscribing a multi-sided figure, a regular polygon either inside or outside the circle we approach the form and length of the circumference of the circle closer and closer as we increase the number of sides of the polygon, so that we can say that the limit of the sum of the sides of a polygon drawn outside or just inside a circle is the circumference of the circle itself. Of course, we cannot actually draw a polygon having an infinite number of sides, but by using a great many sides we can come very close to the figure we want.

In various situations in life it is better to have many points of reference rather than just one or two or three. In some cases the more points we can set down on our chart or map or system of evaluation—the more nearly we can approach an accurate representation of the external reality, and thus out conclusions based on the map—the better the symbols will correspond with the conditions they are supposed to represent. It hardly seems necessary to point out that the closer the map comes to representing the territory, the more the map can help in reaching your objective.

CHAPTER 38   INFINITE-VALUED SYSTEMS

Just as there are two- and three-value systems, there are infinite-valued systems. Now we must measure instead of count. Between two points exist an infinite number of possibilities. To measure these infinite possibilities we must follow the engineering principle of least effort. We will weigh diamonds on a jeweler's scale and use freight scales for railroad cars of coal. For practical purposes, "infinite-valued" may be taken to mean "having a very large number of values." We may not be interested in all those values—after $10.01, we are not concerned with $10.01001. It's just not practical.

We have progressed from single-valued situations where there is no choice at all through systems offering, two, three, several, or many choices. It's true that some problems can be expressed only in terms of one, two, three, or some larger number of discrete choices, but we also have cases that could be called infinite-valued, or at least continuous-valued.

When you measure the size of a table top with a tape measure, it's true that you call off the size in inches, say 40 inches wide and 72 inches long. This is not quite the same as calling a telephone number or pushing an indicator on an elevator. In these situations you have to make your choice using whole numbers only. But, as you know, when you measure a table, it can be 71 1/2 inches long, or 72 7/16, if, if we had a tape measure accurate enough, 72 19/28. In fact, there is no limit to the number of values we can assign to tables having a length of more than 72 inches and less than 73 inches.

Temperature, which we express in degrees, is of course not limited to whole numbers of degrees. Temperature is infinite-valued, meaning we can read it as close as our thermometer and our eyesight will permit. For most purposes it is not necessary to know that the temperature outside the kitchen window reads 35.276 degrees Fahrenheit. It's good enough for ordinary purposes to say, "It's 35 degrees." In determining electrical resistance, potential, etc., and in checking speeds of traffic or machine parts, in reading boiler pressures, light intensities, levels and frequencies of sound waves, in fact in most of the fact-recording of science, we are dealing with infinite-valued functions. "Infinite-valued" means simply that we are not limited to whole numbers but can measure the data as closely as our equipment will permit and our needs require.

"Measurement," as contrasted with "counting," is the key to the infinite-valued orientation. It should be obvious that a man is failing to use his entire problem-solving forces if he uses too coarse a measure. You would not want to use a scale designed for weighting freight cars in the railroad yard for weighing diamonds, since in the case of coal or sand it would be sufficient to determine the weight within a few pounds and there would be no sense in trying to get the exact number of ounces in a 30,000-pound load. But the difference in a small fraction of a carat (a carat is roughly 1/150th of an ounce) would be important in weighting diamonds. On the other hand, you would certainly not want to use a jeweler's scale to weigh out a carload of coal.

Measuring concerns the choice of a suitable unit where the choice is infinite. It might be appropriate to use a steel tape to measure the George Washington Bridge, but for measuring the diameter of a ball bearing, we need a micrometer. It is just as stupid to spend time and energy taking unnecessarily accurate measurements as it is to take measurements that are inadequate because they are not sufficiently accurate.

There may be some confusion in your mind, unless you are thoroughly familiar with the use of technical and symbolic material, as to the relation of maps, symbols, value systems, etc. To the engineer it is very easy to see a choice of several decisions reduced to so many specific points on a diagram. He can also see the choice of decisions in an infinite-valued system as the choice of any point on a smooth curve. The more accurately he measures his data and draws his charts, the more precise an answer he can expect to get from the map or diagram. As we said, it is very important to have a scale and measure that is appropriate to what we are trying to find out.

Another way of putting this, a way that irritates some people brought up in the perfectionist school, is that we follow a rough rule of least effort: We do the job just as carefully as necessary, but no more so. We never shoot for any greater accuracy than is needed. This is important. A bank statement has to read to the last penny. An estimate of the national debt for 1970 does not need to be figured to anything closer than a few millions; in fact, anything expressed more accurately would be misleading, since it is not possible to predict this figure very closely.

In the same way it is a waste of time to measure and record the size of a gymnasium in 64ths of an inch, since all we need to know is the size in feet to the nearest odd inch. Just so long as we keep in mind that the data obtained by physical measurement is not precise, does not need to be precise, and should not be expressed with any more precision than is needed for the job at hand, we do not need to consider the very small leftover fractions beyond the tolerances we have set. So measuring is quite different in principle from counting, for there are no indefinite leftovers when you say there are six eggs or ten eggs.

In mathematical computation there are two basic methods, and it will not surprise you to learn that these are based on the counting and on the measuring ideas. The prototype of the counting method is the abacus, where a certain number of beads represent a certain definite number, exactly, no more and not one bait less. The model for the measuring method is the slide rule, which can give you as much accuracy as its scale and your eyesight will permit, but which never expresses a positive, definite result. In other words, with a slide rule, as in measuring the size of a room, you can get as closely as you need but you cannot say that the result is *precisely* 172.43908 inches. Modern computers represent these two basic methods. If they are of the counting type, we call them digital; if they are of the measuring type, we call them analog.

Strangely enough, the differences in the two types of computations are not so vitally important as you might suppose. The apparent absolute precision of the digital machine disappears when you begin to run into long calculations involving decimals, for the string of decimal places very quickly runs fight off the paper and out of sight, and the very small values at the right hand end of the decimal result become so unimportant as to be entirely negligible.

Furthermore, some types of data that for ordinary purposes we think of as infinite-valued are not really unlimited. For instance, we can magnify an object with lenses, we can make it appear bigger yet with microscopes, but eventually we reach a point where the units (the lengths of waves) by which we see become so coarse that we cannot see any more by further magnification. The image breaks down into discrete impressions, like a coarse screen photograph in a newspaper or like the detail on a television screen.

Most of the data that we treat as infinite-valued is, if we carry the argument to the limit, actually multi-valued. At some point when we break down our measurements to something very small indeed, we reach a stage where it is simply not possible to go any further, either because we have reached the point where the data itself is discontinuous and has to be read in packages or discrete units or because our sense organs cannot perceive the stimulus beyond a certain point except as separate packages.

At some point we arrive at the end of the line, where we have broken up the data into the ultimate, smallest bits. At that point it is not possible to measure any further; nature has no means of communicating any more detail to us. In the case of counting sheep, this point is reached at one sheep; in figuring a bank account, the limit is one cent. With most stock prices the limit is one-eighth of a point and will soon be decimalized. In various scientific studies we are limited by certain physical constraints representing the final breakdown of the data to their ultimate bits.

The reason we have touched on these questions about infinite-valued systems is so that you will understand clearly the nature of what is meant by infinite-valued. What we really means is having a very large (but not necessarily unlimited) number of "values."

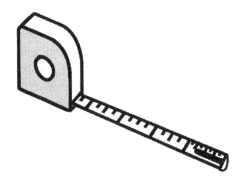

CHAPTER 39   THE GREEKS HAD A PHRASE FOR IT

Phrases we learn from the Greek—"nothing in excess," "measure in all things"—are often pointed to, but we are not really taught their significance. We are certainly not taught to live according to the philosophy these phrases express; otherwise, men would not hitch their wagons to stars and consider themselves failures for failing to reach the moon.

The man with the ability to consider measure in all things can enjoy the amount of success that for him is necessary and sufficient. He can make his choices based on a scale of many values and recognize an infinite number of shades of gray between white and black. This is not a popular methodology with the crowd, which doesn't want to be bothered with qualifications and analysis but wants strong black/white rhetoric rather than careful statement of degree or the earthy fact.

The ancient Greeks fell into some colossal blunders in their philosophy and in their science. The "good old days" of 2,000 years ago were really the very young days of man's understanding.

What is striking about the work they left to us is not what they did not know or what they knew that was not true. It is how much they were able to discover that was useful and significant and valid, especially in view of the limited inheritance of knowledge they received from their predecessors, and the rather primitive equipment they had for making their observations. We can take the good time binding they did for us and put it to work today. That is, we can admire and accept whatever part of their architecture and literature and mathematics and logic we find applicable to the conditions under which we live today in the light of what we know now.

One of the really basic principles of the Greeks can be expressed in the phrase "nothing in excess," and another phrase, "measure in all things." This idea of moderation, of reasonable sufficiency, holds the answer to a great many problems that we all have to face every day. The man who understands this would not be tied to a compulsive need to "hitch his wagon to a star." He would not have to be *absolutely* successful, *absolutely* honest, *absolutely* generous; in short, he would be free of the one-valued orientation, free to live like a man instead of trying to live like a saint. He would live in reality instead of projecting an image of some high-order abstraction and trying to live up to it.

Of course, to some people, many people, the drive for perfection is a good thing. As Browning put it, "What I aspired to be, and was not, comforts me." We are taught to think this way. We are taught that if we aim very high, if we aim at the very pinnacle, we may still come closer to perfection than those who set their aims very low.

However, if the aims are so high, or so absolute, or so vague that there is no hope of realizing them ("a miss," we are taught, "is as good as a mile"), this one-valued orientation may lead to demoralization. When the one right course to the one right objective is contrasted with its either/or opposite number, the slightest falling short of the goal becomes complete and utter failure. The man who is frustrated in achieving his impossible aims feels entirely defeated and is a prey to depression and anxiety.

The Greeks held the key to this problem, but it is as good as lost for many of us, for we have been trained not to use it. In our culture we do not put a premium on "measure in all things." We learn to go all-out, to make up our minds and then shoot the works. We want the top or nothing. This oversimplification, where we apply a one-valued or two-valued method to what may be at the very least a three-valued situation, one that may even be multi-valued or infinite-valued, limits our chances for success.

These oversimplifications are tied up with the process of abstracting we discussed earlier. They are not entirely false, and that is what makes them so dangerous. But they are faulty in that they are inadequate. Tell a man that he is making a mistake to set such a high value on kindness (a very high-order term), that he will feel guilty if he flares up at a child throwing rocks at his car, and he is likely to hear you in a two-valued way: if you don't believe in kindness, you must believe in unbridled cruelty to children.

In the same way, if he occasionally feels justified in telling a small white lie, there are some who feel he has thrown honesty to the winds and will stop at nothing. If I say I am not satisfied that all stocks are acting bullishly, there are friends who will take this as a statement that I believe this is a bear market.

There is something between up and down or black and white or good and bad—or between success and failure. It is possible for a man who has learned measure in all things to enjoy a modicum of success. He can arrive at the amount of success that for him is necessary and sufficient.

Engineers know this well. Since all engineering measurements are approximations, the framework of a problem becomes a study in how much accuracy is necessary and sufficient. It is not at all necessary, nor is it desirable, to shoot for perfection. Inability to achieve the (often impossible) perfection is not necessarily ruin or failure.

We can shoot for a given goal up to a point (modified one-valued method). We can choose this, that, or something in between (modified two-valued system. We can go this way or that way or stay where we are, or some combination of these choices (modified three-valued system). Or we can make our choice on a scale of many values, perhaps operating between certain specified limits (multi-valued system).

These last thoughts are not always accepted freely. It is very hard, as we all know, to change the established habits that were inculcated in us when we were quite young. People will fight to defend old maps and old symbols, regardless of whether they actually represent any territory here and now and regardless of whether they ever did represent just what we were told they represented. Even when people take their map, go to the territory and compare it, and note the changes or corrections it needs, they will still cling to the old map. The picture we have in our memory of the old swimmin' hole may be more meaningful to us than the photograph of that spot as it is today.

We cling to our ideas about family, about sex, about "our" country, about God, about the ways we feel about ourselves and our neighbors as if the maps we hold in our minds were more real than the external realities themselves—so much so that even when these realities have demonstrably changed or are provably different from the map, we still tend to deny the external reality and assert the truth of the map. We know that very often it is better to think of something in degrees rather than in absolutes, but the old habits stick by us. We know better, but somehow we go right on following the old methods.

In some fields there is no difficulty in thinking according to degree. No one would think of limiting the temperature of a room to either hot or cold. These words are too broad, for we would have to assume that if the room is not hot, it is cold, and vice versa. That might not be an entirely valueless report, for as between a room at, say, 100 degrees and one at 20 degrees, most people would agree that the former was hot and the latter not hot and therefore cold. But this does not allow for any very fine discrimination.

Neither does it allow for any personal choice. Since the concepts hot and cold are very high-order abstractions, they may be different for various individuals, and there is no way to compare these maps directly at the very high levels of abstraction. When we measure in multiple or infinite steps, we can assign much closer (and more generally verifiable) values to hot and cold. We can ask how hot? How cold?

This is all very obvious in the case of simple physical measurements such as temperature, voltage, pressure, and distance. The principle is not so easy to accept when we are dealing with love or purity or success, or even valuation of the stock market. Because of the way we are taught to think, the way almost everyone in our culture has been taught to think, we do not like to see things in terms of degree. It is almost as though we had been taught "measure in nothing," or to follow a principle of "everything in excess."

We understand and appreciate the simple, all-out statement much better than we grasp the thoughtful, measured evaluation. This is because the vague, loosely defined generality at a high level of abstraction seems much more significant than the imperfect, measured observations from reality. In our enthusiasm over being able to abstract to high principles, which animals cannot do, we forget that the principles, if they have any validity, must derive from roots based on external reality, so we reject reality, which is the source of truth, because it is not so perfect and so all-embracing and so absolute as the fine, sparkling abstractions. We prefer the glorious glittering generality to the little earthy fact. Speakers will win great audiences orating about brotherhood and holiness and loyalty, where the trained observer who is trying to do a job of helping human beings with necessary and sufficient solutions to their real problems here and now stirs no great emotions and wins no great following.

We would not weaken our position if we tried a little measure in making our decisions. Perhaps then we would not inquire whether an employee was honest or not honest; we might, instead, investigate how honest he was. We would not ask ourselves whether we were a success or a failure but would decide what constituted success for us and estimate the degree to which we had achieved it.

But many people don't like hedgers. They want a leader to speak right out in black-and-white all-out terms. No compromise. No measuring. Everything to the limit. If some Jews were used as scapegoats in Germany, many would not want to know what Jews, or to what extent and degree they allegedly made trouble. Many would (and did) accept the all-out condemnation of all Jews as totally bad, and the remedy proposed (and used) was simply to exterminate, so far as possible, all Jews. This is what the all-out way of thinking can lead to, as it has over and over again in the tragic record of wars, persecutions, massacres, and inquisitions across the pages of history.

People want clean-cut, easy directives in plain loud words like cannon balls. They do not want to hear that "Some stocks appear to us to be weak, but about 60 percent still seem to be moving in bullish trends." What they want is a statement that "Yesterday's market confirmed the up trend. The market will make new highs for at least two years to come. Fantastic profits will be secured by those who buy now." Perhaps you have read such statements in the commentaries and the advertisements of financial experts.

The public thinks it understands what is meant by a bull market. The label does not raise any questions about how bullish or what stocks are bullish. It simply indicates, "Buy now!" Like most absolute directives, such all-out terms carry an unspoken prediction, as though the statement read, "If you buy now, you will make fabulous profits." This is very similar to the implied promises in other directives: "If you honor your father and your mother, your days will be long upon the land which the Lord thy God giveth thee." "If you are honest, it will be the best policy."

We have many of these plain directives concerning how we regard almost every basic problem of life. You can read them or hear them any day in the week (especially on Sunday). They are stated without particularization as to when or where or under what conditions. They are stated as absolutes, without limit and without degree, and it is never explained that they represent not reality itself but the outcome of many stages of logic and inference, crystallized as judgment or opinion. This is too bad. Many of these directives have a solid center of truth. They are not without value. But they may need verifying and restatement in terms of multiple or infinite orientation.

If we really want the most useful answer to a question, then, we do not go to the mass meeting and listen to a speaker repeating, with gestures, the simplified generalized wisdom of the ages. We go to the laboratory and study the facts, and we determine to what degree the ancient principles apply today. We measure. We determine what is necessary and what is sufficient, what is valid in the ancient lore and what we can add or change to make it useful for us here and now. We accept the partial, imperfect answer carefully framed to include no more ground than our data will justify us in including. Where we don't know, we say, "I don't know until we have further facts."

If we look at things in this manner, testing, checking, correcting, accepting only as much from the directives as we can reasonably justify, we will be accused of weakness. Because we cannot or will not come right out and say whether "this" is black or white, therefore we must be unable to make up our own mind. We must be too ignorant or too timid to take a stand. Unless we can plunk all-out that the Egyptians are right and the Sudanese wrong, we are vacillating. There is no room for anything in between, no possibility of a partial rightness or wrongness. We must endorse a bull market or look for a panic. We must pick up one side of the dichotomy and forget the other, and everything between entirely.

Is this the road to better understanding? Is this an approach that is going to help us to understand ourselves and the world around us and how to deal with it? Is it any wonder that there are contradictions between the views of various statesmen and moralists and stock market analysts, if they are each clinging to a simple all-out view and for all practical purposes ignore anything that does not support the view they hold already.

There are no contradictions in reality, you know. When experts declared a bear market in the summer of 1957, Lorillard did not fit the map. It was true enough that some stocks, many stocks, a great majority of stocks, were bearish and fell many points. But Lorillard was pursing a bull market course in every sense of the word, and doubled its value during 1957. This is a contradiction at the high level of bear market, but it is no contradiction at the level of what Lorillard actually did.

If we can just look away from the high abstraction long enough to see the facts, we find no contradiction. The only contradiction is in our too-high, too-absolute statement. If we value the map more than the reality, we must not be surprised to find that the reality doesn't always fit the map. In such a case the reasonable man will change his map, not try to explain away the facts. Notice that it is not necessary to throw away or burn up the map.

Just as we have gone beyond Aristotle in logic, beyond Euclid in geometry, beyond Newton in physics, beyond Freud in psychiatry, we have also gone beyond Dow and Hamilton in understanding the technicals of stock trends. But we do not discard all the great work of Aristotle, Euclid, Newton, and Freud, nor Dow and Hamilton. We simply add the necessary corrections and additions to the maps they left for us, and use these revised and up-to-date maps.

In some cases this may mean correcting erroneous statements. It may mean developing a new hypothesis to better explain what we perceive in external reality. More often it will mean a slight modification of the terms. For example, a whole family of paradoxes in logic can be eliminated by adding to the words "This statement is true in all cases" the phrase "except in this case." Thus, in order to give any meaning to the all-out statements, "I am a Texan. No Texan ever tells the truth," I must add "except in this case." We could still question whether the statement will hold true, but at least it makes sense, which the first does not. But the biggest, most useful change we can make in the old maps is to add the dimension of degree. When we specify how much or how many, we will be so much better off than when we say all or everybody or forever or absolutely. When we learn "measure in all things," we will have "nothing in excess."

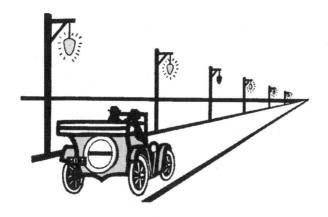

CHAPTER 40   IMPERFECT INFORMATION

When faced by choices human beings long above all for certainty and simple situations. But nature, life, and the market are never reducible to totally clear decision making. There are always exceptions—stocks that go up when all the others go down and vice versa. There are situations where all data appear to be present and clean, but the information is later found to be imperfect. As in life, operating in the market with this in mind can relieve us of the necessity of being right or wrong and give us the option of being skillful, mindful, and practical, of liquidating our losing activities (and stocks) and profiting from our fortunate activities (and stocks).

You can imagine how unacceptable it would be to a person who has been carefully taught to accept a certain value system that some of the basic premises of that system would have to be changed. Perhaps you have read Oscar Wilde's story of the "Birthday of the Infanta" and wept, as I wept, at the spectacle of the little princess, brought up to feel that her slightest wish would be met always and always, faced at last with the inexorable fact that Death was not bound by this directive. She, who could command whatever she pleased, had to face the unpleasant fact that Death could claim her, as it could claim any of her subjects.

When we have been brought up to feel that there is an answer to everything and that the answer, if we only look diligently enough, will explain everything, it is hard to reconcile ourselves to methods that deny the possibility of obtaining perfect information. It is terribly hard to have to build a way of life around such terms as "I don't know . . . maybe," "up to a point," "so far as we can find out at this time," "in all probability," etc. It would be so much easier to have a sure, pat answer, a straight yes or no to all the questions we have to answer.

We can get those pat answers, too. If we want to close our eyes to reality and work in the ivory tower of high abstractions, we can find the perfection that, alas, is not to be found in the world of reality. But it won't always help us if we do this—not when we have to deal with the imperfect and the approximate.

You will find, perhaps you have already found, that the law has a great tendency to take the broad directives stated in the ancient wisdom and apply them to this particular case here and now as if the map made 500 years ago told us all about this poor devil picked up in Hoboken for obtaining money under false pretenses from his father-in-law. The law, by and large, is not interested and not able to make a particular study of all the factors in this individual case. It is necessary to classify it, to convert it into a higher abstraction and chuck it into the pigeonhole with other cases having some similarities.

In every field, especially those concerned with ethics and human relations, we assume that a "perfect" or "ideal" case will serve as a map of all possible cases in present reality. This can lead to a lot of lawsuits, and a lot of other troubles as well. When you begin to treat the market as if it were a single, real thing instead of the highly complex aggregation of individual cases that it really is, you can delude yourself badly. For instance, if in the summer of 1957 we had a bear market, then we would be justified in selling Parke, Davis short.

There was some truth in the conclusion that in the summer of 1957 we had a bear market. If we had to limit our action to buying everything or selling everything, we would do much better to follow the map and sell everything. But we can do better by accepting the partial and imperfect answer that *most* stocks are bearish, instead of taking the all-out course. If we had followed such a plan, we would not have sold Parke, Davis but would have treated it on its own merits for what it was—a strongly bullish stock. We might still have sold a majority of stocks, but not this one.

By accepting the imperfect reality instead of the perfect ideal, we can often do much better. The very word "imperfect" suggests that there is something wrong with the information. Really, all it says is that we don't know everything. Unless we have impossibly high standards, which can ruin us in the end, we do not need to seek a perfect or absolute answer. We can deal with the facts directly, and we do not even need to seek complete information about them. All we need is necessary and sufficient data, which is something else again.

Considering the market again, if you have been brought up to believe in success vs. failure, a strictly two-valued orientation, you are faced all the time with the necessity of classifying the market as strong or weak. You cannot very well stay out of it entirely—this is the third choice, the running away, and nobody likes a quitter, not even you. So you must choose. You must make the all-out choice between black and white. Nothing in between. Either it's a bull market or—what else can it be? It must be, then, a bear market. But unless you have "a pipeline to the Almighty," as John Brooks expressed it in one of his articles on finance in the *New Yorker,* you're going to be torn by anxiety all the time. For one thing, not all stocks move together. The case of Parke, Davis is not unique, not even rare. During a series of crashes in early 1953, Pacific Western Oil made new highs, even through a downside late tape. Ask someone what happened in the market in 1929. He will probably tell you that for several years the market had been advancing spectacularly. That it made its high in early fall of 1929. That it crashed in late October, an the crash continued, to become the worst bear market in all history.

All that is true, in a sense. If we substitute for "the market" the words "Dow-Jones Industrial Average," it is true. Approximately true. It overlooks the big four-month rally ending in April 1930, which many regarded as a resumption of the bull market. It overlooks the steady downward trend of dozens of important stocks right through 1924-1929. It says nothing about the really big stocks, such as Chrysler, which topped out over a year before the crash, and had lost many, many points in their own private bear markets long before the market toppled. It sweeps under the rug the fact that many stocks made new bull market highs in 1930, and a few stocks made their bottoms in 1929, proceeding from there to start genuine major bull market trends of their own.

Then is the statement that the market advanced to 1929 and then crashed and declined to 1932 a false one? No. It is not false. It is true—to a degree. To a large degree. But we will have a better grasp of the situation if we do not distort and color the picture so as to lose sight of all the contrary action.

People get hurt taking things for granted. People get killed because they project a map instead of checking the detail in reality. My father used to drive an open car from a railroad way station at one end of Morraine Road in Highland Park, Illinois, to the dead end of this road where it terminated at the grounds of the Morraine Hotel. Along Morraine Road there were just six overhead streetlights, spaced rather widely. On the hotel grounds at the end of the road were a number of trees, and between two of the trees was strung a guy wire at a height of about four feet from the ground.

One evening he and my mother and two other couples were returning to the hotel down this road. Father decided to "let the car out" and show what it could do. He counted the streetlights as he came down the Morraine Road, intending to stop before the dead end at the hotel grounds. Unfortunately, one of the lights was out that night. The car tore over the curb, into the hotel park, and it was only by sheerest good luck that some of the passengers did not lose their heads as the car slewed just barely past the heavy steel guy wire. It was true, you will notice, that he had passed five lights. But his information was imperfect; he did not know that one of the lights had burned out. Yet he had acted as if his information was perfect and complete. The data were not false but were inadequate.

When we consider factual, observable events, we can get into a great deal of trouble if we insist on looking at only the high abstractions of these events, but this is nothing to the troubles we can get into when we are dealing with uncertainties. The average man does not like uncertainties. He is not trained to cope with then. He will try to sweep them under the rug. He will use any device that will make it possible for him to feel more sure, for he is not willing to accept a "maybe" or an "I don't know" as an answer. So he will resort to averages, to market indicators, to complicated charts of intersecting lines designed to prove that it is either a bull market or a bear market. He will accept almost any kind of nonsense if it is stated with enough assurance. He will buy horoscopes to determine the trend of the market by the position of the planets. If all else fails, he will look for some authority who will relieve him of using his own intelligence by making the either/or decisions for him. But he must have a straight, simple answer, otherwise it means nothing to him.

Do you see how this way of looking at things is out of line with the facts? Do you see how it leads, inevitably, to frustration, anxiety, or demoralization? It's asking too much of reality. It's setting up a make-believe world, and then crying if the world isn't exactly like the make-believe. We know, for instance, that trees in general are round, but we have all seen tree trunks distorted by the trunks of adjacent trees or by a cramped location. It's useful to know that tree trunks are round only so long as we understand that this is an abstraction, and the reality in any particular case has to be looked at. If the tree trunk isn't round, that's that. The territory is the final answer, not our map.

Suppose we're faced with a more difficult situation. We're going to draw a card out of a well-shuffled deck of 52 cards. Which will it be, red or black? A man could go crazy trying to figure this one out. He might consult fortune tellers, astrologers and mystics, but it's questionable whether any of these experts could help him achieve a significantly accurate naming of the next card to be turned. What to do? Do we turn our backs on the question and say (as many do when it comes to the market), "It's all just a gamble"? It's a gamble, yes, but not "just" a gamble. It isn't true that we know nothing of the outcome, and it isn't true that we can't cope with the situation. We cannot name, without fail, always and always, what color the next card will be. And that hurts. It hurts to be wrong. We have been taught to be right, and if we are not, then we must be wrong.

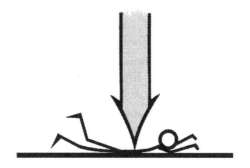

CHAPTER 41   WHY DOES IT HURT SO MUCH?

Money is not everything. What is everything, or damn near, is self-regard. Tie money to self-regard or put them at odds and you will certainly have a pretty pickle. All too often investors identify with their money and their stock positions to the detriment of their self-regard, and their portfolios. If your portfolio is you or its performance is the measure of your self-worth, you will not be very effective as a trader. Wall Street is a good place to test a weak ego with the fire of reality—but an expensive one. To the ego involved, a mistake—a losing trade—is a personal not just a financial pain.

A more skillful way to deal with losses is to accept that conditions have changed and to change your analysis (and opinion). Changing your mind is not so difficult once you have changed your mind to make it all right to change your mind. Once we have re-oriented our minds to this viewpoint, we can go by the territory as it is. If there is a detour on the road to Boston, we just take it—we don't try to drive down a road under repair, insisting that, torn up or not, THIS IS THE ROAD TO BOSTON. Some great trader—I forget who—said, "Trading success is not difficult if you have no opinions about the market."

If the non-material part of your self, the part that thinks and feels and chooses, is, as we have suggested before, the most important part of your living and its preservation and enhancement the first objective of survival, the most important value in life, then anything that attacks or threatens to attack this self must if possible be avoided.

How serious any kind of attack must be rated depends on how we perceive it. An assault by a gangster armed with a knife might appear rather frightening to me. It would probably be much less alarming to a soldier trained in judo. Any kind of attack will be perceived according to both the nature of the attack itself and also to our own equipment for coping with it as we see it. "As we see it" is important, for we all know cases where a big brute of a boy is chivvied around the school yard by a nasty little bully, and we say, "Milhous doesn't know his own strength." So long as he doesn't, he's going to be licked by the little bully every afternoon.

Consider the matter of losing money. If the threatened loss is trivial, say a nickel or a dime, we are not going to feel very badly hurt. If the threatened loss is large, but we have the means of preventing or recovering the loss, we will not be bothered very much either. But if the threatened loss appears large, inevitable, and final, then we are going to worry a good deal about it. The principle would be similar whether the loss was money, love, reputation, or self-regard: If it is trivial, we don't need to bother. If we can avoid the loss, we will do so. And if we actually realize the loss, we all suffer according to the value we have assigned to what was lost: The loss of $100 might be a very serious matter to me but only a small inconvenience to you.

Naturally, the loss that will hurt the most is the loss of that which has the highest value. If you agree that our non-material self has the highest value to each of us, then a threat against that self is the most ominous danger, depending on the degree of threat and our ability to cope with the attack.

If you have watched children playing, as I have watched my own, you know that a large part of their play revolves around competitive situations, as if the purpose of the game was not the game itself but a demonstration of which child is strongest or smartest. The playing often seems to be a contest to determine the pecking order of siblings, and very likely that is just what it is.

If the purpose of games and contests is to demonstrate superiority, this suggests that most children (and a good many grown-ups) have such feelings of inferiority that it is necessary for them continually to prove how smart or how strong they are. This reassures the timid one and makes him feel better about himself. It is probably why so many people like to watch the big TV giveaway programs, for while they cannot win the $64,000 sitting at home and watching, they can, if they are smart enough, name the first governor of the state of Arizona and give the date of the Dred Scott decision, thus proving to themselves that they are as smart as the fellow before the camera and that they would be able to win the $64,000 if they were on the stage. It does things for their self-regard.

It would be hard to check this next statement: One might hazard the guess that (in some cases at least) the public acclaim and recognition, which must in turn lead to a private upgrading of one's own self-regard, may be more important to the winners than the cash or mink coats or trips to Hawaii that they receive as material reward. This is a long way around repeating the old cliche about money not being everything. What is everything, or damn near everything, is this matter of self-regard. Certainly there are many, many times when a man will pass up monetary gain in order to make his self look better: "Let my sister have the inheritance. She needs it more than I do." Why? Because he loves his sister? Yes, but before that love, another: By his generosity he will enhance his self.

In spite of the classic economists, who had a useful though somewhat inadequate map of human motivation, men and women do not always act according to dollar wisdom. When the chips are down, a man will not do for money anything that causes him too serious a loss in self-esteem. What his standards and values are in this matter, of course, depend on his whole background and training; you do not expect the same evaluative abstractions in a dope peddler that you might look for in a bishop.

The question "Why are you in the market?" seems stupid. If we took a vote on it in a number of brokers' boardrooms, I'm sure we would get a fairly uniform answer: "To make money."

Like so many simple answers, this has some truth in it; also like so many simple answers, it is grossly inadequate. For one thing, if the object of being in the market is solely to make money, some of these fellows would do well to get out and get a job in some other line of work, for it's hard to believe that all of the familiar faces that have turned up each morning for 15 years or more to watch the tape until closing belong to men who have made consistent and substantial profits in the market sufficient to justify the expenditure of all those years of time.

Of course, these board room traders, like others in the market, want to make money. But that is not necessarily the only goal, and there is some evidence to indicate that it is not even the principal goal. If making money were the only goal, and if these men had used their own powers of observation over a period of, say, the past ten years, they would either have found out enough about the market to be able to take care of their monetary problems or have decided that the market was not for them.

Apparently, there were other factors. Social factors. There is congenial and familiar company in the boardroom. Matters of habit. After a few years one must become very accustomed to the easygoing camaraderie of the boardroom. For some it may represent, too, a welcome shelter from the problems of home. Certainly the boardroom provides a place where one can pit one's self against the forces of the market, and an audience for whatever victories one achieves.

There is a continual communication of sorts going on in these chapels of commerce. Everyone seems to have rather definite ideas about what "it" (the market) is going to do next. Also, there is a good deal of Monday morning quarterbacking, especially with respect to recent past action of the market and of certain stocks: "Didn't I tell you last Monday, Sam, that we'd get a three-day rally?" "If you'd listened to me, you wouldn't have sold Polaroid." "See that FGT? I bought that, the old stock, last year. It's gone up 200 percent." Somehow these remarks, and many more like them, seem not so much to be directed to the apathetic listeners, who appear to be mostly anxious to get in their own two cents' worth, but to be directed inward, as though to reassure a timid and uncertain man.

The loud, over-assured opinions remind one of the small boy passing a tough gang hangout and muttering under his breath, "I ain't afraid of nobody." Meaning, "I'm scared most to death." I think we can safely assume that a good part of the board room chatter comes under the head of talking to one's self, and that it is for the specific purpose of bucking up that apprehensive self. There is fear and doubt here, not too deeply concealed.

Jones buys 100 shares of Fruehauf Trailer at 24. He will tell you with all the enthusiasm of the true believer what a fine company Fruehauf is, and what excellent prospects they have for the coming 12 months. He will tell you everything he knows that is good about the stock, but he will not tell you anything that is bad. For him there is no bad. His mind is made up. He does not want to be confused with facts. He is not looking for the truth; he has found it. And like a politician or a minister or a trial lawyer, he is not trying to see reality as it is. He is trying to keep himself convinced that his map of Fruehauf is actually a good one. He wants to hear nothing that will upset his all-out judgment.

What he wants and needs is argument to bolster his shaky judgment and make him feel a little more secure. Therefore, he will not read, or he will forget, anything that appears in the *Wall Street Journal* that threatens his faith that Fruehauf is all good. And he will clip and treasure the favorable comments or reports that tend to show that he was in fact right. The data he collects are no doubt true, but they present a very one-sided picture.

Suppose, now, that Fruehauf stock sells off to 18. Will he re-examine the territory and see whether there have been essential changes in the situation "out there"? Or will he, more often than not, cling to the old map of his original opinion and simply go on a search for more evidence to confirm his rightness in that opinion? He may even buy another hundred shares on the basis that if his original conclusion was valid, then this new purchase will lower the average cost of all the shares he owns, so that even a moderate advance would put him back in the profit column.

What is he doing? Is he making an impartial evaluation of a stock? Or is he defending his obsolete opinion in the face of present facts? Is he acting in a way that is likely to make him profits? Or is he setting a higher value on being right than on the money involved.

Let Fruehauf drop to $12 a share. Will this man sell now? No. It would hurt too much to sell. Who would it hurt? Why, it would hurt him, of course. How would it hurt him? Well, it would mean a loss in money. But isn't it clear that the larger loss is not measured in dollars, but in pride? It will hurt less to sweep the facts under the rug, delude one's self, and maintain that one was right in the beginning and is right still, than it will to admit that one was a fool. To put it another way: If he has decided, "The stock is worth $60 a share," and the market says $12 a share, then the market must be wrong. For the sacred map cannot be wrong. It would hurt too much.

Call it fantasy, prejudice, opinion, judgment, or what you will, when the high abstraction collides with bare facts, it is the facts that have to give way if your value system places such a high premium on rightness that your tender ego cannot suffer the slightest setback. Many men cannot afford to take monetary losses in the market, not because of the money itself so much as because of their oversensitive, poorly-trained selves. The humiliation would be unbearable.

The only way that occurs to such men to prevent such painful situations is to strive to be always or nearly always right. If by study and extreme care they could avoid making mistakes, they would not be exposed to the hard necessity of having to take humiliating losses over and over again. And so? And so, too often, rather than settle for a relatively minor loss, our friend will stand firmly on the deck of his first judgment, and will go down with the ship. The history of Wall Street, and of LaSalle Street, too, is studded with the stories of men who refused to be wrong and who ended up ruined, with only the tattered shreds of their false pride left to them for consolation.

How to avoid such unnecessary tragedies? Be always right? You know that isn't possible. Keep away from the speculative market entirely? That is one answer, but it's rather like burning down the barn to get rid of the rats.

There are other answers, and they are simple. They are standing there, right at hand, like elephants in the front hall, if we can only see them. In the first place, there is no rule that we can't change our minds. It's not necessarily wrong or a mistake to believe that Fruehauf stock will go up from $24 to $60. What is wrong is sticking to the opinion after the evidence clearly shows that the conditions have changed. The rational approach is to be ready at all times to consider new evidence, and to revise the map accordingly.

In the second place, it need not hurt so much to have to change one's mind. Unless we are so wedded to absolute standards that we cannot entertain anything that will conflict with what we decided in the first place, we can alter the map to any degree we want, or completely reverse our position. If we have a good method of evaluation, in which we have confidence on the basis of observed and verified results, we will not have to think of these changes of opinion as defeats. They are simply part of the process of keeping our maps up to date. If we plan to travel to Boston over Route 20 and there is construction underway on a five-mile section of the route, we don't try to blast our way through. We take the detour. We go by the territory as it now is, not by the old map. And if the road is blocked entirely and no detour possible, we don't shoot ourselves, or run our car over a cliff; we simply turn around and go back home and try again tomorrow.

It is perfectly amazing how many losses you can take in the market and not get hurt very much, provided you are able to cut these losses short as soon as a change of trend appears. In order to do that, you will have to keep an open mind—not open just to favorable things that confirm what you wanted to believe in the first place, but open to any reports that will have a bearing on the situation, whether good or bad.

The really serious losses come when someone closes his mind and stubbornly refuses to recognize new factors in the situation. Of course, it's not enough merely to keep losses small. In order to keep solvent, one must also have some profits; but profits, too, bring their psychological woes.

CHAPTER 42   PROFITS CAN BE
             PAINFUL, TOO

Profitable situations can provide us with as much pain and anguish as the unprofitable if we work it right. If they are tied to our self-esteem—if we are trading ourselves instead of wheat or GM—a paper profit presents us with a real problem: to take it, book it, feel good, and perhaps see it soar to extremes, leaving us kicking ourselves for exiting too early, or perhaps to see the profit erode away and not be takeable at all. Ego involvement and a lack of a mature methodology can only result in pain and regret for the unequipped and uneducated trader. One thing is certain: If perfection is your standard or goal, art (or machine tools or theoretical mathematics) is the field for you. Not Wall Street.

We have seen how utter ruin can come about when a man perceives any need to alter his opinion as an attack on his ego. He can also be hurt when he is on the profit side, and for much the same reasons.

Let us say that Ed Smith buys a contract of soy beans at around $2.90 a bushel. He has put up a deposit of $1,000 against his contract of 5,000 bushels. Each cent that soy beans advance will therefore mean a gain of $50 or 5 percent.

Let us suppose that soy beans do advance (as they did at this particular time). What is Ed to do when beans are selling at $3.00 only a few weeks later? Obviously, bidders have perceived the possibility of a shorter supply of soy beans or (you could put it) a greater demand. If Ed sells out now, he will have a good profit; in fact, he will have made 50 percent on his capital of $1,000.

It is hard to lose money. But it may well be that the sufferings of the trader who has a big profit are more intense than those of a loser. What to do? To sell the beans means securing the immediate profit. But if one sells them now, what is to prevent them from going higher? Then one would be left standing on the dock, with a strong feeling of having missed the boat. Then again, if they were not sold, suppose they were to react and end up again at $2.90—or $2.80.

This is a problem in commodity trading and in money. But it is also, and most importantly, a problem concerning the self. Unless one can muster some defenses, it's going to hurt too much to see beans go up after they have been sold, and it will also hurt too much to see them go down if one decides to hold.

There are some possible defenses. They will cost more money, perhaps, but they may save the ego. One can always argue that the commodity markets are manipulated. Or that the information underpinning the decision to sell (or not to sell) was inaccurately or dishonestly reported. These defenses make it clear that whatever happens, it's "not me" that was at fault. It's somebody else's fault.

We do this very often in other life situations. We can keep looking pretty good to ourselves if we can externalize the blame. We lost the job because the boss was looking for a place for his nephew. We lost the girl because her mother influenced her against us. We failed in the examination because the professor asked some very unfair questions. In any case, it was "not me."

It appears that some sort of sleight of hand on the part of professional market riggers was to blame. This is not the way to correct past errors or improve one's trading methods. Let us go back to soy beans. Beans, having advanced from $2.90 to $3.00, now run up to $3.15, giving Ed Smith a profit of 125 percent. If the tension was extreme before, think what it must be now. Consider the ups and downs of the emotional barometer as beans react to $3.05, advance to $3.30, decline to $3.20, etc. The fact is that on this move soy beans eventually advanced a good deal more than $1.00, a gain of over 100 percent, in only a few months.

What a wonderful opportunity to take a big profit! Yes, but how many men would have the stamina and assurance to see it through? How many would be able to face the possibility of losing part of the gains? There are, I believe, many market traders who would find it easier, all things considered, to sell out the soy beans when they first reached $3.00 than to let soy beans go to $3.50 and then sell out at $3.20. In this second case, one would make a good deal more money, but it is much easier to sell on the way up than to sell after the price has gone against you for 30 points. In the first case you can always say, "Well, I got my profit; let the other fellow have his," which leaves the self-esteem looking pretty sharp. In the second case one is forced to face the fact that one did not call the turn at the top. And you must realize by now that the difference of a few hundred dollars is as nothing compared with the pain of a hurt to the ego.

It all depends on how you measure your values. If you insist on using a fantasy of perfection for a mirror, you are bound to be threatened by the danger that the reality will intrude itself on the pleasant image. There is no reason you need to regard selling out at something less than the top as a defeat. And if you let yourself be worried into premature selling every time you have a small profit, you will find your equity shrinking as the commissions and inevitable losses mount in your trading account.

CHAPTER 43   PREDICTING THE FUTURE

Most of us predict the future with a great deal of reliability. We predict that school will open at 8 a.m. and usually it does. We predict heavy or light traffic on the freeway and it occurs. We can't predict the price of wheat with absolute assurance, but perhaps we can predict it with a degree of accuracy that is necessary and sufficient for our purposes. We want a plan that allows for inaccuracy in our predictions.

When we think of predicting the future we are likely to think of an old gypsy crone in a screened cubicle at the back of a vacant store. She draws the curtains, decorated with signs of the zodiac, and reads our palm. Others do it with tea leaves, or by the bumps on your head; some use horoscopes or examine the entrails of pigeons (which, incidentally, is called haruspication). For we all have to predict, and there is no limit on what can be used as a predictive method. I could decide to buy stocks when it rains and sell them when the sun shines. I could go long when the Yankees win, and short when they lose. So far as I know, none of the above methods of predicting has any positive value, but you are free to try them, or others.

As a matter of fact, you have better ones already. Your own predictions about things in your daily life are pretty good. You predict future events, and they happen with fair regularity. Mr. Nixon is going to meet you at 1:00 p.m. for lunch. He usually shows up. The school play is to start at 8:00 p.m. sharp. It will, if you allow 15 minutes leeway. So long as we don't insist on absolute predictions, we can do pretty well. For almost everything in our dealings with reality, we can get along if we are willing to settle for something a little short of perfection. It's a matter of degree: how much reliability is necessary and sufficient for certain predictions, and whether we can expect to attain this degree of dependability. If it's a question of predicting eclipses, we can come very close to the exact time and areas of visibility, with a very high degree of accuracy. If it's a matter of predicting the price of wheat futures, we must compromise on a very much less dependable prediction.

The point is simply that prediction of the future is possible. It is not mysterious. It is the carrying out of methods we use all the time without thinking about them.

CHAPTER 44   THE METHOD OF PREDICTION

As someone said, prediction is always uncertain, and especially so when it concerns the future! In situations of self-contained universes where repetitive behavior occurs over long periods of time (e.g., the stock market), we can study the past to see if it gives us a basis for predicting the future. From this study we may construct a method for dealing with the behavior of this universe as we record similar patterns of behavior recurring with necessary and sufficient frequency to give us some statistical reliability in predictions. We then back-test our method on fresh data to determine its performance on recorded history. Finally, as in the case of the market, we may paper-trade the method to see how well it holds up in real time. In all this we are not looking for perfection but for an acceptable level of efficiency.

In order to make good predictions, we have to have a method. In order to have confidence in the method, we must be able to check it to see what degree of dependability we can expect from it. Sometimes, of course, you may be faced with a problem that cannot be repeated, yet one in which you have to make a prediction and decision. The ship is on fire. As captain you must decide whether the boilers will explode, in which case you should order, "abandon ship," or whether the boilers will stand up until the fire is under control, in which case you must not abandon ship. Such dreadful emergencies, however, are not likely to complicate the lives of most of us.

The kind of predicting we are thinking of is the sort that concerns repetitive situations, situations somewhat like others that have arisen in the past, and like some expected to arise in the future. Ruling out all magic and mysticism (though you are free to try any experiments you wish), all we know about the facts in any case concerns the past. The future, which we are trying to predict, remains a closed book.

The first thing to do, then, obviously, is to gather some facts about the past. Some statistics. We can study these and see what sort of patterns these facts seem to make, and whether they point to the likelihood of certain patterns forming in the future. For example: Old Mrs. Carpenter comes down the front steps of her house on Monday morning around ten and walks down the street to her daughter's house. If she does this at the same time on Tuesday morning, and on Wednesday, and on Thursday, and on every single morning for three weeks, I would be willing to make a prediction that tomorrow morning at around ten o'clock Mrs. Carpenter will be coming down the steps of her house to go to her daughter's. I might observe that Mrs. Carpenter made this visit every day except Sunday, when her daughter came to her house, and then I would make my prediction that if tomorrow is any day except Sunday, Mrs. Carpenter will leave for her daughter's house.

Always and always I would be prepared to change my data. Mrs. Carpenter might be taken ill. She might be away for two weeks to visit her other daughter in Kansas. But until I had data of sufficient weight to cause me to change my original view I would feel that the most probable outcome would be for Mrs. Carpenter to appear as usual.

Not always would we predict in this straight-line fashion. Suppose, for instance, that Don is going to see how many bottles of beer he can drink, with a time limit of ten minutes for each bottle. Knowing a bit about Don's temperament and capacity, I might very well make a uniform series of predictions covering the first, second, third, fourth, and fifth ten-minute period. However, based on past experience with beer, and perhaps with Don, I realize that the man's thirst will not continue indefinitely to operate on a straight-line basis. He will slow up and ultimately stop.

Therefore, my predictions will have a little less certainty, I will not back them with side bets so heavily, or I will call for progressively lower odds.

The important thing is to set forth all the relevant facts we can get, leaving out all matters not pertinent to the problem at hand; study what seems to be happening, and what seems likely to happen if we move forward in time, and then make a guess. Some of the guesses we might make are: The prediction can be represented by a straight line at a uniform level (things will continue as they are). The prediction can be represented by a straight line at an angle (things will speed up at a uniform rate). The prediction can be represented by a curved line having uniform rate of curvature (things will advance or decline with a uniformly increasing or decreasing rate of change). The prediction can be represented by a line going in the opposite direction from the record of past experiences (the trend will reverse itself).

At any rate, since we have no direct and certain knowledge of the future, we must study the past, and make the most plausible guess we can about the future. Then we see how the guess comes out. If possible, we check the method (the guess) for some time and observe the results. We note the degree of success or failure in the results of the prediction, and if these appear to be abnormally out of line with what we had expected, we re-check the data. We check the original facts, and perhaps gather more data. We examine the most recent records to see whether there has been a significant change in the patterns and, if necessary, we make a new guess. We then check the new guess, again adjust our method so as to obtain the closest possible fit, and once more project a prediction.

We will not ever expect to hit the bulls-eye on every shot with a perfect predictive method. As in all engineering studies, we are concerned with good, practical, approximate results, and it is not necessary to try to reach an impossible perfection. If we find that the best predictive method we can devise will not come close enough to meet what is necessary and sufficient to solve our problem, then if possible we should leave that problem alone. If all our efforts to develop a predictive method for the stock market or for the grain market do not on testing produce consistently good results to a degree sufficient to pay its own way, we should stay out of these markets, at least until we have found such a method.

It is not necessary, in the case of market operations, actually to risk dollars in the market. One can usually make dry runs by keeping paper trading accounts and so test the method before risking capital in it. Since we are not looking for perfection, we need to consider losses only to the extent that they may affect the overall net result.

If a certain method produces a profit of $800 on one transaction and losses of $200, $50, and $150, the net result is a gain of $400. If another method, using the same capital, gives four profits of $100 each, and no losses, the net result is the same. If we can just re-educate our egos to a point where each small loss is not an occasion for the beating of breasts and the tearing out of hair, it will be possible to evaluate the net results as a whole; in that case the presence or absence of loss items would have no special significance. We can afford to take losses, and losses do not need to hurt too much, if we can operate on a tested and proved method in which we have good reason to have confidence in the net results.

CHAPTER 45   HUNTING

If you have ever watched your children (or yourself) row a small boat, you know how for most people the boat follows a zigzag pattern towards its goal as the rower constantly turns to look over his shoulder to see how his path relates to his goal. This is called hunting, and the process by which the boat is realigned is called negative feedback. Negative feedback usually results in over-compensation—resulting in the zigzag pattern we see the rower take. Constant adjustment, of course, may keep the boat on a straighter course, but at a greater cost in energy. This analogy serves to describe the behavior of markets as they zigzag back and forth searching for the fair market price. Hunting and negative feedback will occur and the trader must choose between many short-term adjustments or a longer-term approach that may expose him to greater profits and losses.

I have watched my son out in the rowboat at Bass Pond, weaving a course like a drunken sailor across the water in the general direction of the Indian Village at Camp Wilder. Johnny will take off at a furious clip, headed out toward the middle of the pond. After a dozen or so pulls on the oars, he will look around, see that he is headed toward the pine grove, and pull harder on the right side. The boat will begin to swing back toward the Indian Village. After another dozen pulls he will look again. By this time the prow has swung too far and he is pointed toward the inlet. He pulls harder on the left oar. The boat swings back and out of course on the other side. Eventually Johnny gets the boat moving in the approximate direction of the Indian Village, but all the way across the lake he is looking around, correcting his course, and swinging first too far to the right, then too far to the left.

The problems of "steersmanship" are familiar enough to anyone who has ever taken out a rowboat, paddled stern in a canoe, or handled the tiller of a sailboat. Even in navigating the placid waters of Bass Pond there are always steering corrections to be made, and these generally will over-compensate, calling for counter-corrections. It is not possible, even here, to maintain a "perfect" course for an appreciable time; where the problem of steering is complicated by choppy water, gusty wind, and perhaps a tricky current or tidal rip, the difficulties of keeping on course are increased enormously because of the need to adjust continually to new and changing conditions.

The process of steering may involve, too, some predicting—an estimate of the size of the next wave or the time of the next likely gust of wind. In such waters we do not expect to steer even as close an approximation of a perfect course as we might hope to achieve in a quiet pond.

In practice it isn't necessary to expect anything like perfection. If we can keep the boat moving in the general direction of the goal, a certain amount of deviation from true course is unavoidable and does not defeat our main purpose. Naturally we will hold as close as possible to the straightest course. How close this will be will depend partly on our own experience and skill and partly on the winds, currents, and other changing conditions we must allow for in making corrections and compensations as we go along.

Now consider a medium-size black part-retriever, answering on occasion to the name Bozo. Bozo has forebears of sporting stock. His formal training has been entirely neglected, but his instincts still spur him to the chase. Let him out of the car on a picnic and he will take off down the road, nose to the ground, tracking—what? A bear, perhaps? A rhinoceros? Who knows? More likely a rabbit. Possibly a cat. If the quarry is in sight, Bozo will charge off directly. For sheer dynamic frenzy there is hardly anything to touch the furious pursuit and the frenzied flight of a dog chasing a cat. In a straightaway run down the road, it's simply a matter of speed and endurance. The dog will follow the cat—a linear function. But if the cat veers sharply and heads across the field, then it's no longer a question of following where the cat has gone. Bozo, or any other smart dog, will cut across in a new direction. In short, he will take a course not where the cat has gone but toward where the cat is now.

This means abstracting at a higher level than merely following. For example, we have in almost any problem of human activity the factor of the pursuit of a goal. The goal may not be a cat—it may be dollars of profit; it may not be a direct course over water—it could be the improvement of the efficiency of coal-fired boilers. But there is usually a definable objective. Again, as with the pursuit of the cat or the steering of the boat, we may not hope for perfection in our method, even though we may look for success to a degree in reaching our goal.

We are dealing, as a rule, with imperfect or incomplete information. We must make the best use of the information we possess. And again, the conditions may change. The cat tries a new angle. The wind freshens and swings the bow of the boat off course. We must change our tactics to meet these changes. There is usually an opportunity for prediction. We can, if we have the experience and intelligence, anticipate with some expectation of success the probable maneuvers of the cat or the set of the tidal rip.

Finally, we have the matter of *hunting,* the very important matter of continual over-compensation one way or the other. The whole principle of adjusting to the "ideal" course, which we keep overshooting and undershooting, is based on applying a counter-force to any swing out of line. If the boat swings too far to port or to starboard we apply an opposite or negative correction. If the engine speeds up beyond the constant speed we want, we slow it down. If it slows down below the indicated speed, we accelerate it. We call this process "negative feedback." In such a system of control we are continually applying a negative force to correct a tendency to run out-of-line with what we want. It is never perfect. There is always a certain amount of swinging back and forth, the hunting we have spoken of, as we try to hold the never-to-be-exactly-maintained true course.

This hunting is one of the unavoidable inefficiencies of any steering. It is a loss of efficiency as inexorable as frictional losses in a machine, or, perhaps a better analogy, like the backlash in gears. It's something we can't entirely avoid but something we try to keep as small as possible under any particular set of conditions. If the hunting swings are too wide—if the negative feedback is too pronounced—the goal may be missed entirely. We would say in such a case that the boat is out of control. If the swings are too small—if the corrections are too numerous or too frequent—we may be paying too high a price in frictional losses, backlash, and diversion of too much energy to the control mechanism. In such cases we may keep headed for the goal, but we may never get there or we may arrive too late.

This discussion must all seem very far removed from the stock or commodity markets. Actually it's only a short step away if we can now apply our generalized observations to specific cases. Consider the market for Christmas trees as you have observed it, trudging through the vacant lot where, for a few days, the air is perfumed with the rich aroma of balsam, strolling through an electric-lighted grove with a couple of starry-eyed moppets in tow. One year you may find a great scarcity of trees and the prices uncomfortably high. This condition will produce a negative feedback in the economics of Christmas tree marketing, for the high prices will suggest a larger stock next year. When next year comes, you will find such a wealth of Christmas trees in the lot beside every corner store that you can take your pick of the biggest and handsomest at your own price. This, too, will set up a negative feedback; oversupply will lead cautious buyers to go slow and in the following year once again trees will be scarce and prices high.

The same principles apply, of course, in the big commodity futures markets and in the stock market. Prices will rise fast on a minor trend. Profit-taking will come in, but it will go too far and then a counter-move begins as buyers rush in. Each move brings its own correction, and each correction tends to overcompensate somewhat.

In technical studies of stock and commodity movements, it is necessary to consider just how much negative feedback to apply in certain situations. Because of the complexity of the problems this becomes more a matter of experience and judgment than of precise mathematics. But the basic question must be answered: whether to adhere closely to every small fluctuation in the trend, which means making changes in position, paying many commissions, taking small gains and small losses; or whether to steer a constant course on the major trend, disregarding all minor swings and changing the course only when the evidence of a change in that trend is overwhelming, which means risking a rather heavy loss from time to time against the hope of taking a large profit. Or should one plan some course between these two extremes, representing an optimum policy? These are the kinds of questions that arise.

The problem we have just roughly sketched is that of the trader who is weighing the advantages of short-term trading against long-term or some compromise or combination of these. There are other problems concerned with the steering of a course in market tactics. And there is always the problem of how much negative feedback to use. Needless to say, the man who has only one course and who uses no feedback but lashes the tiller and goes to sleep is not in a very good position to meet changing conditions of wind and current. Yet this is exactly what some investors do. And if no great changes come about in the economic weather, they may and sometimes do bring their craft to port.

Steering and its adaptive and predictive techniques are at the heart of investment and trading policies. It's always necessary to set a course, that is, to work in the direction of a certain goal or objective. It's necessary to take observations relating the actual course and the planned course, and it's necessary to make changes when these two differ too widely. If you will consider this for a moment, you will see that what we are talking about here is simply the re-examination of a territory in order to verify data on a map, and when necessary to change the map to accord with new features in the territory.

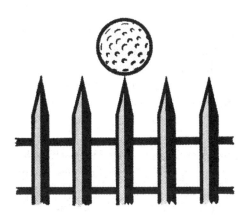

CHAPTER 46   POSITIVE FEEDBACK

Positive feedback is the engineering concept that explains how a mechanism goes out of control when it has no negative feedback, no self-correcting capability. A golf ball balanced on a spike, for example, will shortly fall off because the positive feedback of gravity on its circumference will at some point cause it to fall.

Positive feedback sounds better than negative feedback, but that is a deceptive semantic thing. Whether that is the reason it is so prominent in human affairs or whether its prominence is due to human perversity, humans will exaggerate and exacerbate a bad situation, as in a war against neighbors. It is positive feedback that causes us, having bought a stock, to ignore contrary data and opinion and refuse to re-examine our original decision.

If we looked at each piece of new data as an opportunity to make a new decision instead of as an affront to our original decision, we might overcome the tendencies to positive feedback so prevalent in our human experience, culture, and education.

If we consider some motion, acceleration, torque, trend, habit, or other variable that we want to control between certain limits, we must have a means of correcting the swing as the variable passes the upper or lower limit. The correcting force must be opposite to the movement of the variable. This has been called negative feedback. It is never quite perfect in practice. There is always a certain amount of hunting. In certain situations the hunting tends continually to override the limits of wider margins, setting up wilder and wilder swings until the mechanism simply shakes itself to pieces.

There is something else that could and very often does happen. This is where the feedback is positive from the very start; the mechanism is out of balance from the word go.

Although this is not what we usually think of when we speak of feedback and controls, an ordinary pendulum, as it swings wide, gradually encounters an increasing force from gravity that checks its swing and tends to bring it back toward the center. The pendulum, of course, will pass the center and swing out on the other wide; gravity again will check it and start it back toward the center. Here we have an object in motion that is held in a stable and controlled situation. But if we balance a golf ball on a sharp fence spike, setting it up very carefully so that it is in balance at the start, we know that this is an unstable sort of balance. There will be some slight air current or vibration that will move the ball a trifle to one side or the other; as soon as this occurs, the force of gravity becomes stronger on that side. This will not check the imbalance; it will draw the ball further in the same direction and as this happens, the force of gravity in that same direction becomes more pronounced. There is a positive feedback and the ball comes tumbling down.

This is a long way around to say that you can't keep a golf ball balanced on the point of a fence spike. Yet we get this kind of positive feedback all the time in various departments of our lives and it almost seems as if we were taught this "wrong-way" control method from early childhood. If there is a real danger that the Crips gang and the Bloods gang may get into a rumble that might cost some of them a serious injuries, we don't use a negative feedback attack on the problem.

You can't expect the kids to do it by themselves, but parents, teachers, and public authorities might start by checking their own group. The Crips' parents and teachers might ask, "What are we doing that is obnoxious, hostile, unkind?" The Bloods parents and teachers might, in the same spirit, look at themselves and their own kids to see where their contribution to the trouble lay. Such an approach, or at least an approach in such a spirit, might hold the greatest hope of solving a very nasty social problem. But if adults on both sides of such a question close their eyes to their own shortcomings and those of their kids, and if they seek out and magnify the faults of the other faction, isn't this exactly the same kind of thing that happened to the golf ball on the spike? They are permitting a positive feedback to build up more hostility, which in turn will lead to more trouble, which will be perceived as *their* fault, and so on. An unstable condition, a vicious circle—or rather a vicious helix.

Wherever a bad inter-human situation develops, whether leading towards divorce, assault, or murder, we are likely to find that as the problem becomes tighter there is more and more of a tendency to see only one side of it, to pile up the "good" forces on our side and the "bad" forces on the other. As a matter of fact, this is necessary to protect the ego. No man can maintain a campaign of hate without some justification, and the more unpleasant his own actions become, the more justification he will need. He must continually be able to feel more righteous indignation, and this requires that he must be able to see how "right" he is and how "wrong" is his adversary.

This is not exactly the road toward the brotherhood of man. It seems hardly necessary to add that, in spite of inspiring pictures of peaceful souls gathering in friendship at the meeting house to work for the common good, our political system is in fact a matching of hostile forces in which practically no punches are pulled. It is based on the either/or principle, which permits of no moderation. By and large, the democratic method as it is actually practiced is a study in organized nastiness, as anyone knows who has taken an intimate part in city politics at the ward or precinct level. The politician not only claims for himself the noblest motives, in many cases, it seems that he actually believes he possesses them. He has trained himself to see nothing but corruption and stupidity in his opponent and his opponent's party. If he were not able to concentrate all the "good" on his side and all the "bad" on the other side, he could hardly get up and roar his speech at the rally with a straight face. This is positive feedback; the campaign progresses from debate to accusation to slander to stink bombs and bricks tossed through windows. This is not the way to make democracy work.

One of the great social problems of the next generation (if there is to be a next generation) is to find out how, in human relations, we can put negative feedback to work. For we cannot achieve peace in the city by sending our kids to special schools or moving to a better neighborhood or by drawing lines of discrimination that will keep us from knowing the truth about our neighbors. We cannot achieve peace by living in a compartmented world, shielding our children from normal contacts so that they will not be "contaminated" by those who think differently, cutting out of our libraries books that tend to show that Germans or Japanese or Russians are also human beings with whom potentially we could enjoy friendship.

Somehow, and soon, we must establish communication not with the people who live like us, and think like us, and believe as we do, but with people who have a different view—not so that we can "reform" them but so that we can prevent our own tight little vortex of prejudice and narrowness and hostility from building up explosive pressures. You know that the attitudes of many sick people are due to the same kind of positive feedback we have been discussing. The neurotic, as someone put it, is just like everybody else, only more so. Unfortunately, his controls work in reverse. The very defenses he sets up against the perceived threats of attack intensify his need for aggression, or submission, or isolation. This in turn calls for another round of defenses, the positive feedback or vicious helix.

If our whole social structure is permeated by the kind of perception that tends to make a little problem a big problem and a big problem a tragedy, it is no wonder that people learn to go off on these tangents in almost any field. When this tendency to see only "our" side of a question has been ingrained in people from the time they were infants, it seems only natural that the same distorted views would apply to the market. And they do.

When we buy a certain stock, we want to see it go up in price. We like to read of increased earnings, of higher dividends, of a wonderful, long-term growth outlook. There is no harm in seeing all the good things about the stock. What can be very dangerous, however, is the habit of closing one eye the moment the purchase is executed and looking only for good news. Instead of allowing the negative feedback of caution and informed pessimism to operate to get us out of the situation if conditions should change (as they certainly can), we tend to overlook or even to deny anything that does not support our original hope.

It could be, you know, that the fault may lie in the weakness underlying that original hope. Maybe we weren't too sure in the first place. But once having made our decision and bought the stock, we cannot afford to be prey to fear and doubt. And so we bury our fears and close our eyes to the warning signs along the way from that point on.

This is not anything we do consciously or deliberately, you understand. We simply do not read the bad commentary on the stock. If it isn't good news we're not interested. (If you should doubt this, go into a broker's boardroom some noontime and throw out a few negative opinions about some popular favorite among the stocks. You'll be as popular yourself as a skunk at a picnic.)

If you are reasonably sure of your own judgment in the first place and satisfied that your reasons for buying that stock were sound, you will not need to be afraid to know the truth. Since you are secure in your self-confidence, you will not need to feel that the stock you bought is perfect, any more than you need to feel that you are perfect. You will expect some bad news along with the good news; in fact, if there were only good news, you might wonder what kind of manipulation or promotion is going on.

If the bad news eventually outweighs the good news, assuming you are ready, willing, and able to evaluate both, it will be in your own best interest to get rid of this stock at once. In fact, one could almost say that the bad news is more important to you than the good: Since you are already tipped in the direction of good news, you need the negative, corrective force that can keep your opinion in balance and sound the danger signal when it is time to change your mind.

In reading these paragraphs, you may wonder whether it is a good thing to buy or sell stocks on "news" at all. Perhaps news is not the word. It could be reports on the stock, or it could be technical indications. What is meant here by news is evidence or information of whatever nature on which one bases an opinion.

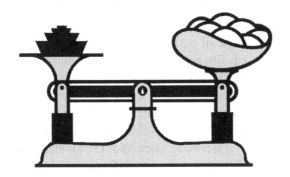

CHAPTER 47 WHAT IS "VALUE"?

We can probably start a hundred year war on the subject of value, but we can shorten the dispute pretty quickly by realizing that value, like beauty, is in the eye of the beholder. Couched in dollars, the value of a gallon of water to a man stranded in the Gobi Desert is radically different from the value to a man sitting next to a tap in New York City. It's the same with General Motors. Its true value (as a high-order abstraction) may be debatable, but its market valuation is obtainable in seconds. You may disagree violently with the market price but you can't change it unless a lot of other investors agree with you, then your opinion has become the market consensus. You can always fight the tape, but you will rarely win. Clinging to absolute standards rather than accepting flexible and variable reality is an expensive lesson the market freely dispenses to participants and students.

For eight years I taught at the evening school at Commerce High in Springfield, Massachusetts. In my classes on The General Semantics of Wall Street, I always allowed a full two-hour session for a discussion of value. I would write the word "value" on the blackboard and ask the class what it means to them, as applied to stocks.

There was no shortage of definitions. In fact, before we finished the board would be covered with notes: Value is what a stock is worth, based on the assets of the company, less the liabilities, divided by the number of shares. Value is the original cost of all assets less depreciation, and plus the estimated worth of goodwill, patents, and other intangibles. Value is the per-share portion of the company's earnings times ten. Or times 15. Or times five. Value is the per-share portion of the dividends times 20. Or times 25. Or times 15. Name it and you can have it. Value is the price of the stock in the market. And so forth.

It is not necessary to list all the definitions and all their variations; one thing was quite clear. There are about as many ideas as to what constitutes value as there are investors in the market. Very well. How do we go about finding the true value of a stock, the "intrinsic" value—not what somebody says is the value but what it really is?

If you start a discussion on this subject you had best be prepared for an all-out all-night session. There are so many factors to be considered: Assets and liabilities, of course. The intangibles. The items subject to depreciation. The items involving a question of original cost or replacement cost. The long-term prospects for the company, and the trends of earnings, dividends, etc., as well as their present magnitudes. The probable tax liability as foreseen in future years. Development of new products, and potential for new markets. And much, much, much more.

When we get all these facts down, and presumably correct as to the ascertainable facts, how much will we assume is a fair return on capital? How much weight will we give to earnings plowed back into development? Who is going to weight all these factors and produce a formula that will give us the final answer as to the real value, the true value, of the stock of this company?

No matter how factual the reported figures, they still leave wide open the question of how to combine these factors. Is a growth outlook more important than a steady dividend? Is a new market for a new product worth more than a progressive sales and development program?

These questions cannot be answered finally the way we can answer a question about the amount of last year's dividends. They concern high-order abstractions, that is, opinions and judgments; when the experts differ (as they certainly do), there is no external reality to measure or count, so there is actually no final court of appeal. One man's opinion, in a sense, is as good as another's.

Not only that. The facts on which we must base the "true" value are from the records of past performance. But people do not buy a stock to get last year's dividends. They are thinking about next year's dividends. However, the figures in next year's report will concern future assets, liabilities, earnings, dividends, and all the rest. We have not seen next year's report. As you know, we cannot predict the future with absolute precision. The best we can look for is an estimate by qualified experts, and the best estimates will differ rather materially. These are some reasons why we have no general agreement as to the real value of a stock.

We could look at something else. We could examine a half-gallon container of water. I have such a container here on the desk before me. It came from the kitchen faucet, and was brought here by pipeline from Cobble Mountain. It is clean, and clear, and cold; and it tests so chemically pure that it can be used, right from the tap, to fill the battery in your car. Our Springfield water is the purest in the east, possibly in the whole country.

What is the true value of this half-gallon of water? I could try to peddle it from house to house and see what I could get for it, but I know what I could get for it. Exactly nothing. Every house on this street has a number of faucets, all connected to the same fine Cobble Mountain water supply. For a negligible water bill each house has what is tantamount to an unlimited supply of this sparkling, delicious water. So its true value as economic goods is so close to zero that we cannot measure it at all.

But last year in certain cities in Texas during a drought, water was being sold in half-gallon containers for 20 cents apiece. I don't imagine it was as cold, and as clean, and as chemically pure as our Cobble Mountain water, but people were willing and anxious to get it, and apparently they valued it at 20 cents. Or suppose you were driving with your wife and three children along a little-traveled road in Death Valley. Suppose the car gave out on you and left you stranded in the hot desert for three or four hours. Suppose you had no water. What would you say was the true value of a half-gallon of water then? A dollar? $10? $100? $1,000? Everything you've got? It could be.

Don't you see that "value" is not a thing? The value is not in the water. Value is valuation; it means how much something is worth to you. Value is a transaction between you and, in this case, the water. You can take a half-gallon of water to the laboratory and you can look at it through microscopes, you can fractionally distill it, you can test it for traces of gold and for radioactivity. You can do anything you want with it. But you will not find the true value, the real value, of the water in the water, because it is not there.

When you look at the stock of the General Electric Company you will not find its real value in the stock certificates. Or in Schenectady or Lynn or any other property of GE. The real value of that stock is entirely a matter of what it is worth to somebody.

Some chapters back we mentioned one of Frank Stockton's stories. There is another of his stories that applies to this matter of values. In "The Queen's Museum" a certain queen had assembled the most complete collection in the world of the most interesting things in the world to her: buttonholes. Plain buttonholes, fancy buttonholes, embroidered buttonholes, buttonholes with crocheted edges, leather buttonholes, buttonholes of every sort. She had built and equipped a magnificent museum so that her subjects could all enjoy this fine collection. When they stayed away in droves, she issued a royal edict that they must visit the museum regularly or go to jail. To a man they chose jail.

It was only through the timely intervention of a band of outlaws that the poor queen discovered that not everyone values certain things in the same way. Some of her subjects felt that fishing rods were the most important things in the world. The main interest of others was horses, or playing cards, or flowers. Eventually she had to realize that it was not reasonable or practical for one person to expect others to have the same value system in all respects.

The term "true value," then, has no specific, definite meaning that can be verified in external reality, not unless we assign particular requirements that we will use as arbitrary criteria of true value; then we are no better off, because the choice of these requirements becomes a matter of opinion and judgment. Value is not "out there." It is "in here." It is a high abstraction, not a thing at all.

But if the market is concerned with values, and if values are subjective and different for each one of us, how can we deal with the market at all? Fortunately there is a good answer to that. It involves, as usual, abandoning absolute standards. We must realize that true value cannot be precisely established as real and verifiable, but we can arrive at a good approximation, a consensus.

Here is how we do that: At any time there will be many opinions as to the value of GE stock. As we have said, it is not possible to settle these differences by appealing to an authoritative source. We each have a valid right to our own opinions. You set a value of $40 a share on your stock. I cannot value it at more than $39. I can order my broker to buy me some GE stock at no more than $39 a share. You can instruct your broker to sell your GE stock at no less than $40 a share. From all over the country orders funnel in to New York and eventually to the hands of the specialists, specifying the limits of valuation people have set on stocks.

You could, if you wanted, set a valuation of $60 on your GE stock. I could make a bid of $25. There is no assurance, of course, that you will sell your stock at $60, or that I can buy mine at $25, but as the bids and offers accumulate, a certain balance is achieved. Orders to buy that match orders to sell can be executed at the price at which both parties agree to sell or buy. Normally we have a situation where there are many orders to sell at various prices above the market, and many orders to buy at various prices below the market, with a small gap just below the lowest offer and just above the highest bid at any time. Thus General Electric may be quoted "offered at 40: bid 39 3/4."

This region between 39 3/4 and 40 is probably the best approximation of the composite valuations of the American people with respect to GE stock that we are ever likely to get. It is not perfect. It may be distorted by some special news item, by overhanging supply, or by various minor technical surges in the market, but at a particular moment the best we can say about the value of GE stock in any general sense is that on the New York Stock Exchange it is now quoted at 39 3/4 bid, 40 offer. The next sale may be at 39 3/4, at 39 7/8, at 40, or at a higher or lower price. But the bid and offer for the moment is the only general measure of the value that we have. It is approximate and imperfect and ephemeral, but it is at least something we can all agree on and understand. It is the nearest substitute for a territory we can get to correspond with the generalized conception of real value.

In this sense the market is a sort of synthetic territory. This market value that we must use as a stand-in for the true value will not necessarily, or even usually, correspond with our own personal valuation. In fact, to some people the maps we must use as a stand-in for the true value will not necessarily, or even usually, correspond with our own personal valuation. In fact, to some people the maps they have constructed in their own heads seem more valid than the whole evaluative mechanism of the market.

You've heard people say, "It's selling now at 39 7/8, but it's really worth at least 60." Perhaps if these people understood more clearly the subjective nature of such words as "worth" and "value," they might alter the way they stated this. They might then say, "It's selling at 39 but *in my opinion* it will be worth $60 before long."

This recognizes that the $60 value is a personal opinion as well as a prediction of the future market value. Otherwise, it would mean nothing. It would be like a child who values her favorite doll at a "million trillion billion dollars." That is a personal valuation; it has very little importance to the rest of us, since nobody is ever going to raise the question, or the million trillion billion dollars either.

Somewhere in the back of a file case with some of the papers from my father's estate there are typewritten stock certificates representing 50,000 shares of the common stock of the Big Blue Lead Mining Co. of California. This corporate property belongs to my brother and me and our wives. I know that there is gold in the mine. Once, when I was a small boy, I saw some samples of pure gold taken from it. I will not bore you with the long history of strikes and flooding and tax liens and recapitalization. Enough to say that whatever gold might be there is likely to stay there a long time. Nobody is digging for it now, and I doubt whether anyone ever will.

I can place any value I please on this stock. I may be able to convince myself that these 50,000 shares are worth $100 each, which indeed I believe is the par value. For I do know there is gold in the mine. And I may develop a plan to try again the difficult job of extracting it profitably. But until such time as someone else shares my enthusiasm and also values the stock at $100 a share, the market value remains where it has been for the past 40 years: at precisely zero. Whatever valuation I choose to put on it is strictly a matter of financial solitaire, for it has no reference out there in external reality.

But please: Do not feel that the valuation you place on a stock is necessarily worthless. If you have good reasons (better reasons than I might have if I were to assign a dollar value to Big Blue Lead), you may be quite right. You may feel that ABX will be worth $75 a share when such and such probable developments occur, in site of the fact that the market now values ABX at only $25. If you're right, that is, if your predictive method is valid, you may eventually see the stock selling at $75, as you expect.

The point here is to avoid confusing your opinion with the consensus. They are not, and there is no reason that they should be, the same. When you express your opinion that ABX will be worth $75 right soon, do not forget that the big, free, competitive, speculative market is saying, "We don't think so. We'll sell you all you want of it—at around $15. You buy that stock at your own peril. If you're correct in your opinion, you will be richly rewarded. If you are wrong, you may lose a good deal of money."

You have a right to disagree, but don't feel too contemptuous of the market. There are other men, some perhaps just as smart as you are, who are also evaluating that stock. It's possible that some of them have just as good reason for valuing it at only $25 as you do for expecting a value of $75.

In a sense you have more than a right to differ with the market. As a speculator (and there are very few investors who are not in some measure speculators), your function is to "speculate"—to observe, to evaluate. It is your actions, along with the actions of many others, that determine the market value of the stock, which, as we have seen, is the best general statement of value we can get. When you buy several hundred shares of a stock, it tends to raise the price. If thousands buy it in large quantities, it will tend to bring the price up to their composite valuation. In the same way, your selling tends to demonstrate that you feel the stock is likely to be worth less than its present market value, and if you and others sell enough, this will force the price down to your composite valuation.

This is the function of the speculator as I see it. If it is not possible to set an arbitrary true value on a stock by formula, or by government commissioners, or by any other method we know, then it must be the market itself that sets the value.

The aim of the speculator is profit, and the work of the speculator is evaluation. His rewards will be proportionate to the success of his predictive methods, in other words, to the general soundness of his evaluation. Furthermore, it is the pressures of speculative opportunity that shape the flow of capital, not the dictates of a committee or commissar but the needs of the nation as perceived by the entire investing public.

We do not find perfection in the free market; like most things in reality, it falls a good deal short of the ideal. But we have to work with compromises unless we are reconciled to moving away to a private ivory tower of fantasy.

CHAPTER 48   ASKING THE RIGHT
QUESTIONS

**In our relations with others and our relationship to the world, it is
necessary not only to ask the right questions but to ask the questions
in the right way. To be more precise, it is necessary to be precise in
the questions we ask. Examining the terms of a question and redact-
ing misleading, anomalous, emotional, opinionated terms can make a
question meaningful and answerable. On the other hand, you might
start a brawl in a bar by pugnaciously asking, "Could Ali at his best
beat Dempsey at his best?"**

You will notice that the same kinds of problems seem to come up over
and over again, not only in the market but in other areas of life as well.
The basic idea of warfare, the contest between the "good" nation and the
"bad" nation is simply the either/or dichotomy carried to its psychotic
limits. The matter of attaining success in life is merely a question of softening the absolute ideal and recognizing that there are degrees of success
as with a great many other things.

   The problem of value is repeated in various forms wherever people
confuse a high abstraction with a thing. We can no more measure value

directly in communicable terms than we can measure love or hope or virtue or loyalty. That is why people get into such terrible conflicts with other people when they try to argue the absolute magnitudes of such intangibles. It is also, and perhaps more important, why they get into such tragic conflicts with themselves.

It is important when you ask a question, whether of someone else or of yourself, to know what you are talking about. That seems plain enough. Then why don't we do it more often? If you have a problem and you want to find the answer, ask some questions. But be sure you ask questions that make sense and that are capable of being answered. Whether you ask yourself or someone else, if you ask a silly question you will get a silly answer.

We might try a few questions, just for size, the sort of questions that people do actually ask. These are just for practice; there won't be any discussion of these particular questions here. Just look them over and see how you would go to work to answer them. In what terms would you answer them? How would you arrive at your conclusions? If there is something the matter with the question, ask yourself just what it is that is wrong:

- How far is it to the sky?
- Do animals think?
- Is it a good movie at the Majestic?
- If there were a bird named a Wargspan, what color would it probably be?
- Has Ed Monson any intelligence at all?
- Do you love me more than Arthur does?
- The French measure length in centimeters. We measure in inches. Which is better?
- What would Jesus say about the present policies of the State Department?
- Will I ever be a success?
- Which came first: the chicken or the egg?
- What is the unforgivable sin?
- If you were I, would you be making more money than I am today?

There is something the matter with these questions. The truth is that they are, for the most part, not questions at all. They have the form of questions, but when I ask myself, "How much does a ghost weigh?" or

"Who would I be if I hadn't been born myself?" these are just strings of meaningless words, having only the form of a question, like a meaningless combination of letters that looks at first glance as if it might be a word.

A question, to have any real meaning, should ask something that is clearly stated, in terms that can be understood quite definitely by both the inquirer and the one asked. If the question refers to something that has no real existence, such as a ghost, it is not a proper question. There is no possibility of answering it with a meaningful reply. Such a question, like other nonsense questions, is like dividing by zero.

As you know if you have jittered over mathematical puzzlers, there is a particularly nasty device by which a perfectly ordinary-looking equation goes haywire before your eyes. The gimmick, sometimes very artfully concealed, is that the denominator of one of the terms, when reduced to its simplest form, turns out to be zero. Because dividing by zero is a meaningless operation in our mathematics, the result also turns out to be meaningless.

There are a number of possible hidden gimmicks in the form of a question, any one of which will render the question meaningless.

To answer the question may call for data that it is not possible to get. We cannot, for instance, give a definite answer to the question of whether John L. Sullivan could lick the present champion. Yet around this silly question have raged a good many barroom brawls.

The question may be stated in such absolute terms that any direct answer would be meaningless. For example: Was Woodrow Wilson a good man or a bad man?

The question may have implications that distort whatever answer you might make, such as the law-court chestnut: Do you still beat your wife? Answer yes or no.

The question may involve high abstractions that, because they are subjective and cannot be quantitatively communicated, are not capable of comparison or analysis: Is your father more patriotic than my father?

The question may lack definition or sufficient specification to permit an answer: How long is a piece of string? Is this piece of wood hard? Is Caroline a superior child?

The first thing to look for in finding the answer to a question, then, is to take a good hard look at the question itself. Be sure that it means something. Be sure that you know what it means. Also, if you are going to put this question to somebody else, be sure that it will mean something to him.

Decide whether there is enough evidence to support a logical and rational answer, and whether it is reasonably probable that such evidence can be secured.

Check the question for terms that are too absolute, and if possible restate them so that they can be answered as matters of degree.

Study the question for ambiguous terms that might mean one thing to you and something quite different to someone else. Look also for emotionally colored terms in the question.

Try to confine the question to maters that can be answered factually, and if possible verified.

Watch out for words in the question that can be defined only in terms of emotion, opinion, or judgment.

Be sure that the time, place, and conditions of the question are consistent, and consistent with the expected answer. What might hold for ancient Athens may not be true for modern Chicago; what might apply to Ethiopia may not be valid for the State of Vermont.

Be sure that the question itself does not confuse the levels of abstraction. For instance: If you were sick, would you go to the doctor or would you hope for recovery?

Watch out for questions that project to external reality qualities as perceived, such as "Isn't that the reddest apple ever?"

Beware of verbal similarities in a question. The question "Is Joe democratic?" can easily be confused with "Is Joe Democratic?" with the possibility of misunderstanding all around, especially if Joe is a democratic Republican.

Be careful, too, of faulty identification in the question. "Is Arthur Brown a criminal?" can be asked just as effectively and much more definitely: "Has Arthur Brown performed any act defined by our laws as criminal?" "Is Martha a Methodist?" might require a searching of Martha's very soul to answer, but "Does Martha attend the Methodist church regularly?" can be answered easily. The question "Am I a sinner?" is not only so absolute that it permits no degree in the reply, but whatever answer might be given will not help greatly in improving one's behavior. Restated as "What have I done that according to my own values appears wrong?" it allows for not only a rational answer, but a start toward corrective steps.

This may all seem a great deal of bother just to ask a question. You may even feel that it isn't worth all the trouble. Sometimes that would be quite true. But if the question is worth asking at all, to use the old bromide, it is worth asking well. Give the person you are questioning a fair chance and he may give you a mighty good answer. This, by the way, is especially true if you yourself happen to be the one you are questioning.

CHAPTER 49   TWO PRACTICAL QUESTIONS FOR EVERYDAY USE

In our culture it is common for our analytical and objective minds to be frozen by educations and institutions that believe they owe their survival to the maintenance of the status quo. Men and women interested in success in life as well as success in the markets can employ simple analytical procedures to test whether prevailing truth (opinion) or scientific and social orthodoxy is factual (accurate). Two simple questions alone can illuminate many dark corners of discourse: to the statement, "This is a bear market," you can respond, "Is that so?" and "How do you know that?" The answers you give yourself or others give you can be eye-opening if examined with an objective mind. The use of such questions and procedures will lead to more objective thinking.

When somebody makes a statement, we can either pay no attention to it (the move away), we can accept it sweetly at face value (the move toward), or we can charge in and tear it to pieces (the move against). A neat demonstration of the three-valued orientation.

Naturally, there are many statements we could brush off blandly without the slightest reaction, since they do not concern our lives in any way. I would not, when sober, question your statement that Myron B. Northrop was defeated by 27 votes for the Democratic nomination for lieutenant governor in the Rhode Island state primary of 1898. It may or may not be true, and as a matter of fact, it probably is not true, but it makes no difference whatever to me. I would not dispute it.

If you said that the performance of Alicia Markova in "Swan Lake" was the most graceful you had ever seen, I would accept the statement politely and pleasantly. I would feel, no doubt, that your opinion was sincere and, of course, I would be aware that there could be no possibility of proving how you felt in any case.

If you tell me that my new driveway runs 18 inches across the boundary of your lot, however, I am going to ask a question. It is not in itself a deeply probing question. It is just something to explode in the general vicinity of your statement like a depth charge, and like a depth charge it may sometimes blow your statement right out of the water. The question is: "Is that so?"

This is a hard, cynical question, one to be uttered with a twisted leer and a nasty snarl. You have touched on something that does concern me. Your statement is not just a matter of opinion; it is something that can be proved or disproved by reference to external reality. So I snarl, "Is that so?"

You may be surprised how often this preliminary attack will settle the issue. It forces whoever made the statement to take a second look. He may find that he had not said just what he intended to say, or that what he said would not really stand up under fire. We might try a few on this basis, just to check the deadly effectiveness of this preliminary attack:

Statement: If you give me a ticket, I'm going to report you to the Chief of Police, who is a friend of mine.
Reply: Is that so?
Statement: It's very easy to make money trading in low-priced stocks.
Reply: Is that so?
Statement: Just open wide, now. This won't hurt a bit.
Reply: Is that so?
Statement: I've got you beat, just with what I've got showing on the table.
Reply: Is that so?

Keep in mind, always, that a good part of the time conversations and arguments are not between you and some other person but between you and yourself. They may not be consciously verbal, either. But sometimes by asking the question in verbal form, you can bring yourself up short, and see just where you are headed for trouble.

You say: I'm going to sell Lukens Steel short. It can't go any higher.
Reply: Is that so?
You say: I can just pick up the money and walk away. No one will ever know.
Reply: Is that so?
You will know.

If it is important, challenge the statement. If you really mean business, follow up the challenge with the second question: How do you know that?

A neighbor calls you and tells you that your Johnny smashed his garage window with a baseball. *Question:* Is that so? *Follow-up:* How do you know that? Did the neighbor see Johnny throw the baseball? Did one of the other boys on the block tell him that Johnny broke the window? Did he decide Johnny must have broken it because he has broken a lot of windows lately?

When somebody sees something with his own ideas, he is abstracting at a low level, close to reality. He can be mistaken—it might be some other boy he saw who looked something like Johnny—but chances are pretty good that he is correct in his statement.

If he got his information from one of the other boys, he is not quite so close to reality. The other boy might also be mistaken, he might mean another Johnny, or he might be lying.

If the statement that Johnny broke the window was based on Johnny's past record, this is not nearly so tight a case; it becomes, then, a matter of inference, of high abstraction, rather than direct observation. Low-level abstractions are more dependable as evidence of facts in external reality than high-level abstractions.

Just consider how much trouble people could have saved if they had questioned themselves on certain decisions based on statements expressed or implied in their own minds:

This gun isn't loaded.
    Is that so? How do you know that?
Ford stock is a good buy at 65.
    Is that so? How do you know that?
Stocks that pay dividends are more profitable than stocks that don't.
    Is that so? How do you know that?
Ballpoint pens can't leak in the pocket.
    Is that so? How do you know that?
One more drink won't interfere with my driving.
    Is that so? How do you know that?
Selling short is more dangerous than buying stock.
    Is that so? How do you know that?

And so on. You could add a hundred, or a thousand, such statements and questions.

You may think we are belaboring a very simple point here. It seems perfectly clear that anyone will ask the simple questions we have suggested. Yet they do not. Very often they do not at all. They plunge right ahead, sometimes into the jaws of real disaster. If the statement seems so obvious that it is impossible to conceive that it is wrong, many of us will not even ask the questions. Such a statement, for the ancients, might well have been, "The earth is generally a flat surface, modified by hills and mountains." They would not welcome your question as to how they knew this. They would not see any need to prove what was so perfectly obvious. Feeling this way, they would certainly reject any suggestion from you that the world might not be generally a flat surface but might be, say, more like a sphere.

It seems obvious enough to some people that stocks that pay dividends regularly must be safer than those that never pay any dividends. Not always true, but they are so wedded to what they believe that their mind is not open to any new idea. In the same way they will stand firm in the belief that short selling is more dangerous than buying stocks. They will defend their faith that blue chip stocks are safer investments than speculative stocks. And that commodity trading is foolhardy. And so forth.

How can a man expect his evaluative equipment to help him and protect him when it is frozen? How can he put his abstractive ability to work to make him better maps when he will not look at the territory, but simply fumbles with the old maps he has always used? In short, how can a man see many angles of a situation if he has shut his mind tight against learning anything new? If you want to improve your judgment and your record of predictive success you have got to go back to the territory of external reality and take a good hard look from time to time. If the territory does not match the maps, you have got to change those maps.

Why do you suppose it's so hard to take a second look? Could it be because we value the old maps so much more than the reality that we will deny the reality if it might conflict with the map? Could it be because these old maps were part of what we learned early in life when the mind was still flexible and receptive, before it had become frozen into a rigid value system? Could it be because we had certain directives pounded into us by precept and by example; by the words of mother and father, the counsel of grandfather; by the instruction we received at church; by the lessons at school; by the example and custom of all our friends; by the laws and folkways of our culture; and by the words of high authority that were passed down to us from our forefathers? Could it be that we have been trained not to look at the facts, but to accept without question what others tell us?

You know that when the map doesn't coincide with the territory, it's not the territory that's wrong. It can't hurt you to know the truth. Not as much as you can be hurt by not knowing the truth. If someone tells you one of your employees is stealing money from the till, it may be very generous and noble of you to show your faith by refusing to entertain the suspicion at all. But if the employee is actually dishonest, it will be better to find out as soon as possible. If he is not dishonest, it can do no harm to explode a malicious rumor. In any case, it will not make matters any worse to take a hard look at the facts.

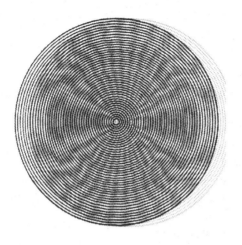

CHAPTER 50   BALDERDASH, UNLIMITED

We can in the study of any subject accumulate so much material—data—that the sheer accumulation overwhelms and defeats our purpose. What matters is our ability to discard irrelevant data and to find and understand the relevant and important facts. In the market above all, it is possible to gather an almost infinite amount of facts—earnings, costs, profit margins, ad infinitum—that only the expert and gifted analyst (fundamentalist) can profit from.

Technicians prefer to depend on the concept that everything known and suspected about the stock is discounted in today's activity and closing price on the NYSE. In other words, technicians declare that the relevant and important data are readily available and are the proper subject of analysis. Put yet another way, the data available as hard numbers from the market are all that is necessary and sufficient to analyze the value (valuation) of stocks.

To some industrious souls, getting the facts means piling up a lot of data, including much extraneous junk and irrelevant nonsense, so that the end result of the fact-gathering is a great bulging mass something like the old Collier mansion in New York.

It's a good idea, before going too deeply into the business of fact gathering, to set some limits on just what facts are to be collected. If you're making a study of libraries, it's probably irrelevant what kind of chewing gum the assistant librarian chews. It's a fact, all right, but it has no particular bearing on the problem at hand unless you happen to be making a merchandising survey for Wrigley.

There are men who collect facts the way a pack rat collects small bright objects. They have clipping files, and reference files, and chart files. They can produce the names of all the directors of a company for the past 40 years. They know the terms of a merger completed in 1934. They have copies of annual reports and the analyses of corporate affairs by various financial commentators.

Some of these data may be important to them. It all depends on what they're trying to do. A research team trying to determine natural magnetic fields at various points on the earth's surface might require certain types of data that would be quite superfluous to a group studying the distribution of earthquakes and the principal fault lines. What might be necessary and sufficient for one type of study might be inadequate (in some respects) and superfluous (in other respects) for another.

As soon as we have decided exactly what we want to find out, and have framed the question or questions we want to ask (and it does not pay to stint on care in framing the questions), we must face the next step in the study by deciding just what kind of data we're going to need in order to answer these questions. In some fields of study, and I would include the market here, the problem is not so much a lack of data as too much. You can get plenty of factual information about the market: daily, weekly and monthly charts, some with volume and ratio comparisons to the averages; dividend and earnings records, percentage advances and declines, etc., etc., etc., almost without end. It's very largely a matter of weeding out the superfluous. We think of students failing in research because they have not searched enough. We blame their failure on lack of information. But isn't it possible that there have been just as many failures because there was too much data unrelated to the problem at hand?

Almost always, in any original study, there is a stage of more or less indiscriminate collecting of facts. If the project is going to carry through to success, there then comes a time when all this stuff has to be organized, and very likely three-fourths of it discarded. This cleaning out and concentrating is just as much a part of the job as the collecting and observing.

A very important part of problem-solving today consists in the preliminary work, such things as stating the problem, asking the questions, determining the data to be assembled, and abstracting from this data the essential information bearing on the job at hand. There has been a good deal of work done just on the method of planning experiments and on the programming of the work to be done by the big electronic computers. You might with some accuracy say that the preliminary work was the most important part of the job; once it was out of the way, the rest was relatively straight sailing. It's pretty much a matter of determining what's relevant, that is, what's important to the job at hand.

Of course, there's always the remote possibility that something apparently meaningless may turn out to be of vital import. For instance, there have been some detective stories and some real cases of crime detection that have revolved around exhaustive examination of every little piece of junk that came to hand. But in general one is likely to solve more crimes if he looks for something that might have something to do with the crime.

If I'm trying to find out what is going on in some stock that has suddenly burst into great activity, it seems unlikely that I'll find the answers by rummaging in the corporate statistics of the past 10 years, for the plain reason that the new activity itself suggests that conditions are now strikingly different from what they have been. New conditions call for a revision of the old maps, or for an entirely new map; you'll not find the new toll bridge on the 1952 road map no matter how hard you look for it.

To a great extent, then, the job of analysis, once the data have been collected, is a matter of sorting the data out and throwing away all of it that is irrelevant. Very often this means throwing away most of it, just as a miner with a great pile of ore will reduce it to a small amount of a concentrate and throw away all the rest.

Perhaps I could cite my own experience here by way of example. In my work as a counselor in stocks and commodities, I follow what is known as the technical method, as contrasted with what has been called the fundamental method of analysis. Briefly, the fundamental operator tries to evaluate all of the factors affecting the stock on a sort of "reason-why" basis. There have been some outstandingly successful traders who worked on this basis, probably because they knew which factors were important and which were not and were therefore able to select the relevant data. There have also been thousands of investors who have attempted to buy and sell according to the fundamentals who have failed, perhaps because they did not realize that it's not possible to know all, and because they were not able to select the really important facts or to relate these facts one to another.

The technical operator, on the other hand, is concerned mainly with the action of the stock and its market behavior. He makes no attempt to find the reasons why things happen as they do but strips the problem to a limited field, namely the observation of the market action alone.

This line of attack was opened by Charles H. Dow and William Peter Hamilton with their discovery that the market averages have a relation to the probable future course of business. Others have carried this work forward: In the early 1930s Richard W. Schabacker applied the technical principles to the evaluation of individual stocks. Later Robert D. Edwards and I elaborated these studies and, I hope, did some further time binding of our own in our book, *Technical Analysis of Stock Trends.*

The technician is still regarded as a strange breed of cat. He ignores, for the most part, the flood of statistics, reports, rumors, tips, production and earnings records, and most of the other fundamental information. He does not do this simply because he is an odd fish, nor because he feels that these facts are not important. He recognizes as well as the next man that they tell the story of what's behind his charts and diagrams.

The technician has elected to study not the mass of fundamentals but certain abstractions, namely the market data alone. He is fully aware that this is not all, and that it does not provide an infallible guide for predicting the future of any stock. He is also aware that what he's looking at is indeed a fairly high-order abstraction and that behind it lies the whole complicated world of things and events. But this technical view does provide a simplified and more comprehensible picture of what's happening to the price of a stock. It's like a shadow or reflection in which can be seen the broad outline of the whole situation.

Furthermore, it works. It's not perfect, but neither is any other way perfect. It's easier on the nerves because it can be made quite definite, subject to rules and policies laid down in advance, and these rules and policies can be revised whenever it seems necessary. They're general enough so that it's possible to compare very different kinds of stocks and see the similarities in their behavior. There's not so much detail that one cannot see the forest for the trees. From my standpoint, this is a more realistic, more practical, way of dealing with the market than any other method I've known.

CHAPTER 51   WE CAN'T GET IT ALL

Our ever restless and dissatisfied culture constantly seeks to know all, to accumulate so much data about any problem or question that solutions appear ready-made from the mass of data. It is, of course, impossible to know all. Just as an Eskimo knows enough about boat engines to repair them, we may know enough (that is, have the necessary and sufficient information) to trade a commodity or stock without drowning in data.

Behind the drive some people have for the indiscriminate collection of data, whether the data be useful or irrelevant, rational or nonsense, seems to lie the idea that if only we have enough information, any problem will become clear. That, of course, is true. We must have the necessary amount of information. But we must also stop at a sufficient quantity. Otherwise the grain of truth will be lost in the barrow of balderdash.

Sometimes a very little clear light on a problem, if it is not obscured by clouds of ambient gibberish, is all that is needed. Volumes of statistics will not solve anything until they have been reduced to orderly arrangement so that intelligent abstractions can be made from them.

Some people have the feeling that if they know everything about "it," all the answers will become clear. The fact is that we don't know everything about anything. We don't know all about a grain of dust. It's too bad that children are taught so definitely that mathematics is the "exact" science. They are drilled in the mechanics of positive integers until it seems as if two plus two equals four were the very foundation of all truth.

Nobody ever tells these children that they are dealing with some very special situations in the world of figures, or that the figures themselves are high abstractions having significance only according to the particular rules of the game we decide to play with them. They are taught that it is always possible to come out with a perfect answer in arithmetic; by extension they may, and often do, get the idea that it is always possible to get a perfect answer to any problem if only you work hard enough.

It must come as quite a shock to them to find, even before they are through junior high school, that it is not possible to get perfect answers in many, in fact most, of the problems of mathematics, and that in other fields it isn't even remotely possible to know it all. Perhaps that's why children are so bothered and frustrated by math—and why so few adults ever really accept the broader idea, the idea of approximations, of partial answers. So they go through life still looking for a two plus two that always and precisely equals four.

It is not possible to express exactly the diagonal of a square in integers. Nor in fractions. Nor in any simpler way than as a function of the square root of two. The ratio of the circumference of a circle to its diameter will not come out even. You cannot get to the end of it. You cannot know it all. The base of the natural logarithms, "e," has no end. You cannot know it all, either.

When we look at a tree, a cat, or a neighbor, we will realize, if we have moved beyond the "two plus two" stage, that it is not possible to get it all. This can be another case of the either/or dichotomy, unless we can take a more reasonable view. For if we have only two values, and if we can't know it all, then we must know nothing. Then we cannot expect to make any practical deal with our environmental at all.

Well, of course, it is simply not true that there is no middle ground. Not only can we deal successfully with things we do not fully understand, but we can deal very successfully with things about which we know relatively little, if that little is of the right sort and properly applied. Some of the Eskimos are said to be very expert mechanics in the repair and maintenance of machinery, such as the diesel and gasoline engines in their fishing boats. It seems unlikely that all of these fishermen are trained engineers, familiar with the construction and theory of these engines and conversant with the chemistry and physics and mathematics involved in their construction. But they know a little, and in the right places. They have what is necessary and sufficient.

There are circumstances where it is desirable to know a good deal about the detail of a corporation's structure, and about its production, management, financing, future prospects. But no one can know *all* about these things. It is not even necessary to know very much about any of them in order to buy and sell the stock of that corporation successfully in the market. I know a number of successful investors whose knowledge of the fundaments is very limited. In much the same way, I know some traders in commodities who literally would not know the grains they trade in if they were to see them. You cannot say they know *nothing* about these grains, but they are not even *trying* to know all. They have developed technical methods that are adequate to meet their requirements. With their limited knowledge, of the right sort for the purpose, they are successful.

So, along with abandoning the drive for absolute success and complete happiness and infallibility, we are going to have to give up the idea of total knowledge about anything or any person. And a bit later we will discover that it is necessary to let go of the ideal of absolute certainty. It seems as they were having to let slip some of the things we have been trained all our lives to value very highly. That is true. We have been trained to value these absolutes too highly. Until we can see that ideals are not things, and until we are willing and able to scale down our ideals to something within the range of possibility, we will never be able to attain any very great degree of success, or happiness, or rightness, or for that matter understanding.

Let's put it this way: When the maps representing our aspirations are too far above or beyond our real accomplishments, we are bound to feel defeated, depressed, discouraged, and unworthy. Durkheim, the great French sociologist, spoke at length on this subject, which we called "the infinitey of the emotions" in his classic work on suicide. The solution to these problems may be to raise the level of our accomplishments, to lower somewhat the absolute quality or our ideals, or a little of both. Until we can bring our own picture of what we should be into some degree of focus with what we actually are, we cannot expect to feel much satisfaction or security.

CHAPTER 52   THE TRUTH, THE WHOLE TRUTH, AND NOTHING BUT THE TRUTH

Absolutes dog our footsteps, do what we will, so to deal with the absolutes that society inculcates in us ("whole truth," "good girl"), we develop the very human capability of selective inattention, of not seeing. As we become aware, we can view these absolutes with more mental flexibility.

Heaven help the man who took the legal oath at face value and attempted to give his testimony strictly in accordance with the oath. If we might quote Pontius Pilate: "What is truth?" The poor puzzled Pontius was beyond his depth, and unless one realizes that truth is one of the nouns of very high abstractive level, one could flounder pitifully trying to explain in terms of things "out there" what properly belongs with maps "in here."

We know already that the whole truth is not possible to comprehend. Not in the literal sense of "all," for we cannot know all about even Tennyson's little "Flower in a Crannied Wall." We can get a practical grasp on the whole truth if we will once again chuck out some excess baggage, if we will stop using words of unlimited or absolute scope, such as "utter" and "complete."

Mathematicians do this by attaching limits in their formulas. We may consider a certain function "between the limits X equals 0 and X equals 1,000." In the same way we can limit "the whole truth" to "that which may reasonably be considered to have a significant bearing on the case at hand."

In this chapter, however, we are not concerned so much the problem of superfluous truth as with the matter of lost or suppressed truth. You may remember the invisible elephant. It may be practically blocking your front door, but you cannot see it unless it is significant to you, and you may not be able to see it even then under certain conditions.

There are conditions in which selective inattention can tune out almost anything. You probably know from your own experience how the pain of a headache can mar your perception of normally enjoyable company at a party. It is also true that when the dentist's beautiful nurse smiles at you in a tender manner, the grinding of the dental drill seems somewhat less irritating. In such simple cases you know how much the attention can be shifted, so much so that certain things are not fully and consciously perceived.

Of course, the really spectacular cases of selective inattention are those that involve the self. We do not like to observe things that make ourselves look small or cheap or stupid or mean or dirty. We will go a long way to avoid seeing ourselves (compared with our own values) as degraded, guilty, or unworthy. In fact, if necessary we will go all the way and deny that what is true "out there" exists at all. We will escape into a world where we are not rejected and where we do not have to reject ourselves. Very likely we will be locked up in a state institution then, but we might be happier than we would be if we saw plainly what would hurt us too much.

As always, it is a matter of values that are too high, too vague, too absolute. Until we can begin to see things somewhat more flexibly, we are likely to be at least a little blind, in the sense that a color blind person is not capable of seeing external reality as completely as one who does not suffer this disability.

CHAPTER 53   INTERLUDE

The author steps forward from behind the curtain to confess that the foregoing chapters have been used to set the stage for the rest of the book, where the market will be used as a laboratory for the application of the principles of general semantics—general semantics being the discipline that concerns itself with the study of meanings and how we improve our functioning in reality by understanding the thing, and the symbol for the thing: the word.

Some years ago there was a rattling good musical show on Broadway, "The Night Boat." It had one or two unusual wrinkles in it. About ten minutes after the start of the show, the curtain came down and a chorus line came out from the wings, spaced themselves across the stage, and addressed the audience in unison: "For the benefit of those who came in late, we simply wish to state . . . ," and then described the opening scene and outlined the plot. The curtain went up again, and the action continued. Near the end of the second act, the curtain was rung down again, the chorus line again took their places before it, and recited: "For the benefit of those who will remain, we simply would explain . . ." and reviewed the situation up to that point in the show. And then the curtain went up again and the performance resumed.

This is a brief explanatory interlude of that sort. Up to this point it is quite possible, yes rather more than possible, that the long-suffering reader has been wondering whether this volume was actually a book on the market, or on general semantics, or on sociology, philosophy, mathematics, or on just exactly what. It has been, as in fact we threatened in the preface, a little of all these things, offered humbly by one who is not a master of any of them, in the hope that between his efforts and those of his readers, a little more understanding on a number of matters might take form.

If your interest lies primarily in the marts of trade, you may have been bored stiff with the seemingly wandering trail of these long discourses. Actually, more than the market is involved, much, much more. The market is important, but it is no more important than certain abstract values that have nothing to do with dollars or shares of stock: love, peace, security, confidence, joy, wonder, contentment, enthusiasm—in fact all of the concepts implied by the founding fathers of this country in the phrase "the pursuit of happiness." All these things are important, for they are the salt and flavor of life.

As we have tried to show in the previous pages, these subjective satisfactions rest in very large degree on the maintenance of an adequate degree of self-regard. Since it is closer to observable reality to deal with matters that can be checked, verified, and demonstrated in such a way that we can call them "facts," it is easier to study the mechanisms of general semantics with reference to a specific area of external reality than to speak in purely abstract terms. By using the market as a theater of operations, we are able to apply highly abstract principles to a particular down-to-earth case in point.

You will understand, it is hoped, that the methods of study and the applications of general semantics are not limited to the market at all. They can be applied in very much the same way to other problems in other areas. They are applicable in home life and in the complicated domestic tangles that arise within the family constellation. Most especially, they can be used to ease the tensions and conflicts that work inside our selves. For if we can see wherein we have been taught too much that is obsolete or absolute (or nonsense), and how we have set as our goals the impossible, the indescribable, and the ridiculous, then we can begin to know how to live more easily and more comfortably, how to take care of our selves more adequately, and how to realize more fully our own potentialities.

It should be noted here that the man who does not adequately satisfy his own self is not well fitted to help others, nor likely to do so. The starving man cannot do much to feed the hungry. The sick man cannot do much to help those who suffer. Unless a man has enough food and enough approval and enough sex and enough money to meet his own appraisal of his minimum needs, he will be a weak, insecure, fear-ridden, and possibly criminal or insane menace to his neighbors.

That is why the basic foundation of general semantics is so important. We have used the market as an example, like a little world where we can test the method; and from time to time we have hinted, by examples taken from fields outside the market, that the applications are much broader. But you will understand that the applications are only the end-result of a basic method of evaluation, and it is the method of evaluation that is important, for it applies in every aspect of life.

"For the benefit of those who still remain," in the chapters to come we will focus more and more sharply on specific problems connected with the market. We will see how the method of evaluation applies to a number of particular problems that the investor or trader will encounter. Only remember: these are all examples of something much larger and more important, namely, a basic method of evaluation that, if you can master it, can help you in every part of your life. It can literally enrich your entire living. Though we know it is not easy to change human nature, you may find that it is worth the effort to study your own human nature and make changes that will be greatly to your advantage.

CHAPTER 54   DATED DATA

Sheep will continue to jump over the spot where their predecessors jumped even when the original obstacle the first sheep jumped over is no longer there. Dated data affect people the same way. Dated data can be historical memories—streetcars, horses, buggies—that if much older some of us experienced (and if younger may have seen in the movies). They can also be precepts, directives, instructions passed on to us by our elders that may be valid and relevant, or may direct us to jump over non-existent obstacles. It is up to us to examine our maps to see if they are hopelessly out of date for our purposes, or still useful.

If you impress something on a recording medium, say your own brain, at a time when there is very little material already recorded on it and the equipment is sharp and fresh and sensitive, it is likely to stick with you a long time, as we mentioned earlier.

You have probably had the experience of meeting an old school or college friend after an interval of years and experiencing a shock when you are faced with the facts that your maps are badly out of date. The roistering, hard-drinking, wise-cracking, gal-chasing boon companion of before has become a well-married, respectable vice-president-in-charge-of-research of a great corporation; today his idea of a really big evening is to attend a panel discussion on "The Future of the Middle East in relation to the impact of Western Democracy." As always, when the map does not correspond to the territory, we must be prepared to change the map. If we retain the old map, as we surely want to retain our good memories, we must date that map and not confuse what was then with what is now.

Perhaps we do not entirely understand Salvador Dali's paintings, however much we may admire his techniques. But the title of his famous "folded watches" picture, "The Persistence of Memory," surely makes a point.

Consider the dated data many of us have about transportation. We think of electric streetcars as something real and important, as indeed they were in every city in the country not so long ago. Perhaps you can remember (or have seen them in the movies) the great lurching cars with their destination signs over the front reading "Meadowvale" or "Main Street" in white gothic letters on a green background, and to one side a huge number. Below the glassed-in front from which the motorman looked out along the track were hung, on each side of the single headlight, signs announcing the wrestling matches at the Arena or the opening of Luna Park. You might, if you are old enough, remember the elaborate folding doors and the high steps, so difficult for old ladies. The smell of wet rubbers and raincoats during a late winter thaw. Very likely you recall the irritated thumping of the motorman's foot on the clanging bell when some truck or ice wagon blocked the course ahead.

Maybe you remember some occasion when a great flash and bang in the front of the car proclaimed the blowing of a circuit-breaker, and the silent period of waiting until the motorman was again able to slide the handle of the controller around and ease the car into motion. You have likely watched the conductor, at the end of the line, trundling the trolley around from the back of the car to the other end for the return trip, as the motorman followed with his brake handle and control handle in his hand. You may have seen the great shower of sparks when the trolley came off the overhead wire and had to be eased back by manipulating the rope at its end, an operation much like playing a fish, in an upside-down sort of way. In your member you may still hear the screech of the trolley wheels as they negotiated the curve into Maple Street, late, late at night.

No more. The trolley cars exist as memories, as mental maps. That's all. Our children do not understand what they were like at all. They have never had the pleasure of racing through an empty car and pulling over the seats to face the other way. For them, the trolleys never did exist at all in external reality. And when you stop to think that the trolley car did not come in until almost the very end of the nineteenth century, and was well on its way out 25 years later, you will realize that this reality that was so close and vital a part of the lives of some of us was only a passing phase. In order to have any meaning it has to be referred to a definite period, a period, roughly, of only a matter of 25 years.

These maps! These early maps! They stick with us. And they are not all verbal maps. Language is so important in our lives that some students of general semantics have given practically all their attention to the verbal aspects. But we make maps that are not verbal at all; they are abstracted from non-verbal sensory data. The maps abstracted by means of one sense may be related to those abstracted by means of other senses, and all of these may be related to verbal abstractions.

However they're formed, just be sure you date them! If such detailed and sharply-defined images are projected from a map more or less casually acquired, just think of the likelihood of other impressions staying with us in matters that were not casually acquired but drilled into us by our elders. These maps stay with us. Where they concern our appraisals of reality, they become part of our value system. Inasmuch as we act and think and feel according to this value system, they are in fact the thing that is our self. But if these elements in our value system are not up-to-date in line with present reality, we cannot expect them to apply.

We must date the maps. If we intend to use them we should examine them, check them, revise them if necessary, and make new maps if that is required.

There is not space here to take up all the kinds of maps that may be in greater or lesser degree obsolete, but that many people regard as true, without date or specification, absolutely and always. We have been taught so many things: about how we should act, what we should regard as good or bad, as to standards of success, as to religious views, as to relations with our neighbors, as to sex, as to the bringing up of children, as to our relations with wives, husbands, parents.

Almost every angle of life is affected by precepts and directives handed down to us from our elders, or through them from our forefathers. These are all what we have called maps. They are the time binding, the process by which wisdom and experience can be preserved and passed along from generation to generation in the human race as they cannot be in the case of animals.

Many of these precepts and directives are practical and fully as applicable today as they were when conceived ten years or a thousand years ago. But if they are not dated, and if one is not willing to re-examine them and revise them if need be, they can do inestimable harm. A map, to be a safeguard, must apply to this place here, under these conditions, at this time. Otherwise you may be driving off the end of an embankment where the washed-out bridge used to stand.

Of course, too, we have assumed that all of the precepts and directives were, in fact, valid, practicable, and honest when originally conceived. There is also the possibility that at least some of them may have been nonsense to start with, or may even have been plain, deliberate deception from the start. This is not a great probability, but it must be weighed.

What is more likely is that the precept or directive may have referred to some special or temporary condition, not generally or always applicable. Or it could be that the original precept or directive had a symbolic meaning, that it was not intended to be taken literally but only as an analogy or metaphor. In this case, of course, we are dealing with a confusion of the averages in the market, forgetting that the averages are not the real actions of specific stocks but a high-order abstraction. High-order abstractions, as we will see, can be very useful so long as we label them definitely for what they are and do not try to apply them where they would be meaningless.

Now, let us take a look at a few dated data, things you and I were taught quite early and that we still tend to project only reality and read back as if they were really "out there."

CHAPTER 55   "BUY GOOD, SOUND STOCKS"

Investor, good. Speculator, bad. All of us know that. Or we did until we started reading this book. Now we know that both terms are abstractions: The "investor" who bought New Haven became the "speculator" (or worse, gambler) who frittered away the family fortune. The story of the New Haven and its moral is aptly illustrated in an aphorism of C.S. Lewis: "The safest road to hell is the gradual one—gently sloping, without sudden turnings, without milestones, without signposts."

There are so many books on how to buy stocks. You can send in coupons with $3 or $5 and get lists of "Stocks to Buy Now." Investment clubs are formed to study which stocks to buy. Even the New York Stock Exchange (and we can forgive them for not trying to buck a precept that has almost the force of religious authority) publishes brochures and advertisements explaining how to set up an investment program by buying "good" stocks.

Some of us, who were exposed to a "sound" and "conservative" philosophy, take this so much for granted that it goes without saying. "Buy good, sound stocks" seems perfectly obvious and perfectly plain, like saying that "Honesty is the best policy" or "Haste makes waste." We don't attach any dates to the directive nor do we ask when, where, or under what conditions it applies. Nor do we ask even what it means. It could be as meaningless as one of those dead-level abstractions like "Virtue is good," where we simply reword the same idea without explaining it at all.

A case in point would be the man who consults his physician about a very sore toe. After his foot has been examined and perhaps X-rayed, the patient may be given instructions for the soaking and bandaging of the ailing member. If he seeks further information and a diagnosis, he may be told that he has acute "digitus ulcerosus," which, looked up later, turns out to be Latin for a sore toe.

If we mean by "good, sound stocks" those that will probably result in a strengthening of our financial position and give us security and income, then we certainly do want good, sound stocks. But if we mean here "the stocks of good, sound corporations," then we should say just that. The two statements are not identical and may not mean the same thing at all.

It is quite possible for a stock to be highly profitable and to provide great security and enormous income, although it may be the stock of a highly speculative development venture in uranium mining. And, as you may know from your experience in recent years, the stock of the most staid and solid company can droop and sag and perhaps collapse utterly in the course of time.

There is a confusion here between General Manufacturing, the stock, and General Manufacturing, the company. If it is the stock we're dealing with, we can observe its relation to corporate affairs, but we should not make a faulty identification.

Back at the start of the century there was a good sound stock Jesse Livermore tells about in his book, *How to Trade in Stocks*. It was the stock of a New England company financed and operated largely by New England businessmen. It enjoyed a steady commerce and had a monopoly in its field. The stock, regarded as a blue chip, was widely held by trust funds, insurance companies, wealthy investors, and rich widows. Its name was New Haven, and it was the stock of a great network of rail lines throughout New England known as the New York, New Haven & Hartford. Near the turn of the century it sold at around $250 a share.

Let others speculate in copper, or textiles, or machinery. For the conservative man New Haven represented security. Such a man (and his name was legion) did not speculate. He bought good, sound stocks. Period. If New Haven advanced in the market he would not sell, for he was not a gambler. If New Haven declined, he would not let it worry him; he might, indeed, call his broker to pick up a few additional shares.

But suppose, as Livermore suggested, New Haven drops off to $150. What does one do then?

Why, if this is a good sound stock, should one be disturbed? There is no need to do anything. Let the traders in the market buy and sell, but the physical properties are still there, the rails and cars and engines, the stations and tunnels and bridges. The true value has not changed.

What if the stock drops to $100? No matter. The public is simply unaware of real values.

Do you see what is happening here? Do you see that a map without a date is being treated as if it were the territory? The map is being given greater weight and value than the territory itself! These investors were not only confusing the physical company itself with the stock of the company, they were also attributing a value to the stock. Worse, they were quite unaware that this value was an abstraction, a matter of opinion, and that the very fact that the market price had dropped 150 points was presumptive evidence that collective opinion had changed with respect to New Haven stock. Having the somewhat inflexible value systems of the Proper Bostonian of that period, they were unwilling or unable to take another hard look at the territory; instead, they continued smugly to have faith in their obsolete maps.

If New Haven should drop to $50? It did. Did they change their opinions? They did not. When New Haven was selling at $25? And at $10? And at $5 a share? "At just what point," Livermore asks, "would these investors realize that they, like all other investors are, in fact, speculators?" In other words, how far out of line must the reality become before they realize that the old map has to be changed?

New Haven, as you know, went to $1.00, and then to $0.50. After Livermore's death I saw New Haven quoted in sixteenths; this was just before the stock was de-listed, wiped off the board, pending reorganization.

Who is going to say that the original valuation of New Haven at $250 a share was wrong? At the time, under the conditions then prevailing, it may have been a most reasonable and realistic appraisal. The fault was not in the original map but in hanging on like grim death to an obsolete map that no longer represented the territory in external reality. Things had changed.

When things change, we have to change opinions. We said "hang on like grim death," and grim death it was for many. A young man in my adult evening class came up to me one evening during recess, when we were having a smoke in back of the school building. We had just been discussing this New Haven case. He told me the story of how his grandfather, not trusting the vagaries of the Younger Generation, had left his estate almost entirely in the form of New Haven stock and had so entailed it that it was forbidden to sell that stock under any conditions. This was in line with the implications of a map that showed New Haven to be a good, sound stock, and the purpose of the provision was to prevent the children and grandchildren from frittering away their patrimony in speculation.

The case was taken to court during the years while the New Haven coasted toward total collapse, in a futile attempt to break the provisions of the will. But the will could not be broken, and the family inheritance vanished in thin air.

There is not only an unwillingness to face the fact that things are different now. There are also factors related to preservation of the ego. To some people it is a hurtful thing to have to change an opinion. Such people may cling to a faith, directive, precept to the very bitter end rather than make the supreme sacrifice of going out and taking another look at the facts.

It does not need to hurt that much—not unless you have such a rigid conception of "rightness" that an opinion you have once formed becomes something sacred and eternal, not ever to be questioned or examined again.

There is another way the idea of buying good, sound stocks can hurt us. There are many angles to our value systems, and they involve not only matters of ethics and conduct but how we value our selves in relation to the clothes we wear, the house we live in, the kind of car we drive, and even the stocks we own.

There are people who feel that it is better, or at least more respectable, to own shares in a high grade conservative utility like commonwealth Edison than to muck around with more speculative issues, such as Polaroid, which has been expanding and developing very rapidly in recent years. They are perhaps confusing the fact that there is more risk or leverage in certain stocks with some abstraction connected with respectability. Some writers have noted that unearned or inherited wealth carries more prestige and snob appeal than earned wealth.

Admitting that when we look for extraordinary gains we must expect to take extraordinary risks, it is strange to see how much moral implication is read into the situation, quite unconsciously, by a great many people. Somehow it is considered more respectable, at least more solid, to clip the coupons on 2 percent bonds than to speculate in Canadian penny stocks. Yet this seems more related to social snobbishness than anything else.

The have-not young man will have to get into something with opportunity to increase his capital or he will never be in a position to lounge on the deck of his yacht and clip bond coupons. Conversely, the very fact that Mr. Pot Belly is able to sit in the window of the Union League Club and ponder the tax-exempt features of certain new debentures is evidence that he has already "got his." By semantic extension, therefore, he is higher up the social ladder, is better than most of us, and what he does must be right.

Perhaps this map, which so many of us have held at one time or another, ought to be torn right out of the book. If you are going into the market, you should recognize that you are a speculator, both in the original sense of being an observer or evaluator and in the sense of being, to some extent, a gambler. While you can strike almost any balance you choose as to the amount of speculative risk you want to assume, this is a matter of degree, not of principle.

It is similar to the case of the two men who were arguing over the approachability, or at least the availability, of a certain young woman strolling along Fifth Avenue. A bet was concluded between them, and one of the men accosted the girl:

"My friend and I have been having an argument about the moral standards of women today. Could I ask you a question, a rather frank question?"

"Why, yes, what is the question?"
"Would you be willing to sleep with me if I paid you $10,000?"
Pause.
"Yes, I think I would, for $10,000?"
"Well, would you sleep with me tonight for $10?"

"Naturally not! What do you think I am?"

"Excuse me, but that really isn't the question. I know what you are. What we're talking about is the price."

Some years ago I visited my father in Connecticut. During the evening he gave me a little fatherly advice on financial planning, investing, and the like, and finally said, "What you've got to decide is whether you're an investor—or a speculator."

You'll notice the either/or dichotomy. One apparently is expected to be either an investor or a speculator. One cannot be both. One cannot be even a little of each. There is no in-between.

Notice, too, that the words "investor" and "speculator," though they sound like common nouns, actually represent rather high-order abstractions. In order to mean anything specific, they have to be defined. When we use words that we have not clearly defined, even to ourselves, then we are very likely to find ourselves talking nonsense, as indeed I believe my respected parent was doing on this occasion.

As often happens with these either/or situations, you will realize that there was to my father, as there is to many people, a moral color to the words. "Investor" not only purports to be the name of a thing, but it is the name of a "good" thing. It calls up pictures of solid citizenry, honest taxpayer, faithful husband, intelligent parent.

"Speculator," on the other hand, suggests a weak-lipped, amoral ne'er-do-well, someone who is dissipating the family fortunes in wine, women, and song. He is the fool who is so soon to be parted from his money. How could it be otherwise? He has appeared in so many newspaper stories, so many sermons, so many lectures on sound finance, and so many heart-to-heart talks. He is, in the person of poor old Uncle William, numbered among the family skeletons. "Investor" is a good word. "Speculator" is a very bad one.

At any rate, on my return from father's, I related our discussion to my wife. She asked, "What did you tell him? How did you answer him?" I told her I couldn't answer that question. If I had to make an either/or choice, I had already made it—and of course, it was the wrong one, from father's point of view.

CHAPTER 56 "I'M ONLY INTERESTED IN INCOME"

Perhaps there are still investors who are only interested in income. If there are, they will shortly be extinct, so we should study them quickly to see what we can learn before they disappear. The equity of an account—original capital plus/minus market activity minus commissions and fees plus dividends is the high-order abstraction that allows us to focus on the valuation of our portfolios. Only accounting hairsplitting—which must come after the fact—separates capital and income conceptually.

This is a sort of footnote to the preceding chapter. It concerns much the same line of thinking we have already discussed, those rigid opinions about the market, about stocks, and about investment generally, based for the most part on what grandfather always said, or on what has been gleaned from some other high authority by way of a substitute for direct inspection of the facts.

The particular shibboleth in this case is "I'm only interested in income." Like several other attitudes we've examined or will examine, this makes it very clear that the speaker is not interested in speculative profits. It implies that he has no high opinion of those who make their living, or try to make it, in speculation. By making it quite clear that one is not interested in the day-by-day or week-by-week fluctuations in the price of a stock, one can underscore the solid conservative policy one follows. The impression is given that one's securities are so unimpeachably secure that the waves of market action can beat on them for years without eroding away one iota of the real value.

Whether anyone else is aware of this super-confidence or not, it serves the purpose of making unnecessary any mental efforts on one's own part. All that is necessary to understand the current position is a pencil and paper and the dividend record for the past year. Out of this frame of mind comes the abhorrence of dipping into capital, for in this view capital becomes something fixed and unchanging, a great defensive structure like the Rock of Gibraltar, in itself the protector and the treasure, not to be violated, not to be chipped away, but to be preserved as a sacred trust and passed on intact to one's children and their children.

As a result of this outlook the descendants of wealthy families have grubbed along for years on the pitifully small and often shrinking returns of the once-handsome family fortune. As it is nibbled at by the tax collector on the one hand and by administrators, advisors, and lawyers on the other, while all the while the forces of long-term inflation deplete the exchange value of both principal and income, it is small wonder that in the end there is very little left to show for the original inheritance. In these cases it is not a matter of eating one's cake and having it, too. It is more a case of not ever getting to eat the cake at all.

G. M. Loeb, a partner in E.F. Hutton & Co., in his excellent book *The Battle for Investment Survival* takes up this matter of the separation of income and principal. He feels that it is not possible to maintain income in one category and principal in an entirely separate one. The two are inextricably related. For example, when a stock selling at, say, $20 goes ex-dividend in the amount of $1, we do not expect to see the stock open the following morning at 20. The probabilities are that it will open around 19, perhaps 19 1/8 or 18 7/8. The dividend that has been taken out is reflected immediately as a depletion of capital; this is true whether or not the dividend is made up by earnings during the following quarter.

It would be possible for a stock to go on paying dividends for months and years, even while the price continued down, down, down. This would raise the interesting question of whether in fact the dividend was actually coming out of capital, so that in drawing out and spending the dividends, one would be dipping into capital right along. Of course, this may be stretching things too far; there will be auditors and lawyers who will prove that it is not possible to pay dividends out of capital. Yet how about one of my students, who told me that he had held an important chemical stock from a purchase price of nearly $60 a share to around $18 over a six-year period? During that time he had received dividends regularly, some at the rate of $2 a year, others at the rate of $1.50, totally about $10 a share over the entire period—while the market value of the stock declined some $40.

We could say that the decline of the stock had no direct relation to the payment of the dividends, and that may be true. But it is as if the dividends had been deducted or taken out of capital along with other decrements. At any rate, the net result was that this man had very considerably less than he started with, even counting in the dividends received—and the stock was a genuine blue chip, at that!

We cannot abolish the distinction the tax collectors set up between income and principal so far as our tax returns are concerned. But in all other ways we can consider income and principal as one if it will help us to a more practical financial philosophy. It is like the higher abstractions we have spoken of so frequently before in that it wipes out differences but provides us with a clearer picture of the situation as a whole.

If we do this, we will not be likely to draw out income complacently each month while our capital skids down the scale in a bear-market slide. Nor will we feel that a moderate cash withdrawal from time to time is a quasi-criminal insult to our ancestors and an attack on our descendants. When we receive income we will simply credit it to the account, just as a margin clerk will do in keeping his records.

The dividends will simply increase the equity by so much. An advance in prices of the stocks held will also increase the equity. Both will be measured in the same account, and in the same way. When money is drawn out of the account, it will be debited and will decrease the total equity. A decline in the prices of the stocks in the fund will produce the same effect: a decrease in equity.

We have used the word "equity" here rather than value since it has a specific meaning: It is the value in dollars of everything held in the account as of a certain time. It takes into account, therefore, all additions, whether dividends or deposits from other sources, all withdrawals from the account, and all accrued changes in dollar value due to changes in market prices. (The question of accrued versus realized values will be taken up a few chapters hence.)

In practice, what this means is that we will not try to keep our capital account in one place or in one set of books and our income account in another. This is a case where we have nothing to lose, and a good deal to gain, by abstracting at a higher level, that is, by merging these two accounts into one.

The reason this point of view is so hard for some to come by lies probably in our puritanical education. It is linked nebulously with the general feeling that working is good and with the acceptance of responsibility as it concerns capital. Thus, income could be regarded as some sort of return for goods delivered or services rendered, while increment is likely to be preceded by the word "unearned" and suggests to many people a rather reprehensible getting something for nothing.

It is the old either/or again. Two values: a "good" one and a "bad" one. We reject the bad one and accept the good one.

It seems hardly necessary to point out that, regardless of whether your 100 shares of XYZ were inherited or bought from the proceeds of your hard labor, the return you get on this stock so far as it concerns you cannot realistically be segregated according to some bookkeeper's formula. Whether a stock advances 10 points in price and pays no dividends, advances five points and pays $5 in dividends, or remains at the same price and pays you $10 in dividends, the result as it touches your financial status outside of taxes is precisely the same.

CHAPTER 57 "BUT STILL I INSIST ON MY DIVIDENDS"

Some words achieve the status of a shibboleth or a talisman. They can be used as a magic wand to settle any controversy. "Dividend" is an example of such a word. Time was that no "conservative," "prudent" investor would have tolerated stocks that paid no dividends—until Magee conducted a rational study comparing dividend-paying with non-dividend stocks and determined that over the long term the net return on the two groups was little different. This is a story not just about the term "dividends," but about the nature of a talisman.

If a man is not used to exercising his mind against new and unfamiliar situations, he is very likely to go through life depending on a whole body of directives and precepts picked up in the family circle, from teachers, friends, etc., and from books, without ever going out to look at the world and see what it's really like. The good advice and rules for living he accumulates from others may be, and probably are, on the whole pretty good. It may be just because they usually work pretty well that he never bothers to question anything that has come to him from a trusted authority.

Yet a statement can be an untruth without being a lie. It may be obsolete, vague, inapplicable to a particular situation, or mistaken. It may be partly true, that is, inadequate. In any of these cases, none of which could be described as lies, the statement could get you into a peck of trouble if it's acted on without question.

It sounds so cynical to say, "It may be true, but I want to take a look for myself." Some people would resent anyone wanting to verify statements they have made. You're supposed to keep your eye on the map all the time and never peek at the countryside itself. They will tell you, "It stands to reason"—meaning "It isn't necessary to prove it out there; you can prove it right inside your own head."

Case in point: Two important, well-known stocks, both listed on the New York Stock Exchange. In January 1950 S.S. Kresge, a conservative, investment-type stock, showed a record of steady earnings, well above $3.00 a share for a number of years. It also had a record of steady dividends at the rate of $2.25 to $2.50 a year. The stock was selling for $43 a share.

At the same time, January 1950, Baltimore & Ohio Railroad, a speculative and erratic issue, showed an irregular record of earnings and no dividend payments for a considerable period of years. It sold then for $12 a share. Which to buy? The good, safe, steady-earning, dividend-paying Kresge? Or the chancy, non-dividend-payer, the B&O? How many bankers, how many trust administrators, how many prudent men would have even considered BO as against KG? Doesn't the answer seem obvious.

Over the next six years S.S. Kresge moved down in a steady trend, reaching $25 by the end of 1956. During this same period the Baltimore & Ohio climbed to $46. Which turned out to be the better buy?

You could say this is an exception. Perhaps so. But some years ago I made a study of nearly a thousand stocks over a period of several years, comparing the value received in dividends and price increment or decrement at the end of the period with the price at the start of the period. I separated the stocks into two groups, those that paid steady dividends and those that paid none, omitting entirely those that paid dividends irregularly.

The results of taking this look at reality were surprising. There was no net advantage in this period to buying the stocks in the dividend-paying group. The non-dividend-payers did just as well, in fact a shade better. If we compared the final price plus dividends received in the first case with the original price, it averaged a bit less than the final price in the second group, the non-dividend-payers, compared with their original price.

The vehemence with which some people will defend their feeling that dividends are necessary and are the essence of investment wisdom makes one wonder whether it's really a matter of investment wisdom at all or merely an opinion related to value ideas about "common sense," "prestige," "conservativism"—and "prudent men."

A good friend of mine, a successful paper merchant, practically went into hysterics when it was suggested to him that he might consider buying a stock that did not pay dividends. "I'll tell you one thing," he roared, "I'll never buy a stock that doesn't pay a steady dividend."

Would he, do you suppose, sit contentedly and draw his dividends while the market value of his stock drifted down, and down, and down? Would he refuse to buy the stock of a concern engaged in such tremendous development that it might be several years before the fruits of the effort could appear in the form of dividends? It's simply amazing how the connotations of a word can blind us to the real facts of a situation.

CHAPTER 58   PUT THEM AWAY IN THE BOX
AND FORGET THEM

**One of those old maps of abstractions—"good" stocks or "safe"
bonds bought and held (put them in the safety deposit box and forget
them)—is one of the most insidious of investment philosophies. Buy-
and-hold without regard to market action is as irresponsible to the
facts as outright gambling. In fact, it's a passive form of gambling. If
the vicissitudes of the market don't devalue the portfolio, inflation
will. Bond salesmen (for example, the U.S. government) will not be
overly punctilious in explaining the risk of inactivity to you.**

Very often you will hear arguments that are just plain silly being seriously
advanced to support something that someone already believes. Motor
stocks, you may be told, must be good investments because the automobile
is here to stay. Aircrafts must be good investments because we are entering
a new age of air travel. You have heard these and a thousand like them.

In the first place, such statements are terribly superficial. They overlook the fact that the price of the stock has already been determined in a
highly competitive market, and that the basic character of the business
has already been appraised very thoroughly, long ago. If a stock must be

good because the company represented is in the food business, that was as true ten years ago as it is today, yet the stock has probably made enormous moves since that time.

Along the same lines, you will often hear that certain stocks, or all stocks, are seasonal, likely to go up in the spring and decline in the fall. If this is true, it would be worth acting on but the evidence to support it is for most stocks not convincing. If any general seasonal trends existed, they would be discounted, and the discounting process itself would smooth out and destroy the seasonal cycle.

Perhaps a great many people forget what they mean by "good" or "sound" when they speak of stocks. Probably they are thinking of certain kinds of business as good or sound, but even this is a matter of opinion and judgment. Certainly the railroads today do not look quite so good or quite so sound as they did 40 years ago before the trucking business took up the work of mass transportation. Yet some investors, and some brokers, and a great many bankers will continue to consider S.S. Kresge a better investment than General Cigar, in spite of the fact that Kresge has gone from 45 to 22 in the past eight years, while General Cigar has moved from 14 to 49.

Wouldn't you feel that the proof of this particular pudding, that is, enhancement of capital, was an essential part of investment planning? Or do you feel that it is more important to conform to the "prudent man" standards than to look at the real facts?

There is another question involved in this matter of investment versus speculation. It revolves around the conservation of capital as seen by a bank or a court of law. In their eyes the primary objective is to preserve the same value in dollars in an account as were in it at its inception. This is a good objective compared with a policy of not caring whether dollar capital was preserved or not, but it is hopelessly inadequate. Would you consider it a satisfactory performance if a trustee after an interval of 20 years turned back to you the same number of dollars he had originally received, plus, of course, the 2 or 3 or 4 percent income received during that period? Is the almighty dollar to be so rigidly valued that we overlook the realities in the case?

We like to think of the American dollar as a solid rock amid the raging waters of economic changes. But the dollar, at least in our times, is not strictly defined in terms of gold or any other commodity. It is an abstraction, a map, and like any map it requires a date to make it fully meaningful. If you had put away $100,000 20 years ago for the purchase of a house now, you would find that these dollars would not buy you anything like the home you could have bought then. You would still have $100,000, the same number of dollars you had in the first place, but this is a case of faulty identification, because the dollars today are not the same as they were 20 years ago. Even if you had invested these dollars in government bonds and had accumulated all the interest on them for the entire period, you would still not have enough dollars at their present exchange value to buy as good a home as you could have bought with the original capital. The promotion of government securities has not been frank in pointing out the rather steady depreciation of dollars, and therefore the substantial losses that buyers may sustain on this account.

The U.S. government has not been entirely frank either about the tax liability of its securities, or about the real value (in terms of purchasing power) of the proceeds of its bonds. We have spoken of partial truth; that is, truth that is slanted not by falsification but by concealing or neglecting to state part of the essential information.

We have been told that government bonds are "the safest investment in the world," meaning that the precise number of dollars specified will be paid after, say, ten years. This is a lie by implication, unless the listener is aware of the speculative risk in dollars; unless he realizes that an agreement to pay over a certain number of undefined "dollars" means very little unless we have some assurance that these same dollars can be converted into definite quantities of particular commodities. The whole weight of government propaganda has been thrown behind the drive to stress one side of the story, to present a half-truth, a distorted truth, as if it were a complete picture. We have not had a ruinous runaway inflation, but put yourself in the position of someone who bought German mark bonds just before the post-war inflation of the 1920s. You would have received back precisely the principal and interest agreed upon, but they would be worth nothing.

The difference here is only one of degree: The man who overlooks the necessity to increase his dollar capital in line with the march of inflation is simply letting inflation eat up his life savings. If he sets great value on the precepts of high authority, he will not even look at the facts. He will value the map; what he has been told, more than the reality; what is really happening.

CHAPTER 59   THAT OLD DEVIL MARGIN

Good words and bad words. We recognize them instantly, just as we recognize the good guy and the bad guy in the movies. Even at this late date almost all investors know that "margin" was one of the villains of the 1929 crash (and of other crashes). Speculators (bad) use margin and usually come to a bad end. The semanticist wonders how borrowing to buy stocks (i.e., using margin) is different from borrowing to buy a house.

It is certainly true that our friends can hurt us more than our enemies, for we are prepared to deal with enemies but we are easy prey to the well-meant blunders of our friends. It is true, as we have just seen, that the truth, if it is not the full and forthright truth, can hurt us more than a lie. We can deal with lies by challenging and disproving them, but it is much harder to deal with a truth that merely omits to state some essential facts in the case.

We are often told that trading on margin is an evil. That is a truth, too, in a way. Plenty of people have lost their hard-earned savings in margin accounts. Perhaps you could say, with about the same kind of truth, that automobiles are an evil, since every year brings its thousands upon thousands of mangled bodies in the nation's accident toll. The evil in anything is, of course an opinion or judgment. It is not, strictly speaking, in the thing at all, since it is of the nature of a very high abstraction. It is hard to measure evil, since the amount of evil in any situation would depend on the value system of each particular observer.

As in other situations involving high abstractions, it may be easier and more fruitful to ask the question in a different form. We could ask: How is a margin account likely to lead to trouble? Or we could ask: What is the nature of the trouble and what are some of its principal causes? Then we might get an answer that would help us to avoid these troubles, or at least to estimate the dangers.

Some of your friends will tell you they pay cash for every stock they buy, and that they "wouldn't go on margin, not on your life!" They will remind you of what happened in 1929. This is a simple matter of dating the map. For the 1929 margin picture is quite obsolete, and in order to talk intelligently about margin it is necessary to consider today's margin requirements, today's market action, and the rules and regulatory machinery of today.

Many of the very people who will scornfully reject any idea of trading on margin (making it quite clear that you are no better than a cheap tinhorn gambler) are setting aside a large part of their family earnings each week and each month to keep up the payments on their houses, their washing machines, their TVs, and practically every other major possession they have. Except that we use different words, how is it basically different to buy a house on borrowed money than to buy stocks on borrowed money?

One could say that the purpose was different. The buyer of stocks on margin is putting up a smaller amount of money than he would if he bought the stocks outright, in the hope that with an advance in price he will make a correspondingly greater profit. Yet not the least of the arguments for buying a home is the feeling that real estate values are increasing, so that the increment of speculative gain will more than offset the cost of interest and other charges on the mortgage.

People can kid themselves. Oh, how they can kid themselves! Call a purchase a sound investment and they will buy your house, your deep-freeze, or your 40-volume set of The World's Great Literature. Call it a speculation and they will avoid it like the plague.

You see, we have good words and bad words. As we abstract, we lose the details, and in the highest echelons of abstraction we lose all details and often settle for the simple either/or orientation. It makes everything so simple if we have just a good and a bad, no in-between. Like the Westerns your children watch, no one has to be a very keen judge of human nature to detect the dangerous character of the slinking, leering, degenerate horse-thief. No one needs to be very sharp to recognize the fine upstanding quality of the clean-shaven stranger from Montana.

Speculation is bad to most people because they have been taught to attach a "bad" label to certain operations. Buying stock on margin is speculation. Therefore it must be bad. Buying a color TV set on time, on the other hand, is an investment in family togetherness, therefore good.

There is no discrimination in this sort of thing. The labels tell the story. We don't have to look at the facts at all. So the most conservative financial operation involving margin will be automatically labeled bad, and the over-extended purchase of the shoddiest piece of junk for the home will be labeled, and considered, good if the salesman can talk fast and smooth.

The fact is that it all depends. Just as it is wise and practical for many families to buy their homes and perhaps some of their household equipment on borrowed money, it may be wise and practical to trade in stocks on margin. It is not in either case a matter of either/or. It is a question of evaluating the relevant circumstances and striking a reasonable balance.

It is not necessary to go out on a limb. That *would* be bad. But if we know what we are doing (and I am assuming that you are interested enough to do a little studying), and if we do not over-reach, there is no great danger in the operation of a margin account. It is, once again, a matter of measure in all things and nothing in excess.

So far as outright ownership of stocks being safer than holding stocks on margin, that is one of those half-truths that can hurt you. For a great many people who have never been thought of buying anything on margin have lost a great deal simply buying good sound stocks for cash and putting them away in a box. These losses have been not only on account of the fluctuations in the stock market but also, as we pointed out a few pages back, because of the fluctuations in the dollar market.

CHAPTER 60 NOT JUST A MARKET OF STOCKS

In America we have come to realize that the value of everything—stocks, dollars, D-marks, commodities—is in constant flux. One way to look at these relationships is to say when the market is very elevated that dollars are cheap, because it takes more of them to buy IBM than it did several years ago. Likewise, a market at bear lows reflects a strong dollar, because it takes fewer of them to buy stocks.

Cash itself is speculative. The value of cash, in relation to everything else, can change enormously. You cannot hide from the reality of speculative fluctuation simply by pretending it isn't there. Your house, your stocks, even the cash money in your pocket fluctuates in value continually, if by value we mean what it will buy.

If you want to tie yourself up to a somewhat circular definition and define a dollar as a dollar, without specifying the dates on your map, then you can achieve a purely verbal, and purely artificial, stability. Many Germans, during their disastrous inflation, stuck by the slogan "Mark bleibt Mark" until the whole house of cards came tumbling down. In any realistic sense, however, all things that have monetary value are continually being revalued with respect to one another, and dollars similarly are in speculative flux with respect to their purchasing power or convertibility into other goods or services.

It is an artificial device to measure everything of monetary value in terms of an undefined dollar. By undefined, of course, we mean not freely convertible into a specified amount of a standard commodity, or an index, composite, or average that would represent the equivalent of a dollar in goods or services.

We use the artificial device of assuming a real dollar of fixed value. It is a convenient way to make stock charts, for one thing; if the price scale were being continually adjusted for every jiggle in the supply of potatoes or fluctuation of electric power output, it would be nearly impossible to keep a chart at all.

Everywhere we turn there is by implication the idea of a fixed-value dollar. The Community Chest drive has a scale showing the number of dollars pledged each week. The corporation report shows the increase in "value of product" year by year as measured on a uniform (or perhaps logarithmic) scale of dollars. But nowhere is there a footnote to explain that when we speak of dollars we are not talking about a fixed and unchanging thing. To be strictly accurate we would have to specify "dollar, 1948" or "dollar, 1958". Not the same. A matter of dating the map.

Not all stocks move up or down at the same time, and the value of dollars is continually in flux with respect to stocks and to goods and services. The picture, then, like almost everything else in reality, is a lot more complicated than we like to think of it. But unless we can get some fairly solid contact with reality, we can get badly set back on our heels when our high abstractions fail us.

When stock prices go up generally, as they did in the years preceding 1956, I wonder how many people make the mental reservation that at least some part of the advance must be considered as merely due to the shrinkage in the purchasing power of the dollar. If this is true to a degree, then the lower the purchasing power of the dollar goes, the higher we may look for the stock averages to do. To a degree there is an inverse relation here: As stock prices go up, dollars go down, and vice versa: As stock prices come down, dollars go up. This isn't just hypothesis, it's an observable fact.

There have been large fortunes made by certain men and women who have been sometimes referred to unkindly as vultures, who "buy" their dollars when dollars are very cheap; that is, when one can get a great many dollars for 1,000 shares of stock (when stock prices are high). Then, when the cold hand of depression squeezes the inflationary breath out of the economy, when the dollars are of such high value that just a few dollars will buy a lot of stock, then these vultures can take their dollars from the safe deposit boxes, or cash in their debentures and their bonds, and trade money for enormous quantities of the now-nearly-worthless stock.

You could say that they sold stocks near the top and bought them near the bottom. But I would rather you think of it in a little different light, since it is a matter of relativity anyway. Try to think that they bought their dollars when they were cheap and sold their dollars when they were very dear.

It should be noted that the designation "vulture" is a term having moral connotations. It is a label with a strong coloring of disapproval. It is a metaphor, a symbol, or a map. Also, it may not be entirely a fair picture, certainly not if you assume that the free market is in any way desirable. Finally, it is nowhere near as easy to be a vulture of this sort as it might at first appear. One can lose one's shirt, and many do, trying to foresee the speculative moves of dollars or of stocks. As Robert D. Edwards put it, "There is no easy money in Wall Street."

We are not endorsing or condemning the vultures. The only purpose in mentioning them at all is to point up the fact that the market is one of fluctuating dollars as well as fluctuating stocks.

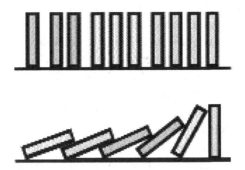

CHAPTER 61   CORRELATIONS AND CAUSES

The market goes up. The market goes down. Why? Dozens of pundits are employed by the media (and brokerage firms) to explain the unexplainable. And, incidentally, the irrelevant. The chairman of the Federal Reserve ate eggs for breakfast; he hinted at an interest rate change. Traders were bored.

"Why" is usually unknowable and does not have nearly the importance of "how." Or of observing detail and extracting relationships and correlations from it.

"Why" is for philosophers concerned with the meaning of meaning. "How" works better in the market.

When I was a boy there was a wonderful green-covered book, a book about mountainous tidal waves sweeping in a solid wall of water across whole villages. About the laying-down of the sediment over uncounted centuries, and how the rocks were formed from it and raised and folded and twisted to make the hills. About volcanoes blasting cinders and flame, while rivers of lava swept down their sides to bury entire cities. Stories of how the earth was made and of the sometimes delicate and often violent processes of nature.

The book was titled *Madam How and Lady Why*. It was explained that in this book we would meet and come to know Madam How rather well. She was quite accessible, and if one would only take the time and trouble one could learn a great deal from Madam How. But Lady Why was quite another sort of person. She was she. She kept herself out of sight for the most part. Most people never saw her at all. Just occasionally, someone who had learned to understand the ways of Madam How might briefly get a fleeting glimpse of Lady Why.

You remember some pages back we spoke about the attribution of qualities, how we project on reality the maps in our own head and "see" that the book is red or that Sally is a pretty girl. Among the high abstractions we project on reality is the concept of cause. The question "why" implies a cause, and we look for causes everywhere.

You can get into a good deal of trouble trying to assign causes for everything. As you know, once you begin tracing the sequence of causes and effects, you can build up a chain proving very neatly that everything in the world is the result of a series of causes stretching back to the creation, and that the whole future of the universe, down to the smallest detail, is already determined by the present state of affairs.

This idea of predestination isn't quite as popular as it was back in the nineteenth century when it was a rallying point for what might be called the "cog-wheel materialists." Of course, the universe was a lot simpler then than it is now, because people didn't know as much as today. Serious scientists seem too busy finding out what is really going on to spend much time on what begins to look like a rather silly game of playing with verbal maps.

Some people limit their choices. They set overly high standards for themselves. They expect the impossible from life. They ask the wrong questions: Why was I born? Why am I unlucky? Why is Grandma so cranky? Why can't we ever save any money? Why did soybeans go up today?

Some of the questions involving "why" that we ask ourselves and others aren't proper questions at all for the reason that they don't mean anything. "Why are there so many stars in the sky?" is a question so vague that there is considerable doubt whether it means anything all. Certainly if an answer is expected, it would have to be rephrased.

There are not only nonsense questions involving "why" but others where it would be necessary to specify a particular level or degree of "why." For instance, Abigail asks me why the car slows down as we approach the Sumner Avenue railroad tracks. I could answer this at several levels similar to the various levels of abstraction that we have discussed before:

Answer A: "Because the brakes tightened on the brake drum."
Answer B: "Because I pressed my foot down on the brake pedal."
Answer C: "Because I wanted to slow down the car."
Answer D: "Because it is safer to slow down when approaching a railroad track."
Answer E: "Because I want to drive safely at all times."
Answer F: "Because I love you and want to protect you."

You will notice that, just as in the other series of abstractions we have studied, the low-level abstraction is specific, definite, and narrow. It covers very little ground, but like a close-up photograph it is sharp and clear: "Because the brakes tightened on the brake drum." That is why the car slowed down, it's true—a correct answer at a low level of abstraction. Each of the other answers is also true, at a progressively higher level of abstraction.

Even the final answer is true. But it is a much broader answer, in much more general terms. It covers more ground but it is not nearly so definite, for it could include anything I might do to show my love and protect my child. It could cover teaching her how to cross streets safely, fighting off an attack by hoodlums, going out to the drug store to buy medicine when she was sick, earning money at my job, almost any of the hundreds of functions a father is supposed to perform.

The drawback of low abstractions is that they do not generalize and therefore do not point up the similarity of various different situations. You will notice that the highest-order answer, F, does do this; it includes and summarizes many of the duties of a father. The drawback of the high abstractions, however, is that they are vague. If I tell my little girl that I have done something "because I love her and want to protect her," that might mean any number of things. It doesn't particularize.

Now if you ask me why soybeans went up today, I could tell you it was because the bidders in soybeans seemed more numerous and more anxious to trade than the sellers. A fairly low-level answer. If I told you it was because the administration was believed to be leaning toward firmer price supports, that would be a somewhat higher-level answer.

You will notice that here, as in the previous example, the first example was a very earthy, specific, hard look at what was observably happening. The second answer was a broad abstraction that, although it contained larger implications, was also considerably more vague as to its precise meaning. Of course, the question "why" in regard to soybeans could be answered in many other ways, each quite possibly correct at some level of abstraction.

As always (and as we have seen before), there is a place for high abstractions, for low abstractions, and for all grades between. The important thing is to know what we are doing, and particularly not to confuse the levels at which we are thinking or speaking. Since the causes of things, as we understand them, very often represent the outcome of many stages of abstraction and logic, we should realize that these causes are not of themselves realities like the physical soybeans but are maps in our minds. We should understand this when we project these causes and attribute them to external reality.

All of this business is part of the game of chasing the coy, evasive Lady Why. We are never going to catch up with her, not really, and we must be satisfied with the occasional flash of understanding, the fleeting glimpse. Like almost everything we have touched, we have got to settle for something less than 100 percent.

In this case we have to settle for a great deal less. It will probably be more productive to give your attention of the most part to Madam How. If you can establish that certain events have happened, and have happened in certain sequences, then you have the basic mechanism for a predictive method and you can tell Lady Why to go hang.

Mariners certainly knew this, or at least acted on it, when they sailed the seas centuries ago. They set their courses by the stars. They did not know why the stars appeared to rise and revolve across the dome of the heavens, but they certainly knew how to make use of the fact. This was the necessary and sufficient data for them to plot their voyages.

Yet the most persistent question one encounters in the boardrooms of brokers is Why? Why did Crucible Steel cut its dividend? Why doesn't New York Central advance? Why didn't the rails confirm the industrials?

If you examine these "why" questions carefully you see that there are many possible, and equally true, answers. Without meaning to exhaust the possibilities, we could try restating the questions, turning them into "how" questions. We could ask, "How do stocks usually act when the dividend is cut?" We could ask, "How is New York Central acting now, and how has it acted for the past three weeks?" We could ask, "How much would the rails have to move to confirm the industrials? And how much significance could we attach to such a confirmation on the basis of past experiences?" The chances of getting a definite and useful answer to questions like these are better than for the first series of questions.

Also, consider this: When we shift from the "why" attitude to the "how," we begin to get away from the cause-and-effect idea. You will see that the last three questions, the "how" questions, do not require the attribution of cause at all. They simply ask for someone to take a hard look at a territory that can be inspected. Because the "why" questions so often lead to nonsense, or confused levels of abstraction, or vagueness, or cause-and-effects answers that concern the relation of maps to territories rather than the activities in the territories as such, we avoid the "why" question whenever we can. It is possible to get into a good deal of trouble with "why" questions, especially if you don't understand the pitfalls of the cause-and-effect relation.

I could take you out in the back yard and show you a pear tree that blossoms gloriously quite early in the spring. For several years, shortly after it blooms, a pair of robins have come and built a nest in the fork of the tree. I could observe the flowering of the tree and the building of the nest and say, "The robins come because the tree has bloomed." In other words, I have observed that repeatedly a certain event follows another certain event, and I draw the conclusion that the one causes the other. Post hoc, ergo propter hoc.

A more scientific way to think about the tree-and-robin's nest problem is to forget the "why" entirely and simply accept the fact that one event is correlated with the other.

We can do this in many departments of life. We can do a good deal of useful predicting right at the operational level, on the "how" level, without ever asking of nature or society the question "why." Why does she love me? Or, for that matter, Why doesn't she?

What a question! How many lovesick teenagers have nursed their aching hearts over that vague and perhaps unanswerable question. Of course, it might be because of halitosis or pimples, but then it might be because of hundreds of other embarrassing physical disabilities or personality shortcomings, too.

A smart teenager might win the lady if he would change his question and drop the "why." At any rate, he would probably feel better. He could ask himself how she acted, what she did, what she said. These are matters of observable fact. He could plan how he might act to please her more, how he could overcome his own awkwardness or acne or whatever. He could treat the problem tactically at the operational level and not worry about the attribution of causes.

You will understand we are not thinking just of teenagers and their girl friends. We are thinking of all the many different situations in life where people go around wringing their hands and asking "why," when they could often do so much better in meeting their real problems if they would start asking "how," and taking a look.

We are thinking about the market, which certainly embodies many of the problems we meet in other places. In the market you don't as a rule need to ask "why." Particularly if you are one who follows technical methods, you will not so often be looking for reasons as for correlations. If you find that certain kinds of stock, gold mining stocks, food stocks, or utility stocks, tend to go up when the market averages are going sharply down, put that down in your notebook; make a map of that in your mind. Never mind why these stocks act that way. It is not necessary to know why, and except as a matter of general interest it can be just so much excess baggage to know why.

What you do want to know is whether this tendency is a general one, one that has been observed on a number of previous occasions, and whether the evidence of the correlation is strong enough to justify your acting on it. As a basis for the final judgment and decision, the material you need to answer your question can be obtained by checking the facts in external reality.

In technical analysis, as in many kinds of research in such varied fields as engineering, medicine, and sociology, it is possible to a good deal of work by means of charts and diagrams. These are abstractions on paper, what we might call externalized abstractions. The charts in themselves are not capable of answering questions that start with a "why," but they often can and do answer questions that begin with a "how." Charts will show you correlations that you might not see without them. They can help you to make your judgments as to the reliability of these correlations, and the degree of dependability you can attach to them.

So again, our study calls for throwing out some very superfluous cargo. We can unload most of our "whys," and we can reduce the primary question-asking largely to matters of "how." We will look for correlations, and only after we have gathered our "how" data and established correlations will we begin to exercise judgment in making the decision on whether to act on what we see.

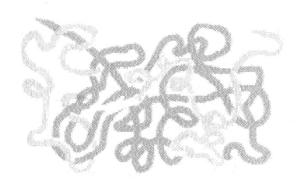

CHAPTER 62   THE "FUNDAMENTALS"

Fundamentalists are investors or analysts who believe the study of the company can bring success in trading in the stock. Fundamentalists are generally depreciative of technical analysts (and vice versa).

Technicians feel that fundamental analysis is fundamentally flawed. It seeks to explain stock market behavior. Technical analysis is not concerned with explanations, which are speculation. It is concerned with what is happening and what might happen—that is, with facts that everyone is in agreement with, such as the closing price on the New York Stock Exchange.

The great body of investors have always subscribed to the idea that by knowing all about the stock they can make money in the market, or at least protect their capital.

There are several things wrong with this. In the first place, they are not going to know all about the stock. That would be simply impossible. Certainly they are not going to know all about a complicated situation like Gulf Oil or U.S. Steel merely by thumbing through the annual report or reading a few news releases off the tape. They are not going to know all by sitting around a broker's boardroom and exchanging opinions with others of their ilk.

As a matter of fact, they don't need to know all—but whatever they do know should be pertinent to the problem at hand. Unfortunately, although they talk about the stock, what they study is the company, as though the company were the stock. They pile up vast quantities of data pertaining to corporate affairs but seem to have very little interest in the stock in its natural habitat, the market.

Such investors, and I am using the word here to include all traders, like to refer to themselves as students of "the fundamentals," no matter how superficial or irrelevant their agglomerations of fact may be. It should be plain enough that there are important factors that affect the stock that are not directly connected with the corporation's internal affairs.

The most important of these factors, perhaps, is the fluctuation in the value of dollars. During the 1946 market collapse there was considerable consternation in the ranks because apparently there was no reason for the decline; in other words, there seemed to be no weakness in the business of the companies represented by many of the tumbling stocks that would account for the break in prices. But one of the most obvious weaknesses of the fundamental method is that it does not adequately consider the action of the money market, the political and psychological environment, and all the forces that may operate on the prices of stocks beyond the specific records of the company whose stock is being studied.

This does not imply that fundamentalists are ignorant of these factors. Basically, technicians believe that fundamentalists are not as well equipped as they are to consider these questions. Also, the fundamentalist is likely to pin his evaluation on the past records of the company's business, on the assumption that either things will continue as they have or they will change in line with a trend.

These assumptions are not entirely worthless. They become dangerous only when we attribute an absolute quality to them and leave out entirely the possibility that things can change. We have to date our maps. We have seen how it is not possible to verify new features in today's territory no matter how carefully we look at yesterday's map. Yet we have all seen people, confronted by a tremendous breakout or collapse in a stock, rush to the Standard & Poor's data sheets to see what could account for the sudden change in value.

We must assume that the stock was competitively valued last week or last month, and if there is now a radical change in its behavior, this represents something that was not there or was not known before—and therefore we are not likely to find it by looking it up on yesterday's map.

A more realistic way to go at this situation (if you must have "fundamental" reasons) would be to find out and evaluate what new factors have come into the picture. Of course, by the time you have found out what they are, you may be reasonably sure that the market has found out, too, and has already revised its map—and its price tag.

Not that these fundamentals are all wrong. Not that they are without value. The trouble comes in their inadequacy, and because people will attribute almost magical powers to a whispered rumor that XYZ is going to buy out PQWR or that TUV has a new process for extracting gold from seawater. After all, there have been some very successful men who operated largely on the strength of their understanding of the fundamentals. But these men were not of the same breed as the average lunch-hour trader or boardroom hanger-ons.

There is another word to be said about (and against) unqualified adherence to the fundamentals. They seem to "explain" things. You will remember the difficulties we had in seeking out Lady Why, and that it was often necessary to compromise on meeting Madam How. For instance: We see a sudden whoop on the tape in MNO, and as the stock pours across the ticker in 1,000-share lots, we scurry for *The Wall Street Journal* (this morning's issue, which was prepared last night; the information is already to some extent out of date) to see why MNO is going up. We know how—we can see that right on the tape—but that is not enough. We have to find out why.

If you look diligently enough, you can find out why. You can find reasons. If MNO goes up sharply today you will find the reason for the move in tomorrow's paper, in the columns of every commentator and analyst who mentions it. If it goes down you will also find out why.

Let us say that the Near East situation flares up today into a really threatening war-scare. If the market should go down at the time of this news, tomorrow's papers will tell us why: because a war would mean curtailment of consumer goods, the closing of many plants now making civilian products, shut-down periods for conversion to armament work, government restriction or control of profits, higher taxes, the danger of a physical attack on the country, and on and on. But if the market should advance strongly on the same news, tomorrow's papers will still tell us why: because the prospect of war would mean immediate stepping up of military orders, the production of uniforms and equipment, full civilian employment to meet these new demands, an increase in rail traffic, government limitations on strikes and other work tie-ups, and on and on.

Take it either way. You have your answer why. The Monday morning quarterback is never at a loss for reasons why Harvard won the game, or lost it, or tied.

Isn't this a sort of silly playing with facts? To take the truth and twist it around so it will tell you why something happened? Is it necessary to know why? You must realize that "why" refers to causes and causes can be taken at many levels of abstraction. We have to know just what level we are talking about if we want to get a useful answer. It is often much more useful to study *what* is happening and *how.* Then we can very often ignore the question "why" entirely.

One danger of seeking out the reason why, even supposing we have made a valid analysis of the case and have, in fact, come up with a sound reason, is that we then tend to close our eyes to all the other factors that may be operating in the same affair. There is no rule that says there must be one and only one reason for something happening, in the market or out of it. More often than not there may be several, or many reasons, some of which we may not be able to discover and which if known might not help us a great deal in deciding what to do next.

The methods of analysis that are known as technical are not concerned very much with the "whys." They do not look for *the* reason, or even the reasons. That accounts in large part for their effectiveness, and it certainly accounts for their unpopularity with a public that is continually asking the futile question "why."

CHAPTER 63   ACCRUED *VS.* REALIZED

Paper gains (and losses). Realized gains (and losses). Accrued gains (and losses). These are inventions of the devil to bewilder investors who are willing to be confused. Worse, it is not only private investors who wander into this maze of concepts. Billions of dollars have been lost by institutions that have not marked to market their portfolios or assets and liabilities. Isn't that a reassuring thought for the private investor who can use the concept that it is a paper loss he has, not a real loss?

Hard cheese. Or hard onions, as you will see in the story of the commodity trader who bought onions. What is important, whether you call it accrual or mark to market, is knowing the truth about your portfolio right now—then having the fortitude to do something about it, right now.

Some of the really serious barriers to an understanding of the market are so fragile one wonders that they can shut out so much insight. It would only take a couple of good hard looks and a little work with pencil and paper to smash some of those barriers entirely.

One of the most formidable of these rice-paper screens is the matter of realized gains and losses versus accrued gains and losses. This question seems as baffling to the average investor as a kitchen chair upended at a berserk circus lion by his trainer, but it is no more difficult to figure out than a kitchen chair.

As you may know, there are two principal methods of business accounting, either of them acceptable in tax reports and other financial statements. In accounting on a cash basis, income and expenses, gains and losses are considered only as they are "realized," that is, at the time that money is received or paid out. On an accrued basis, unpaid bills and uncollected accounts receivable are included. This basis takes note of the debts we would have to pay and the benefits we would receive if the business were to be entirely liquidated by settling all accounts. If I buy 100 shares of a stock at 20 and it advances to 22, I have an accrued gain of two points, or $200. If I sell it at 22, I will have a realized gain of $200, less commissions.

There is a certain school, which sometimes seems to include about 99.44 percent of investors, that seems to believe not only that there is something less tangible about the accrued gain but that it is purely imaginary, not to be given serious weight or consideration at all. A disciple of this philosophy will tell you that the $100 is "only a paper profit," meaning no profit at all. But it all depends on what happens to meet the needs of his own ego; he will switch from accrued to realized and back again, or confuse the two, whatever will most effectively build his self-esteem. If it is your stock, the accrued gain is no profit at all. If it is his stock, he is likely to tell you he has a profit of two points on XYZ. But if he has an accrued loss, he will revert to the view that it is "only a paper loss" and therefore no loss at all.

Consider a case like this: Your friend has bought 100 shares of ABC at 20 and 100 shares of XYZ, also at 20. ABC has advanced to 23. XYZ has declined to 17. Feeling as he does that the accrued is not so genuine as the realized, he can sell the ABC and take a profit of $300, less commissions, and if you ask him how he stands he can quite truthfully tell you that he had a nice gain in ABC and no loss in XYZ.

This, of course, is true if we use his unconscious choice of the realized method of accounting, but it has in it some elements of high abstraction. It is necessary to know, and most especially for your friend to know, just exactly what he is talking about, especially when he is talking to himself. Otherwise he is headed for a peck of trouble, and this is the kind of trouble that has thrown many an investor for a fall.

Suppose that ABC had been sold at 23. He has a nice profit on it (realized). So far as XYZ is concerned, in the first place he doesn't recognize any loss, since accrued losses mean nothing in his way of thinking, and in the second place he is confident that XYZ will come back. This is a map, his judgment of XYZ made from whatever data he had at the time he bought it. It may now be an out-of-date map, but it would be painful to think about that, so he does not.

What he does, in fact, is to support his original judgment by every means he can. He will talk with his broker, who will as a rule reassure him that XYZ is a good, sound stock. He will talk with friends or boardroom companions who may also own the stock, and they will strengthen one another's faith in the tottering stock through collective self-defense. He will read whatever he can find that gives good news and promising predictions regarding XYZ but (quite unconsciously) he will not see anything of a pessimistic nature. As a matter of fact he is not likely to encounter much that is pessimistic; the men who give our corporation news are not paid to give out gloomy statistics.

This leaves him feeling pretty good. He will continue to feel good even if XYZ drops a point or two more. Of course, if XYZ continues to slide and reaches a soggy $5 a share, you and I know that he has a loss, whether he recognizes it or not. He will not, even then. He will very likely have bought more of the stock on the way down, and now with XYZ down to 25 percent of its original value, he will tell you seriously that he is not a speculator and is holding it for income because it is a good, sound stock. We will not ask the question, "How stupid can people get?" That would be unkind. It would be unkind because this man did not ever have the training to see what he was doing to himself. The real question is, "What can we do to prevent this kind of tragedy?"

In order to answer the question of how to prevent getting frozen into bad situations because of inability to recognize accrued losses, we must take a little different view of the case, though not greatly different. As we said at the beginning of this chapter, the difficulty is not insurmountable.

Let us take the liquidating value of the account as a whole, as it actually is at a given moment. This is the accrued basis, of course, but it is not a move away from reality. It is a facing up to the real facts. If we take the case just given, where ABC had advanced from 20 to 23 and had been sold at 23, while XYZ is still held, having dropped from 20 to 17, then except for commissions your friend would come out just even if he closed his account at this moment.

If XYZ drops to 5, he must consider that the value of his account, if he has to close it out, has shrunk, and he would then have a loss on the accrued basis of $1,500, less the net amount of the profit on the sold-out ABC. It certainly would have been better, on this view, if he had actually sold the XYZ when it was at 17. Then he would have been somewhere near even. But if he is going to cling to an old and outdated map of what XYZ is worth in the face of the hard facts, then he is going to ride it down all the way. Unless he changes his method of evaluation he will continue to accumulate losses that will sooner or later have to be accepted as real and that will be much larger than necessary. Unless, of course, his judgment is so good that the stock he has ridden down from 20 to 5 actually justifies his faith and does come back—and you know how often that particular thing happens.

Even if his faith were entirely justified, would it not have been better, far better, to have sold out the stock when it broke to 17 and then bought it back at 5? In that way he could have bought more than three times as many shares for the rise when it did come. But people do not like to take losses. They put so high a premium on being right that they will be too seriously hurt by even the smallest loss. They will ride a stock down the toboggan for many, many points before they will admit to their broker (or to themselves) that they were wrong.

Great heavens! They don't even need to admit they were wrong! Their original judgment may have been quite correct, but the conditions have changed. All that is necessary is to change the map or make a new one on the basis of the present conditions. That should not involve any loss of self-esteem, certainly not so much as the ultimate loss of over $1,000. But, as we have said before, nothing takes precedence over the self; and a man will go down to ruin if his value system is so poorly geared to reality that he cannot make a slight adjustment in his opinions without feeling small, stupid, and incompetent.

There was a man in a nearby city here in Massachusetts who went into the commodity market for the first time a few years ago. He started off, quite reasonably, by buying a contract of wheat and a contract of onions. His hope was, of course, that both contracts would advance and bring him a tidy profit. As a matter of fact the wheat did advance a few cents, and because he was timid and anxious to bolster his unsteady confidence, he sold the wheat, thereby taking a realized profit.

The onions, meanwhile, dropped a bit. In the course of a few weeks, wheat advanced a few cents more. The onions, however, slumped off a few cents more. And a little later the wheat shot up quite actively, while onions continued their downward course.

The novice trader bought himself a second contract of onions, in the pleasant hope that by averaging his cost he would be all right on the first substantial rally. But the rally was not quite so substantial as he had expected. Onions broke down and made a new low.

Wheat continued its advance. Eventually there came the end of the contract, with wheat soaring to the skies, without our friend aboard, and onions bumping along the bottom at giveaway prices.

The expiration of the contract caught this inexperienced trader unprepared. He was issued a notice calling for his acceptance of the onions, onions standing by now on a car in a hot freight yard in Chicago, with many, many more fresh, juicy onions pouring in constantly from the bumper crops of many farmers. He was, of course, forced to sell, and sell at once. Either that or take a carload of onions rapidly wilting in that freight yard. His loss was staggering.

I heard this true story from Victor C. Lea, manager of the Commodity Department of Paine, Webber, Jackson & Curtis. "Now where do you suppose this fellow made his big mistake?" Lea asked me. Then he answered his own question, though I knew the answer, as you must, too: "Why, he made his mistake when he took his profit on the wheat instead of taking his loss on the onions."

This man sold out the contract that was doing well by him. He killed the goose that laid the golden eggs. He was right about wheat, and sold it out, but he held onto the onion contract, which was disappointing him from the start. He valued his rightness so much, his perfect rightness, that is, that he refused even to consider changing his mind, and backed the losing contract all the way to the gutter.

What he had done was to set his map against the reality. He refused to date his map and revise it or make a new one. He had set so high a value on his ego that the loss of hundreds of dollars was as nothing compared to the hurt of making a slight concession. "The science of commodity trading," Lea told me that same day, "is the science of taking losses." By this he meant that in order to prevent any such disaster as the one just described, a man must be able to keep an open mind. He must stand ready to throw the old map out the window as soon as it no longer represents the territory as it is today.

By thinking in terms of accrual, rather than limiting one's point of view to the realized, it is possible to see losses and gains in a different light. When one can do this, he can take many small losses without fear or depression, if he has an overall plan that will give him the reasonable assurance of a few large gains.

In certain types of trading this is basic. A trader must take losses freely and often, perhaps as many as seven losses out of each ten transactions he enters. If he tries to curtail or eliminate these relatively inconsequential losses, he may be heading toward a far more dangerous situation that could cripple him or wipe him out by a single overwhelming adverse move.

CHAPTER 64   UP IS BETTER THAN DOWN

The market has, in addition to occasional pleasures, an intense frustration for technical analysts and investment advisors. Try as they might, they cannot, for the most part, convince their clients that selling short is a necessity in the markets. This may be because of the evidently universal human opinion that up is better than down, or it may be due to medieval superstition, but the ability to think in terms of being long or short is a bright line between professional, effective investors and those who are less successful, or failures.

You may remember some years ago the movie *The Third Man,* the picture in which Anton Karas made magic music with his zither. In the early part of that picture there is a scene where an Austrian, trying to explain to an American who is looking for a friend that the friend is no more: "He is gone—to heaven (pointing down)—or to hell (pointing up dramatically)." This confusion with an unfamiliar language was good for a sure-fire laugh. Naturally. We all know where heaven is. Heaven is up, and hell is down.

Of course, when we consider the nature of the physical universe, it becomes a little difficult to make this stick. Down might mean in the interior of the earth, though that hardly seems remote enough for a truly cosmic hell. Up must mean in the direction of the sky, but the sky is in all directions.

We could engage in heated discussions on this intriguing problem. And just how long would it take us, depending on our previous education and training, habits of perception, etc., to realize that this is just a game of playing with verbal maps, and has no more relation to physical realities than how many angels can stand on the head of a pin?

It is all right to assign directions to heaven and hell so long as we understand clearly that these are symbolic, that they pertain to the world of thought and not to the world of things. It is when we confuse the high abstractions with physical observations that we begin to talk and think nonsense.

One of the most cogent comments on this tendency of people to confuse things with ideas is to be found in the twelfth chapter of the Book of Mark, where Jesus draws the line between the laws of the land and his ethical concepts: "Render to Caesar the things that are Caesar's, and to God the things that are God's."

The confusions we make! Consider the words we were discussing, "up" and "down." They have been clothed with symbolism and metaphor until we are not even aware of their implications. In the ordinary sense, that is, the direct-observation, low-abstractive, down-to-earth sense, "up" can be defined as "in a direction contrary to that of gravity," and "down" as "in the direction of gravity, or towards the center of the earth." These are primary definitions taken from *Webster's New International Dictionary of the English Language,* published by G. & C. Merriam Co. of Springfield, Massachusetts.

You will notice that "up" and "down" in these primary senses are purely geocentric terms, having no meaning with respect to the solar system, or outer space, or the universe. Or to man's destiny, aspirations, moral values, or anything else except to indicate a direction away from or towards the center of the earth.

We must assume that these primary senses were the original meaning in which the words were used. But "up" is generally toward the light, toward the great visible dome of the sky. "Down" leads to darkness and obscurity, yes even to the grave. Stars are on high, birds fly aloft, clouds are above us, the sky itself is up. "Down" suggests the dank miasma of caves, the unhealthy fungi of subterranean chasms, the fiery bowels of the mysterious underworld.

Man has "raised" himself from the quadrupedal posture, but he must sometimes walk carefully or he will have a downfall. Indeed, man was created only a little lower than the angels, but mankind nevertheless did have a fall, a fall from grace in the Garden of Eden. Man tries to avoid low thoughts and to concentrate on higher things. He "lifts up his eyes to the hills." He hitches his wagon to a star. For every man wants to rise in the world. He hopes to have a superior record. He may be elevated. He hopes to get to the top. In that case we must consider he is a high-grade man, and we will look up to him.

We do not like to see a friend on the downgrade. We hope he will avoid low companions, and will not descend to crime. For if he is at the bottom of the heap, downtrodden, an underdog, he will be depressed and downhearted. If he has stooped too low, we may look down on him. A man who is down at heel is not likely to be in high spirits.

Does any of this sound familiar? Isn't this our old friend either/or in another situation? The up-and-down dichotomy can be as damaging as the success-failure dichotomy, and in some ways perhaps even more so, for it is so often charged with emotion and relates to the most absolute and at the same time the vaguest of high abstractions. As so often happens with words that represent the extreme opposites of a scale of values, we simply wipe out everything in between and assign coefficients of either 100 percent or zero to any situation.

This is underscored by the adjectives and adverbs we use so often along with the up-and-down words. We say he is utterly downcast, absolutely up in the clouds, completely down in the dumps, or definitely high-minded. If there were any doubt about what we meant, these words make it clear that what we mean is "all-out." No measuring. No estimating of degree.

You will realize that a great many of the expressions mentioned in the past few paragraphs, almost all of them in fact, do not refer to the direction of something in relation to the center of the earth. We are talking in terms of symbols. We must be careful not to carry symbolism too far. We must not mix things that do not belong together.

Notice the strong judgment content in so many of the up-and-down words. We have spoken before of the tendency we have to set up an either/or situation and then reject one side, leaving us with only one acceptable choice. It is the down words that represent what is bad. And we reject them. Nobody wants to sink. Or to go into a decline. Or to fall down on the job. But we do very much want to be on the upgrade, to move up in the world, and to be held in high regard.

You will understand that the ideas that are so neatly represented by these up-and-down words would not in all cases be easy to describe directly. The metaphor is a short-cut by which we can roughly get across to others (or even to ourselves) how we feel about the success of failure of someone, or his social conduct or his physical condition. Just so long as we know what we are talking about, and realize that we are not talking about direction with relation to the center of the earth, we will be on fairly safe ground. When we forget that these terms are not territories but only maps, when we use "up" and "down" symbolically without realizing that we are dealing with symbols, then we may look for trouble.

You may know that a great many men suffer from a variety of phobias, sometimes to a degree that can seriously interfere with their ordinary life and work. These phobias appear to be related to the confusion of verbal symbols (metaphors) with physical realities. They are very often connected with this particular metaphor, the up-and-down dichotomy. A man who is afraid of high places may be reacting to "high" in an entirely different sense; he may be shrinking from frustrations he has suffered in attempting to make the grade in reaching a "high place," perhaps in his business. Similarly, a man who feels trapped, let us say by his job, or in his home life, may react with a fear of closed rooms, tunnels, caves, and the like.

We are not here primarily concerned with psychoneurotic symptoms. We are concerned with the market, but without this rather long discussion it would be hard to explain the peculiar attitude of 99 out of 100 investors towards short selling.

The short sale of a stock is, as you probably know, a transaction by which you borrow the stock from someone who owns it, and then sell it in the open market. This leaves you owing so many shares of the stock to the person who loaned you the stock. If you sold the stock at $50 a share, 100 shares would come to $5,000 (leaving out the cost of commissions). If the price of the stock should drop to, say, $40 a share in a few weeks or a few months, then you could buy back the stock at that price, at a cost of $4,000, and return the stock to the person from whom you borrowed it. Since you received $5,000 when you sold the borrowed stock and bought back the stock for $4,000 when you returned it, you have a profit of $1,000 on the transaction. The more the stock declines after you have sold it, the cheaper you can buy it back, and the more gain you will have. If the stock advances in price, you will eventually have to buy the stock to return to the owner who loaned it to you, and in that case you will have a loss.

In effect you have reversed the usual order of the dates of purchase and sale. You have sold before you bought. You are making a trade in which your objective (in the future) is not a higher price but a lower one. The short sale is in almost every way the reverse of the purchase of stock on the long side. When you are long a stock, you may receive dividends on it. When you are short, you must pay the dividends to the owners of the stock.

On the face of it, there is no obvious moral angle. Buying stock and selling stock short are both operations made in the ordinary course of business in a free competitive market. They are part of the speculative or evaluative side of the market, regulated in much the same way by the rules of the exchange and by the Securities and Exchange Commission (except that the regulations pertaining to short sales are somewhat stricter than those applying to long purchases), and the objective of the speculator in either case is to make a profit. Then why is it that there is such general reluctance, even aversion, to selling short?

It might be because the market is generally a bull market. This is an extraordinary statement. However, it has been true for over half a century and probably for longer. It is also a somewhat misleading statement. If you examine the long-term charts of the Down Jones Industrial average, you will see that since 1900 the trend or course has been upwards about two-thirds of the time and downward only one-third of the time. Thus followers of the Dow or any other trend theory, if they neglect to look at what is happening, could easily say, "Well, if the market is going up two-thirds of the time, it would be smart for me to always be in long stocks, for the probabilities are in my favor. I would not want to sell short since the odds against me would be two to one."

Unfortunately, during the one-third of the time the market is declining, it tends to come down very fast, about twice as fast on average as it goes up. So while it is true that the trend is up most of the time, the slope on the relatively short down moves is much steeper than on the longer advances. In other words, the gains if a whole year can be wiped out in six months, and sometimes in six weeks.

Looking at this another way, if the down moves run much faster, it's possible to make money quicker on the short side, when these opportunities present themselves, than holding stocks long during the bull market periods. Actually, of course, stocks do not all move together. Some stocks have their bull market moves when most others are going down, as Lorillard and a number of other stocks did during the bear market in the summer and fall of 1957. But what we have said for the market as a whole is also true of individual stocks: With all their irregularities of trend you can say as a broad generality, they come down faster than they go up.

Yet it seems to the average investor who has not looked at the chart records as if the sensible course was to buy stocks and hold them for the long-term advance. His faith in this advance allows for no interruptions, no exceptions. He has a one-way mind. He is thinking in line with the good, or acceptable, direction.

There is another reason people avoid short sales. They will tell you that it is more dangerous to sell short than to buy stocks "because a stock cannot go down below nothing and you can lose only the price of the stock, but there is no limit to how high it can go, so your risk of loss is unlimited." Bob Edwards answered that one some years ago when he said, "Nonsense. You can lose exactly the same amount either way: You can lose everything you've got, and no more."

If this statement is not precisely correct, it is at least approximately so. The margin clerk will see to it, for his own protection and the protection of his firm, that you are closed out when your losses have reached a certain point. This would be true whether you were long or short. There is no greater danger in being short of a stock on margin than in owning a stock long on margin. "Ah, yes," someone will say, "That is true, on margin. But I am not on margin. I buy only good, sound stocks, and I do not have to sell them, no matter what happens. Since you cannot sell stocks short outright the way you can buy stocks, you could be frozen out, whereas I cannot be frozen out."

That argument sounds much better than it really is. The man who bought SK outright in February 1953 at 43 or more and saw his investment go down to 2 5/8 in December 1957 still had his stock. He was not wiped out. But he was so seriously crippled that he might almost as well have been wiped out. He has a Pyrrhic victory, no more than that. Actually, he had gone heavily into SK when Studebaker was at the high levels, say investing all of his available capital in the stock, he would at the end of 1953 be considerably worse off than a trader who had put only 20 percent of his capital into the stock and had been closed out with a total loss. Suppose, for example, that the trader had bought SK on margin at near the top, that is, above 43, and had sold it (or been forced to sell) at around 25, at which point he had sold short. He would still have had the opportunity to profit greatly on the way down, and might indeed have recouped most or all of his losses by 1957.

CHAPTER 65   THE UP-AND-DOWN OF IT

Is it possible for the sun to be located below us rather than above? What a strange idea! It certainly puts a dent in our idea of reality. What if short sales were seen as an exchange of a certain number of shares of stock for a certain number of dollars, and the short seller expected to profit when he could get more shares for his dollars at a lower share price? Is the sun shining from below for you? A little disorientation is a good thing to stimulate the mind.

We're accustomed to think of "up" as good and "down" as bad. But we are not always consistent. It is good for stock prices to go up, but we overlook that this means that the exchange value of dollars is going down—though we know well enough that this may be a symptom of inflation, and inflation is bad. We think of buying stocks and sharing in the prosperity of a mighty America.

Sometimes people buy wheat and potatoes and soybeans in the form of contracts for future delivery. When these prices go up it is not good in the same sense as industrial prosperity being good. It can mean a disaster to the agriculture of the country. If the crop is blighted, destroyed by frost, flood, drought or insects, or if a condition of scarcity threatens, that will be reflected in higher prices or—bull market, if you will. On the other hand, if the heavens smile and the cornucopia of nature's bounty pours out a generous harvest, that is a bear market in commodities and prices tumble. But is this a bad condition?

Actually, we might be much better off if we did not use the strongly colored and absolute words "good" and "bad" with respect to stock and commodity prices. The question is not one of goodness or badness; it is simply a matter of setting a fair value on what is being traded.

We have not quite finished the discussion in the previous chapter about short sales and why so many people avoid them like snakes. There is another up-and-down angle to that question. I would like to show you a photograph of a tank or boiler that has been hammered in several places to produce bumps raised on the surface, or dents sunk into the surface. This demonstration is most striking in the unretouched photo, but since that cannot be reproduced here, perhaps a drawing will convey the idea.

You will notice there are hammered places, two of which appear to be bumps raised on the outside of the tank and three of which appear to be dents hammered in. Now turn the page upside down and look at the tank again. How many bumps do you see, and how many dents? Do you know why this is so? Why do you see what were bumps as dents and what were dents as bumps?

If you study the picture for a minute you will realize that the way you tell the bumps from the dents is by the shadows around and in them. Since the shadows are caused by the cutting off of the sunlight, the appearance of the bumps and dents depends on the position of the sun. Now the sun is ordinarily overhead, and the light comes either vertically or at some angle from above. When you turn the page upside down you see the bumps and dents in a different light. If you assume (as we all do) that the sun is coming from above, that is, from position X, it will reverse the appearance of bumps and dents and we will have the illusion that these have changed place. But the picture as originally shown was made with the sun in position O, and to give a fair representation of bumps and dents as before, we would have to see the sunlight as still coming from position O after we turned the page around.

This we cannot do. We cannot easily picture the sunlight as coming from below. Therefore, since our mind cannot accept a sun down there, we put it up here in position X—and get a faulty interpretation of the hammer marks on the tank. It is a typical case of how our old, learned habits of perception will override our intellectual grasp of a situation. We know better but we still see it the old way.

This is very much the situation with short sales of stocks. When we buy stocks long, we exchange a certain number of dollars for a certain number of shares, which we intend to exchange again, if all goes well, for a greater number of dollars when stocks are worth more with respect to dollars. To be consistent we should realize that when we sell stocks short, we have exchanged a certain number of shares of stock for a certain number of dollars that we intend to exchange again, if all goes well, for a greater number of shares of stock when dollars are worth more with respect to stock.

In other words, to be quite consistent we should measure our gains on the long side in dollars and on the short side in number of shares of stock. But we forget to "turn the sun over," and so we measure both longs and shorts in terms of dollars, which leads to some of our inconsistencies and confusions regarding short sales.

For instance, consider a point we touched on before, that one could only lose a definite amount in a long position but there was no limit to the theoretical loss one could have on the short side. That argument does not hold water when you reverse the entire picture, including the sun. Look at it this way: If you buy a stock with dollars, the number of dollars you can receive for that stock when you close out the transaction is limited by zero at the bottom, and there is no definite limit at the top. The price could not go below zero dollars, and could go as high as any figure you wanted to name.

When you sell a stock short (remembering to reverse everything in the picture), you have bought dollars with a certain number of shares of stock. The number of shares you can receive for those dollars when you close out the transaction is limited by zero at the bottom, and there is no definite limit at the top. The number of shares you could buy could not go below zero, and could go as high as any figure you wanted to name.

If you have followed this, we have eliminated the paradoxes by looking at both purchases and short sales realistically, one being the opposite of the other. If you have trouble seeing this, please realize that it is not an easy thing to turn the sun around. It takes more than logic alone to change the habits of many years; it calls for practice and the acquiring of new habits of perception.

The most difficult point in learning to accept and use the short sale is probably due to the powerful mindset that operates with so many people that up is better than down. The prejudice of the perceived virtue in anything containing verbal up-ness as contrasted with the evils of anything containing verbal down-ness is so strong that it overrides reason. That is one reason so many people feel with regard to short sales that high-minded men should not stoop so low.

CHAPTER 66   POLITICS AND ECONOMICS

Ossified society and particularly its elected representatives (politicians) will always value the label and the map over the territory. In order to satisfy the needs of petty demagoguery, they will attack the rich, the speculators, and the windfall profiteers—even while they enjoy the economic benefits of the free and speculative markets these actors create. Consider carefully the true meaning of "speculator": Instead of an economic rapist, he might be the willing acceptor of risk that the market needs, to control risk for traders with different aims and intentions.

It is not the purpose of this chapter to start a Great American Movement to reform the tax structure. Anyone who has had much contact with politicians knows that any such campaign will run aground not only on the inherent economic stupidity of the breed but also on the pressures that are brought to bear on these men by their own constituents. After all, politicians in our kind of democracy are not selected by a winnowing of the most able citizens but seem to attain their high offices too often by winning a sort of popularity contest.

Under these conditions, although you may occasionally get some kindly men, and some able men in resolving human problems, you do not look for many who are strictly and dispassionately analytical. Almost everything in politics is a compromise, and both the theory and the practice of politics require that the politician keep an ear tuned at all times to the rumblings and murmurings of his own constituency. If he hopes to be re-elected, he had better listen carefully, and work toward legislation that will most nearly bridge the gaps between the various demands of the voters back home.

On certain subjects the politician is pressed very hard to conform to public opinion. As a rule he will yield easily enough, since as a rule he is of the same culture as his home environment and shares the general attitudes of his neighbors. You do not expect a senator from Mississippi to take a strong stand against white supremacy. You would not be surprised if a congressman from the corn-raising states should come out for a more generous program of corn price supports and aid for corn farmers. In our big cities a simple and surefire campaign was always possible (this was some years ago) on the promise of a cheap transit fare.

Generally speaking, an attack on the rich is always in order, and regardless of how well heeled our representatives may be, or how lush may their private lives be, it is often necessary for them to appear in the raiment of the proletariat. You will see them at the State Fair in shirt-sleeves, munching hot dogs and throwing rings to win a Kewpie doll. They will turn up in the picture section of your newspaper pitching hay, wielding a riveting gun, or operating a subway train—just plain ordinary guys, no better than anybody else. It is good politics to attack the rich from time to time, it marks one as a friend of the common man, and there are more of him.

A good many of our tax policies seem to be framed in some such atmosphere as this. Whether the indiscriminate bonuses and benefits to veterans (as opposed to really adequate help where it is badly needed) come under the head of calculated exploitation or arise simply because the politicos themselves share the same muddled sentimentality they are appealing to in the constituents is a moot question. The fact is that our elected representatives will necessarily represent the prejudices and partialities of the mass of voters.

You get echoes of these attitudes especially in tax matters. Sometimes it looks as though the tax program was framed more with an eye to how it would look to the dullest-witted voter than to his real welfare. Exemptions, deductions, special benefits, and expenditures of public funds, all seem slanted to dressing up the package so that it will look much more generous to the common man than it really may be; in fact, sometimes the package is made to look better than the budget or the facts could possible substantiate.

There are just three of the many points concerning taxes that we would touch on here. One of these is trivial, but revealing. It is the manner in which dividends and capital gains are treated in certain state tax returns, our own Massachusetts forms among them. Any income or gain derived from ownership in stocks is treated as unearned income and so designated. It is not permitted to claim ordinary personal and family exemptions, nor any of the customary deductions, on such income. Neither is it permitted to charge against it any of the expenses that might be incurred in securing income from investments.

Furthermore, it is taxed at a considerably higher rate than "earned" income. In spite of all the politicians' cant about free enterprise, the encouragement of private enterprise, and "sharing in the ownership of the tools of production," it is made quite clear that the owner of a single share of stock is, to that extent and in that respect, a pariah, an absentee landlord, a profiteer, and an oppressor of the poor.

We have seen in so many cases that a certain thing under one name is good and under another is bad. It is particularly true in politics that we change labels very fast. One moment intrepid business initiative is good. The next moment, under the name speculation, it is bad. As usual, the maps are all anybody ever looks at; as usual, there are only two labels, good and bad. As usual, the territory may be quite different from the maps and labels, but the voters don't know that.

A second example of the political mind at work is the capital gains tax. This tax is so set up that it benefits the long-term investor, apparently on the assumption that one who buys a stock and puts it away in a box is likely to be a hard-working honest citizen who is sharing in America's future by accumulating his savings in equities.

There is still, of course, the possibility that he may share also in what politicians call unearned increment, though this may be merely the compensatory adjustment of dollar values made necessary by the inflationary policies of the politico himself. This unearned increment is, of course, looked at somewhat disapprovingly, but it is a little hard to condemn it out of hand, since it involves the portfolios of too large a number of constituents.

The hand of the tax collector falls lightly on the long-term investor. But for the short-term speculator there can be no consideration. To the politician, the assumption of purely speculative risks is merely a form of gambling without the mitigating circumstances that make bingo (for a worthy cause) a virtuous enterprise. The very word "speculation" is a powerful weapon that can be turned against an opponent in a campaign. It is a bad word; taxing the hell out of speculators is as much a part of the politician's credo as better schools or investigating the local transit company.

This is the place where you and I should face this issue squarely. Speculation is not incidental to the market; it is not a fault in the market; it is not something to apologize for and minimize. A free market is a speculative market; the one term implies the other.

Speculation is the process of evaluation by which the price of stocks or commodities or real estate is established between men. Without speculation there can be many types of economies, but it remains to be proved that any of the substitutes for a free competitive market can provide the type of economy that we feel has contributed to the health and growth of our nation.

You will understand that we are not speaking here of manipulation or fraud. The word "speculation" has been applied to these, but we are not referring to these abuses. There is nothing inconsistent between a freely speculative market and one in which there is regulation to prevent the artificial moving or pegging of prices. In fact, in the sense in which we use the word, speculation, to do its job in the public interest, must be policed against dishonest practices. It is the free action of supply and demand in a speculative market that results in the democratic determination of price.

Such a market will automatically take all the factors affecting price into consideration. It will weigh every report. It will consider every news item bearing on the situation. It will discount every foreseeable event in the future. No board, commission, or commisariat, no matter how sincere or how able, could collect, compare evaluate, and integrate all of the factors involved in a market situation as searchingly as the collective body of investors acting in the speculative market. We, who profess to believe in democracy, should realize that it is this mechanism of free evaluation that lies at the very heart of our economic freedom, even if our politicians do not realize it.

The third point in connection with the attitude of the political mind relates to short sales. This is another of the many verbal shibboleths the politician shares with his constituents. So far as impartial studies can determine, there is no great depressing or inflationary effect on the market due to short selling. There are a good many serious students of the stock market who feel that short selling is a necessary and desirable function of the market as part of the evaluative process. In commodity futures markets the short sale is simply and plainly the other side of a long purchase, since for every purchase of a futures contract there must be precisely equal and opposite complement—a short sale.

You would think that the politicians, if they were economists or statesmen, would recognize this obvious fact and tax both sides of the transaction alike, but if you know the political mind, you also know that it is often more concerned with maps than with territories. The label "short sale" on the map is a bad label. Therefore you will find a most peculiar discrimination here.

When two men meet through their respective brokers to conclude a transaction in commodities, one buys for future acceptance and the other sells for future delivery. But the buyer and seller are not treated equally tax-wise. Apparently the badness of the word "sell" and the word "short" imposes a stigma that must be penalized. Long contracts held for over six months are considered long-term capital gains, and taxed at the low rate. Short contracts held for over six months are not treated as long term but as short term.

There is no particular reason for you to disturb yourself about this ridiculous situation. If you are a commodity trader, you will be long part of the time and short part of the time, and your tax liabilities will average out. Besides, you will seldom have the opportunity to be continuously long or short of a contract for so long a period as six months. The only reason we are mentioning this here is to point out the predilection of people generally, and politicians in particular, to value the map or the label more than the territory. If the facts are inconsistent with their opinions, they will not hesitate to throw away the facts and act on preconceived opinion alone. It is this habit and predilection that we are trying to overcome, not only in the market but in every activity of life.

CHAPTER 67   A VARIETY OF DEVICES

No mechanical method for beating the market has yet been developed, so the search continues for the philosopher's stone of our time. Many studies, analytical tools, and graphic representations can contribute to our appreciation of the market, but none of them can take the place of intelligent observation and practical experience.

There have been innumerable systems and mechanical methods proposed for beating the market. Few if any of them have consistently produced the profits hoped for.

It is not very surprising that they are so uniformly disappointing. In the first place, if there were a simple system for beating the market, a plan that could be produced in printed form and advertised and sold at a modest price, so that the average man could assure himself of big and reliable profits all the time, the thing would be a contradiction of itself from the start. If everyone knew what all stocks were certainly going to do all the time, their own actions in trying to take advantage of this knowledge would defeat their own end.

For example, if I knew, or had reasonably good ground to believe, that XYZ would advance 25 percent in price in the next month, I could buy some of that stock and make myself a tidy profit. But if everybody, or nearly everybody, had the same information and felt as I did, there would be such a scramble for the stock that I could not buy it at the price I had hoped for and might have to pay nearly the ultimate price at which I had hoped to sell. Also, of course, those from whom I would have to buy the stock in order to gain any advantage from the move would presumably also possess the valuable information and would not want to part with their stock except at a price that would give them most of the hoped-for profit.

Whatever is generally known or believed, whether good or bad, is discounted immediately in the price of a stock. Therefore, any method of dealing with the market successfully more or less presupposes some knowledge or some understanding or some device that is not the common property of everybody.

Millions of sheets of paper and tens of millions of hours have gone into study of the market in an attempt to discover some consistent and dependable relations that can be used to predict market value and that have not already been entirely discounted by general use. Some mechanical systems are obviously worthless. Others seem to have a certain limited usefulness. Others will show flashes of brilliant success at times, giving the illusion that they are in very fact the answer to all the market's problems. These last, however, can be especially dangerous, since the illusion of infallibility can lead to very serious losses when a series of adverse moves eventually comes to pass.

The market is probably too complex to yield its treasure to any simple formula or system. It calls for experience covering many possible contingencies. To put it another way, it is doubtful whether there is any system that can guarantee that a fool cannot lose his money in the market, and doubtful whether there is any method that will automatically produce profits for the operator without any thought or study on his part.

On the other hand, if a man will use the experience and advice of others only to the extent that they check out in his own tests, if he will use his own eyes to make his own direct observations, and if he has the patience and imagination to abstract from these data some valid meanings, then he can hope to acquire the experience to cope with this delicate and complicated mechanism. "If a man would realize that this is a business and give it the same effort he would devote to any other business (I am quoting Bob Edwards), then he may reasonably expect to make for himself a fair return according to his ability."

While I am inclined to be very skeptical about simple mechanical market systems, I do believe that there is a great deal of value in studying the various factors that affect the market and the way these operate, alone and in combination. It is not quite fair, and not quite realistic, to raise the standard protests: "Well, if you're so smart, why haven't you got all the money in the world?" and "If a man knew a method of beating the market, he wouldn't be telling others about it, he'd be making money with it himself."

So far as the first of these is concerned, you don't really believe that all men value money beyond everything else in the world, do you? Granted that we all like to make money, and most of us would like to have more than we do, still, it's hard to believe that everybody wants all the money in the world. There are other objectives, one of them being to have the regard and approval of others, and the most important of all being the possession of adequate self-esteem.

As to the second protest (and I think I can speak on this, for I have met a number of serious students of the market), it certainly isn't true in good many cases, and I would suspect that it isn't true for most men who are really interested in the subject.

There are, of course, all kinds of investors and traders. But the men who are doing the most constructive thinking are not concentrating on beating the market to the exclusion of everything else. Furthermore, many of them teach or lecture, some do advisory work, and in my experience they have few secrets and in general are delighted to discuss the work they are doing quite freely and openly.

Why? I suppose because they are human; because they are proud of their work; because they enjoy sharing the fun of their own work with others who are interested; because they like to display the results of their researches in the same way a sportsman likes to display his catch; perhaps because they enjoy passing along something that may be of help to someone else, and in general because this market work is for them a great game, a game in which they can pit their minds against the mechanism of the market just as an engineer can match wits with the forces of nature or general with the complexities of a military campaign.

There are certain devices that have been used in various and in different combinations, with more or less success, to evaluate the market. Though we do not recommend adopting any simple mechanical device as the beginning and end of market research, this is not to say that these inventions are of no value. One of the most important, because it opened up new lines of thinking about market problems, was the Dow theory.

This was probably the first thoroughly organized attempt to look at the market in terms of market action alone. Charles H. Dow did not actually complete the job; William Peter Hamilton picked it up and carried it through. According to Dow theory, the averages of representative groups of stocks indicate the major trend of the market. The presumption is that this major trend will continue until a reversal has been signaled by the failure of rallies or declines in the trend. There is not space here to outline the Dow theory in detail. It has been explained many times. Several chapters in the book *Technical Analysis of Stock Trends* deal with Dow theory.

The Dow theory, in spite of its overall good record, is by no means 100 percent satisfactory. There are a number of reasons why it is difficult or impossible in practice to obtain anything like the theoretical results it can show. Nevertheless, like the pioneer work in any field, the Dow theory served a purpose. It opened up the whole field of technical inquiry into the habits of stocks as they act in the market, a field in which Richard W. Schabacker extended the idea to the analysis of each particular stock as a separate entity. Schabacker, you might say, applied the principles Dow had crystallized as a high abstraction to the more practical application as a lower abstraction.

There have been a number of studies based on technical action or on some particular angle of technical study. In connection with trend studies there have been systems developed by which stocks were purchased on moves up and sold at pre-determined objectives (in terms of percentage advances, projected distances measured on charts, arrival at resistance areas, etc.). There have also been systems based on buying stocks on each decline, increasing the holdings as the price went further down, and selling on the advance from the ultimate bottom. Both these systems contain something more than a grain of validity, but the half-truth can be dangerous, and the mechanical application of these methods has not been strikingly successful.

Various timing devices have been brought forward such as wave theories and cycle theories. These methods include some of the best of the market studies, and some of the very worst. Surely the worst are those that depend on pure astrology, in which investment is supposed to be conducted according to the various aspects, conjunctions, oppositions, and positions in the various houses of the zodiac.

Among the best are the studies of harmonic analysis such as those of Edward R. Dewey and his associates in the Foundation for the Study of Cycles. Although there appears to be considerable theoretical validity to mathematically-derived cycles as applied to the market, they re not easy to use as practical tools for profit. But there can be no question as to the integrity of the men who are doing research in this field; the work speaks for itself.

There are a number of methods of market operation based on various published data. Some of these use price action alone. Some consider volume. Others take into account the outstanding short interest, or the relations of round-lot and odd-lot short sales. The action of odd-lots in general has been studied with interesting results. Studies have been made of new highs and new lows, and also of advances and declines. Sometimes these data have been weighted and combined to produce indexes, or plotted against one another to show the relative action.

All sorts of graphic methods and statistical methods have been applied. We have moving averages and other smoothing devices. There are many different ways of charting market information using arithmetical, logarithmic, square-root, and other scales. Almost any of these methods in intelligent hands can be a help in seeing what is going on in the market, but none of them can automatically take the place of intelligent observation and practical experience.

CHAPTER 68   CAN ANY MAN PREDICT
THE FUTURE?

Asking such a question in itself may seem foolish. We generally understand that no one can predict the future and we understand, in another light, that we all predict the future in our lives, over and over again. What we don't understand, but should, is an analytical way of looking at predicting the future, so that when we make predictions, we can test them ourselves by asking, "What are the chances that is so?" and "What is the evidence supporting the opinion as to the probabilities?" Predictions of the future may be evaluated on a measurable scale and analyzed considering probabilities.

There is a question implied in all attempts to analyze the market. Obviously, there is no need to find out what the past of any stock might be, since that is a matter of record, easily available. We know the present price (the market value) of the various stocks. The only material gain one can look for in making a commitment in a stock lies in dividends to be paid in the future, or in the price of the stock at some future date. So the question of market study boils down to the larger question, Can any man predict the future?

I have tossed this question to a group in a classroom or during a lecture; right at the start of the discussion without any comment or explanation, just the bare question, Can any man predict the future? or, more operationally, Do you now anyone who can successfully predict the future?

This is not intended as a gag or cheap wisecrack. It is a serious question, and a rather important one. As a rule, when you ask this question, you will see heads shaking slowly from side to side. No one, it seems, knows anyone who can predict the future.

Very well. It just happens that I do know someone who can and does predict the future. I predict the future—regularly, and successfully. I know someone else who can and does predict the future, regularly and successfully. You do.

When you get up in the morning you go to the front door and open it. You expect to find something there. You have made a prediction, a prediction that the morning paper will be lying on the front steps, or at rate within a certain radius of eight or 10 feet, depending on the throwing arm of the newsboy and the speed of his bike.

After breakfast you go down to the corner and wait for a bus. Suppose a man from Mars came up to you and asked you what you were doing, standing there in the rain on a street corner at 8:15 in the morning. You could tell him that you were waiting for a bus, and if he expressed some surprise, since no bus whatever was in sight, you could explain to him patiently that the bus was due at 8:20.

What is this but a prediction of the future? Why, if you will check your activities through the day you will find that your schedule is nothing but one prediction after another, all, of course, related to the future. At 9:15 the mail will arrive; at 10:00 there will be a meeting in Jones's office; at 12:30 you will meet Sanderson for lunch, and so on. You know that next week your wife will be going to a college reunion, and that in August you will take a two-week vacation in Maine. These are predictions, and like all predictions they refer to future events.

You may even predict years ahead. Timothy is going to Cornell and study engineering. You yourself are going to retire on your 58th birthday. These are all pretty good predictions. You expect they will come true. If you predicted that you would win the Irish Sweepstakes, or that your wife would have quintuplets in her next pregnancy, or that junior would eventually become president of the United States, those also might come true, but you will realize that there are great differences in the dependability of various predictions.

When we ask, "Can any man predict the future?" that isn't a very good way to ask the question. It is not an either/or situation. As in so many, so very many, of the problems of life, it is better to measure and evaluate as a matter of degree than to look for a snap yes or no answer. Instead of saying yes or no, we can begin to assign values to the predictions—not necessarily precise values but at least indicative of the order of reliability, ranging from a value of close to zero for the prediction that you will be elected the next pope to a value of close to 100 percent that there will be a total eclipse of the sun, lasting 27 minutes, visible in Northeastern Asia and Northeastern America and over the Atlantic Ocean on July 10, 1972.

There is, of course, the possibility that you will actually be elected pope, though it is perhaps a remote one; there is also the possibility that the eclipse will not come off as advertised, though that also seems a long chance. In between, we have all degrees of reliability.

The chances of the morning paper not being somewhere in the vicinity of the front steps might lie somewhere between one in 10 and one in 100. The prediction could fail because the newsboy was sick or because his bike had flat tire, because the truth with the papers was delayed, because a heavy wind had blown the paper into the next yard, or because the newsboy had chucked up the route entirely. The expected bus might now show for a variety of reasons: an accident, a traffic jam, a new driver, ad infinitum. But the probability of the bus not arriving at approximately (note that "approximately") the right time would probably lie between one in 10 and one in 100—in spite of the general opinion that buses never arrive anywhere on time.

If you had to make a guess whether the paper would be delivered or not, or whether the bus would arrive at about the time expected, or whether the mail would come in, or whether Jones would have his meeting, or whether Sanderson would meet you for lunch, your best guess would be that these things would occur. To put it another way, if you took the opposite point of view, you would be wrong more often than right. (Some of these seem so simple when we begin to talk about them, one has the feeling that this is all a waste of time. It is hard to realize that it is these "obvious" truisms that people will push past, like the elephant in the front hall, not seeing them. It is failure to understand and act on simple points like these that have led to financial ruin, family breakup, suicide, murder, and war.)

You noticed that we said probabilities may approach zero or 100 percent. Most of the predictive situations are multi-valued or infinite-valued; they do not ever attain the absoluteness of "impossible" or "certain." However, if you pick up a book and let go of it about 30 inches above the floor, you can predict that it will fall to the floor, and the prediction is very close to certainty. There are physicians who will explain to you that since the various molecules of which the material of the book consists are in motion, and not all are moving in the same direction at any particular instant, some of the molecules are likely to be moving up or away from the floor at any moment. If it should happen that at the instant you let go of the book, a majority of the molecules happened to be moving up, it could be that the book would crash into the light fixture on the ceiling. This is not very likely to happen. It is vastly more probable that the book will fall to the floor.

Sir Arthur Eddington used as an example of the near-infinite improbability a room full of chimpanzees who have been trained to hit the keys of typewriters. It is quite possible to train chimpanzees to type, and it is also quite possible that in due course one of the apes would happen to type the word "go" or the word "we" or even a three-letter combination like "cat" or "boy." Perhaps now and then one of the apes would come up with five or six letters in succession that would make sense. Eddington suggests, as a measure of improbability, the proposition that the apes might type, without error, all the books in the British Museum. (Several years later the *New Yorker* ran a grand little sketch describing the laboratory with its rows of desks, each equipped with a typewriter and a stack of paper, and at each desk a chimp industriously working his way through Thackeray, Dickens, Trollope, and Sir Walter Scott.)

We all can and do predict the future, with varying degrees of success. A large part of our activities and all of our plans depend on these predictions. The question of prediction of the future, then, resolves itself into evaluating the degree of probability, and this, of course, also involves evaluating our method of evaluation.

You recall we mentioned two valuable questions to ask others or yourself regarding almost any statement. Is that so? and How do you know that? can go a long way towards weeding out nonsense and un-sanity from our daily lives. Now we have to add another dimension to these questions. In considering predictive situations, we must ask, "What are the chances that it is so?" and "What is the evidence supporting your opinion as to the probabilities?"

This makes things a good deal more difficult, for we have to estimate not only the probability factors relating to the event itself, the chances of its happening or not happening, but we must also weigh the dependability of the predictive method we are using. Thus, we should be aware that in forecasting eclipses we are dealing with something much more precisely predictable than next year's potato crop. We should know that even in the matter of the potato crop it makes a good deal of difference who is doing the guessing. The chances are that a man who has spent his life studying the agricultural economy of Aroostook County will give a better answer as to next year's potato crop than you or I.

This is important. The principle is broad and applies to many other cases besides potatoes. We have here a situation where the question, How big will the potato crop be next year? cannot be precisely answered, or with any great certainty, and so a good many people will throw up their hands (as they do about the stock market, about elections, about their own span of life, and other things), and will say, "Nobody knows."

If you must have an either/or answer, that is the right answer. But we don't have to settle for an either/or answer. We can make some sort of estimate of the potato crop or respond to any of the other questions mentioned. The reliability of the opinion will depend to a large degree on the experience of the person making the evaluation. An expert on the economics of potato production does not know all the answers, but he can give an answer that will, year after year, come closer to actual production than the estimate of someone who knows nothing about it.

You will notice that we are not talking about being right in any absolute sense. It is even possible that the stupidest dolt in the world may stumble on a lucky guess as to the potato crop, or the score of Saturday's game, or the result of the election. But on balance, over the long pull and in spite of inaccuracies and failures, the informed observer who has a systematic method of evaluation will average better on his predictions.

One of the very serious blocks to success in the market or elsewhere is the too-high value we put on being right. If more attention were put on developing the basic method, we could afford to be wrong part of the time without any serious loss. The investor who is going to change method every time he has any degree of failure will be changing method radically, or abandoning it, every few weeks. His wild hunting for a perfect method will prevent ever arriving at a method that will stand up over the long pull.

The result, as we have seen it in everyday life, is the type of investor who sends money to some advisory service that is going to tell him how to beat the market. At the first failure he quits and sends another subscription to some other financial wizard for another system, and continues, perhaps for years, looking for something that is simply not possible.

In the end, having an either/or point of view on most things, the investor will probably decide that nobody knows anything about the stock market—that is all luck and that nobody can predict the future. For all his trials and losses, he has learned nothing, and is no closer to having a sound method of dealing with the market than he was in the first place. As a matter of fact, he is discouraged and demoralized, not so much because of what the market has done to him but because of his own lack of understanding.

There is no need to spend much time extending this point to other applications: the case of the psychoneurotic, shopping around from counselor to counselor, psychiatrist to psychiatrist; the maladjusted businessman who tries every new course in personality and inspiration and adaptation in order to discover the magic formula for confidence, popularity, and the big job. These are all variations of the same pattern; at the base it is the inability to study the roots of a problem. The difficulty here is not so much an inability to use the low abstractions of direct observation of a particular case as an inability to generalize, to make higher abstractions. When we discussed the basic process of building up successive layers of abstraction, we pointed out that while the lower abstractive levels provided specific detail about the here and now, the higher abstractions made it possible to see the relations of things, and to get a generally broader, though less detailed, view.

It is only through these higher abstractions that we can arrive at generalized conclusions. It is only by means of logically structured chains of abstraction that we build a method of evaluation. Therefore, we need low-level abstractions, high-level abstractions, and a number of stages in between. But it is important to know what level of abstraction we are using.

CHAPTER 69   THE METHOD OF EVALUATION

Was it Bertrand Russell who said it was centuries before man learned to recognize the common factor in a brace of pheasants, a pair of gloves, and a fortnight? While we must often focus at the lowest level of fact and event, we must be able to draw back from different and similar situations or facts and draw conclusions and generalizations from our experience and observations. Only with this ability to abstract and reason can we hope to develop a method that will allow us to deal skillfully with a multiplicity of situations.

The method of evaluation, as distinguished from "situational" tactics, is the basic tool of prediction. Unfortunately, people do use very high abstractions when they could more usefully take a hard look at the facts—as, for example, when they talk about juvenile delinquency, sexual deviation, political corruption, or racial desegregation in such general terms that it is hard to know just exactly what they are thinking about.

On the other hand, they tend to look only at an isolated problem when they could more usefully tackle that problem by considering other problems having essential similarities. Thus, a man will worry himself sick about a bad personality clash with his boss but fail to see that this is only one case in point of his general inability to get along with people.

In much the same way he will rack his brains to find a way to meet the installment payments on the new car but fail to realize that his basic, generalized trouble is the lack of a financial plan. Even if the payments on the car were taken care of, it would merely postpone trouble until the next crisis came up.

Again, he will lie awake nights wondering whether to sell his Lockheed or not, but will not even try to frame a policy that will help him next month with Socony Mobil, and next year with Chrysler.

There are times when we should look for differences, keeping in mind that everything and every event, in spite of similarities, is unique in some respects. There are other times when it is important to look for similarities. So long as we do not make the mistake of considering "similar" to mean "identical," we can draw some valid conclusions by means of these similarities.

This is the method of evaluation. It does not always give us the precise, exact, absolute, infallible answer to a question. Until we can recognize that precise, exact, absolute, and infallible answers are not possible in all matters, and that to attempt to operate as if they were is to court disaster, we cannot formulate method of evaluation that is worthy of the name. We are looking for something that will help us to make predictions on which we can base plans of operation that may be expected, on balance and in the long run, to be to our benefit.

You will notice that the last paragraph is rather carefully worded. We did not say that a good method of evaluation would give us predictions that would be always right. Nor did we even say that it would give us predictions that would be usually right. Strange as it may seem, there are cases where the optimum evaluative method gives us a majority of wrong answers.

For example, in commodity trading a great many speculators have lost heavily on balance or have even been wiped out although a majority of their commitments were right, that is to say, profitable. Conversely, there have been cases where a commodity operator has made net gains on balance year after year, in spite of taking losses on most of his trades. This, of course, is possible only if the average net gain of the profitable transactions is larger than the average net loss of the losing commitments.

It is possible that some successful traders in stocks may have methods that lead to a similar paradoxical proportion of gains and losses.

The point here is that the optimum method, the method that leads to the most generally beneficial result in the long run, is not necessarily the obvious choice. Unless you are able to generalize at fairly high levels and then apply your conclusions systematically and with confidence that you have arrived at the best method you can find (until you develop a better one), you are going to be disappointed. You will never feel any security in what you are doing, and you will never be able to accumulate any solid body of experience that can help you in the future, for you will be driving from one special situation to another special situation.

In such a case, of course, a man is not seeing the similarities. He is not applying what he has seen previously, perhaps under somewhat different conditions, to a new situation where he is obliged to make a prediction. For such a man prediction means little. A blind guess is as good as anything. Or, as they say, "It's all a matter of luck."

You have probably had the feeling all the way through this book that we keep jumping from one stage setting to another. If only we would stick to Wall Street and talk about nothing but evaluating and predicting stock values!

But the whole point of the "general" in "general semantics" is that we are hoping to learn, by means of higher abstractions, the similarities between quite different situations. Unless we can see that the reasons Milhous cannot hold a job may be related to the reasons he can't quite get along with his wife and children, we are missing the point. The factors that enter into politics may turn up in a little different shape in law or in finance or in religion or in mathematics. I believe it was Bertrand Russell who said something to the effect that it was centuries before men learned to recognize the common factor, the similarity, in a brace of pheasants, a pair of gloves, and a fortnight (all, of course, are examples of the number two).

When you have worked out general methods of evaluation, you will find they can be applied to many different kinds of problems. You will not, of course, overlook the particular circumstances, and you will take these particular circumstances into account in applying the method. But the method is of far-reaching importance. Without it, you have nothing solid on which to build.

CHAPTER 70   BUILDING THE METHOD

In order to succeed tactically, we must be firmly fixed at the lowest level of abstraction, feet located in the territory. In order to succeed strategically, we must draw back from the territory, strip it of tree-like detail, and consider it as a forest, finding relationships and correlations, similarities and differences. Observation of the particular is followed by analysis of the data, production of synthesis, and generalization by hypothesis.

Go back in your mind to what we discussed in the early chapters on abstraction. When the camera is moved back, away from the scene, it takes in more territory but shows less detail. In order to see the broad outlines of problems in a general way, we must move back. We must be prepared to sacrifice some of the detail. We have already spoken of one detail we must discard: the attempt to make perfect predictions. We must give up absolute rightness, absolute success, and absolute knowledge.

In return, we will get a panoramic view in which we can see the relations of things to one another. But before we finish we may have to throw out a lot more than we have so far. Talk to the average trader about Baltimore & Ohio and he will produce from the files of memory quite a

lot of specific material, much of it true. He can tell you the present price
of the stock, the price at the 1957 low, also the 1957 high, the earnings
trend for the last year or so, the dividend situation, and probably quite a
lot of assorted data and scuttlebutt about the management of the company, the effect of present and projected taxation, the prospects for the next
five years under present trends in transportation, the proportion of gross
business coming from freight and from passenger traffic, and on and on.

If you should happen to mention that the 1958 market situation in
Baltimore & Ohio seemed very similar to that of, say, Loew's, Inc., in
1946, our trader might look startled; he might express himself pretty
strongly to the effect that there is no similarity between Baltimore & Ohio
and Loew's, Inc.

Of course, you could knock this down at once with a very high
abstraction, namely that they are both American corporations. But there
are more definite (lower-level) abstractions than that and these show similarities. The two stocks have about the same number of outstanding
shares. They have sold at these dates in about the same price range. They
both had a big advance a year or so previous to these dates, made rather
similar top formations, and declined very rapidly. Both showed signs of
recovery as of the dates given.

Our friend, in short, has overlooked some quite obvious similarities.
Or if he has noticed them at all, he has brushed them aside as having no
significance. If we draw the daily charts of Baltimore & Ohio and Loew's
(and keep in mind that a chart is a map, an abstraction), we can show our
friend at a glance the very similar market action in these two stocks during a two-year period.

He is practically wrestling with the elephant now, for it is right square
in the doorway and he can't get around it. But he squeezes under it, and
fails to notice it. "So what?" may be the reaction. "So what, if a movie
stock 12 years ago had the same shape chart as a railroad today? Does that
make Loew's the same as Baltimore & Ohio? Are you trying to tell me
that because you have a pattern of marks on a sheet of paper I ought to
buy or sell stocks according to how you read those marks? Look, mister,
I'm going to stick to studying the rails, and I'm going to find out what
gives with Baltimore & Ohio. I don't want any part of your charts."

If we want to find out what will happen in a certain situation in the
future, we can look at situations in the past that have relevant similarities
and see what has happened. Sometimes it helps. If in comparing the
records of various events in the past we find certain consistent similari-

ties between them, we may be able to extract some general principles that will help us to frame an estimate of probabilities in the future. We are not speaking of causes now. Not the "why" of things. Just the "how." We are talking about correlations.

Let us suppose that you are wistfully looking at some stock, QRS, that has run up in price from, say, $8 a share to around $50, all in less than six months. There is not much use nursing your regrets or asking why didn't you buy it when it was selling at $8. It may be a little late to buy the stock now, at least unless you know exactly what you're up to.

But you can ask yourself, "How did this stock get up to $50 from $8?" You can draw a chart of the price action, showing the time on the horizontal scale and the price levels on the vertical sale, and you will have a picture of the advance in QRS. It is not a picture of the business of the QRS company, and it tells nothing whatever about the products of that company, the makeup of its board of directors, or the prospects of a 3-for-1 split in July. It's simply a record of the price advance plotted against time.

If we kept daily chart records of several hundred stocks, as some do, when we compare these charts we might find several cases where a spectacular advance like the one in QRS had occurred. These might be in the stocks of very different sorts of companies. The stocks might be in widely different price ranges. They might be taken from the records of different years. But if we took the charts having a similarity of a sharp move up, we could look for correlations. Instead of standing at the brink of the future trying to peer ahead into the darkness, we would be able, through the magic of map-making, to look back at the origins of these stock advances.

We could, in effect, put ourselves back in time and stand at the brink of the future when these moves started, and we could trace clearly what happened from then to now. We could check whether there were any conspicuous similarities in the chart pictures as of the time these big moves started. If we found that a considerable number of sharp, spectacular moves had sprouted from a long period of dullness, perhaps several years of inactivity when the price did not move much one way or the other, then we might check further. We might make a predictive guess. We could guess, for instance, that when a stock that has been inactive for several years suddenly sprouts into great activity, moving up slightly on big volume, this is the kind of situation from which a number of big, spectacular moves have emerged.

This is not really a finished prediction, let alone a predictive method. It is just a guess, based on a few observations. It remains to check other charts, including some that are now making this sort of move, and to watch whether any of these do follow through in patterns similar to the older examples we have observed. If they do, and if there is a profitable degree of correlation on balance in buying these early breakouts, we have a rough predictive method.

Note several points here:

- The charts do not tell us why any of these moves take place. The charts on which we based the original guess may have been taken from a number of different years. Therefore, assuming we will check the guess to be sure the conditions still apply, we may strike the dates off the charts.
- The charts may represent the stocks of many different kinds of businesses. Therefore, we may strike the names of the companies off the charts.
- The stocks may have been selling at widely different price ranges. Therefore, we can strike the price range off the charts.
- The stocks may have had greatly different capitalizations, so some of them may have shown much more volume than others. We are interested in the relative activity, day by day and week by week, but we can strike the absolute numerical scale off the chart.

In order to cover more ground, in order to see more clearly the similarities, we have in this case deliberately abstracted to a point where our chart now shows no date, no corporate name, no price, no numerical volume scale. We have reduced the situation we are studying to its bare bones.[1]

---

[1]Cost of living indexed bonds to the contrary, nothing has changed since this comment was written. The eclipse predicted by Magee in the 1950s actually came to pass in the 1970s.

CHAPTER 71   THE METHOD IS BUILT FROM
THE BARE BONES

The technical method effectively strips the available information on a stock to its bare bones, raising the investigation to a high level of abstraction in order to find the most important data for the purpose at hand. It is as if the other data we have discarded—earnings and dividends—did not exist. The chart is the technician's high-level abstraction, enabling him to analyze, compute probabilities, and make decisions free of the clutter of irrelevant details. What do Fruehauf Trailer and IBM have in common? They have their charts in common.

When we first started discussing relevant data, it may have bothered you that we made such a point of discarding extraneous facts, keeping just what was necessary and sufficient. Now you can see how important this is.

Unless we are able to abstract, to strip away the facts of everything except precisely what will help us to make a simplified, generalized guess, we are going to be confused and bogged down in a morass of detail. The question we took up concerning stocks breaking out of inactivity is just one possible study. There are hundreds and thousands of similar questions, as many as you want, that can be put to the test. But before you can set up any predictive mechanism, you must scrape away and discard everything that is not needed.

We can use charts (or diagrams, or tables) to answer a great many questions. But the first step, and a most important one, in setting up each question is to decide just what it is we are going to look at, and to limit the data to be collected accordingly. We can inquire what happens after a stock is split, whether there are any observable relations between dividend rates and stock prices, how the rail stocks in general compare with the utilities in general. We can investigate the action of low-priced stocks as compared with high-priced stocks. We can look at the action of certain stocks during times of market panic. We can analyze what happened to various stocks in the period 1929-1932 or 1985-1998. But in each case it is necessary to strip away extraneous material so that we can see clearly the thing we are studying.

This type of technical study is quite different from the kind of statistical analysis in which the main purpose of the charts or tables is historical and is intended to fill in the detail for a comprehensive examination of each particular situation. One of the reasons it is so hard for those who are not familiar with technical method to understand the high value technicians give to charts is that they do not understand the purpose of the charts as high-level abstractions. Sometimes the thing we are studying is only a small part of a larger picture; then we may have to build up a collection of parts and construct a highly abstract organism—as artificial, if you will as Frankenstein's monster, but much more useful!

The picture we have of economic man is such a robot. Hans Vaihinger has written about the "as if" situations, where we habitually use a fiction "as if " it were the truth, knowing full well all the time that it is fiction. We know, for instance, that men do not act precisely the way we would expect them to act according to classical economics. This is partly because each man is different from every other man, and partly because the economic forces are not operating in a vacuum. There are family ties, personal loyalties, and individual ambitions that do not always tie in with the motivations of classical economics. But though economic man does not really exist, he does have a reality. The reality is that in certain situations segments of mankind collectively tend to act "as if " the picture of economic man were real.

In law we have a counterpart to economic man. We have the "prudent man," an extraordinarily stuffy phantasm but a creation that suffices as a substitute for reality in certain "as if" situations encountered in legal matters, especially those connected with banking and finance. The prudent man is the fall guy for trustees. When their performance is lamentable, they can point to the imaginary prudent man and claim he would have done the same.

We have many such "as if" setups in scientific work. There are many cases where certain known and admitted facts are deliberately disregarded in order to study other facts. We sometimes assume a constant temperature or constant pressure when we know these are not really constant under the conditions of an experiment. We disregard friction or backlash or any number of other inconvenient factors in order to get at the bones of some particular aspect of nature.

We collect these abstract, over-simplified pictures of idealized portions of reality, and we construct methods based on what we can deduce from what we have seen. The conclusions will be tentative, subject to re-examination, revision, or rejection. They will be partial rather than absolute, and will express predictions in terms of probabilities rather than certainties. Yet the conclusions will be as free as we can make them from highly colored or absolute judgments.

If somebody should ask me, "What is most likely to happen in the case of a stock whose chart has been making the kind of formation we call an ascending triangle?" I would say, "It's most likely to break out and move up substantially, probably at least a distance equal to the open side of the triangle." If they ask whether this will surely happen, I would have to answer, "No, not surely. Just probably." If they ask if this is good or bad, I would have no answer, because such a question has no meaning at all in this case; we would have to know good for whom or bad for what.

In stripping extraneous matter from our studies and reducing everything to the few simple, answerable questions that we have selected as a basis for our inquiry, you will notice we have left behind a good deal of trouble. We have chucked out our absolute ambitions and ideals. We have tossed away the goal of perfect results. Instead of storming the gates of Valhalla, we have settled for a very ordinary kind of success, in a limited degree, in a narrowly bounded area. If we can do this, we can eliminate a good deal of the unnecessary strains and tensions of life.

We know there are going to be problems. There are going to be losses. There may even be some downright defeats. But if we can stop worrying about impossible objectives, vague aspirations, and conflicts that have no existence save in our own minds, we will usually be able to handle the real problems. This is true in many areas of life besides the stock market.

CHAPTER 72   PUTTING THE METHOD
TO WORK

The field or discipline of general semantics occupies itself with facts (in the real world) and abstractions (in the mind). It seeks to impose orderly thought processes on the relationships of these in order to allow its practitioners to better predict and cope with situations that arise in the real world.

Stored up in our minds there is a vast collection of information: what we have seen or experienced, what we have read, what we have been told, and all the logical combinations we have made, resulting in attitudes, opinions, prejudices, and judgments.

There are people who seem to carry around a great deal of pure information in a rather unorganized form, so that they are full of facts but have very little ability to predict. There are others whose abstracting at higher levels has gone on for years without much comparison with reality, so that while they can voice predictions on almost any subject (often loudly and vehemently), the results of these predictions don't check out too well.

The discipline that has become known as general semantics is concerned with organizing factual material and its derivative higher abstractions in such a way that the relation between "in here" and "out there" is continually maintained on a current basis. The raw material of knowledge is consciously organized, and the relevant portion of it can be focused on whatever particular problem concerns us. We know what happened in the past, we have noted certain correlations, we draw some conclusions, and then we can make an informed guess on the probable outcome of some new situation with an enormously better chance of success than someone who has not organized his mind in this way.

When a patient recites his symptoms to a doctor, there is a process of "re-call" going on in the doctor's mind. He brings into consciousness some of the things he learned in medical school bearing on cases with these symptoms. He remembers articles on the subject he has read lately. He recalls some of his own cases that seem similar. He considers the history of other cases like this, their outcome, and the kinds of treatment that seemed to benefit them. On the basis of all these, plus his observation as to the condition of this particular patient here and now, he makes his diagnosis, prescribes treatment, and makes a prediction or prognosis, at least to himself, as to the probable course and duration of the ailment.

Change a few words and this is exactly what a lawyer does for his client. It is what an engineer does in solving a problem. In practically everything we do we take stored-up data from the past and apply the conclusions we can make from it to a problem in the future. Our solution is a form of prediction, whether it is that an action for damages of $500,000 will probably be successful, or that a cantilever bridge built according to such-and-such specifications will withstand any storm likely to hit this county.

CHAPTER 73   HABIT CAN BE A PITFALL

Sheep ranchers know that in a large flock of sheep, jumping an obstacle is self-perpetuating; that is, if you cause the first sheep to jump an obstacle, all the sheep behind will leap the obstacle, whether it is still there or not. So runs habit in the animal kingdom, of which, alas, we are a part. We will persist in unskillful and self-defeating habits unless all our will and energies are marshaled to lead us to be aware and mindful to do the skillful thing—to liquidate the position losing money in a skillful way—and buy the probability of a promising new situation (perhaps to short the losing position we just abandoned on the long side).

There was once a story about a woman who visited a fortress in Spain. It was a large establishment complete with parks and shaded walks, with benches along the walks. At the main gate to the grounds and at each of the other gates there was a sentry, and sentries in front of the administration building, the armory, and the powder magazine.

The lady visitor noticed that there was a sentry pacing a short post along one of the walks, back and forth in front of one of the benches. As she watched, another soldier appeared, saluted, relieved him, and continued to walk the same post before the bench.

The visitor asked the lieutenant who was guiding her over the grounds just why a sentry had been placed at this spot, which was not near any of the buildings or entrances. The lieutenant replied that this was one of the regular posts and so far as he could remember there had always been a sentry at this spot. However, he would be glad to check the orders at the main office.

On checking these it appeared that the original order had been issued several years earlier just before a new commandant had been appointed. It was merely a copy of a previous standing order calling for a sentry at Bench Number 23. A further search of the records went back five years more to when the previous order had been issued. The old commandant had been taken suddenly ill and had been replaced by another. Just a day or two before his illness the original order had been placed—an order calling for a sentry at Bench Number 23, "which has just been painted." Through the accident of a new commandant coming in, all orders, including this one, were simply reissued. Inadvertently this temporary order was issued without qualification and became a permanent standing order.

For over 10 years a sentry had marched back and forth in front of Bench Number 23, and there was no machinery to cancel it. The soldiers who marched asked no questions. The superiors in charge merely followed their standing orders. The clerks simply carried forward the standing instructions. The commandant had other matters to think about. This thing, once useful, had long outlived its usefulness, but there was no one to spot the anachronism.

We do this sort of thing to ourselves, you know. This sort of situation comes up in business all the time. Somebody starts a system, say, taking down the subtotals of expenses for Department 16 and carrying them in a special file. Perhaps somebody was making a special study at one time, or maybe the government had called for a detailed report on this department. In the course of months and years the old clerks would teach the new clerks, and the old managers would train the new ones. This would become just part of the routine, somebody's job, and the blue cards and the green cards would pile up in the files and nobody would ever use them. They were just part of the overhead, and as fixed as the laws of the Medes and the Persians. Just a sentry marching back and forth in front of a park bench.

If you think this is a stupid exaggeration, permit me to give you an actual example. Some years ago I served on a municipal committee in charge of public relations for the City of Springfield. Under our jurisdiction came the annual Municipal Register. This turned out to be a large volume of some 400 pages of small type and tables of figures produced at a cost of over $10 a copy. It ran the city a few thousand dollars each year for printing and binding. It also turned out that there was no law that required any such report to be printed, though the Municipal Register had actually been issued each year for nearly a century.

On checking the various departments it was found that although each department of the city government had a file of these reports, none of them ever used them for any purpose, since the particular records of each department were kept in the department's own files. Neither the mayor nor any member of the Board of Aldermen or the Common Council ever consulted the book, although each of them received a copy.

The public library reported that no one ever requested to see the Municipal Register at either the Main Library or any of the six branches. The local newspaper reporters covering city hall said they got their material from their own files or from particular departments as needed. A number of copies of the report were sent each year to the City Clerks of other municipalities, but it is hard to believe that these City Clerks were any more anxious to plow through the deadly pages of these reports than the people in our own town.

As a matter of fact, no one could read the report intelligently even if he had tried. Tables of figures often carried headings like "Committed during the year: Sewer Construction—1935 Docket Mass. 1242R." Since the only way to get any further light on this would be to go to a department head, who might or might not see fit to explain, the information hardly contributed much towards the enlightenment of the citizenry or a towards a more economical city government. In a city of 150,000 our committee was able to find just one person who had ever looked at the book, a reporter who said he had once or twice looked up some figure in it. The Springfield Municipal Register was, by any standard, one of the most completely unreadable and unread books ever published.

The happy ending to the story seemed to come when the committee substituted a free circulation book titled *Our Home Town* that reported city affairs in such a way that citizens lined up in queues two blocks long to get their copies, and that won a lead editorial, "A Bell for Springfield," in the *Ladies Home Journal.* The citizens were hungry for information, hungry for bread instead of stones from the City Fathers.

The cost of the new book was just under 50 cents a copy as against $10 for the Municipal Register. But believe it or not, after two years of *Our Home Town* it was replaced by the Municipal Register in its old form, and the old-style register has been published regularly every year since as the city's contribution to public enlightenment. This was the sentry again, of course, with a new quirk, the reversion to the old habit even after a definite break had been made.

You'll find Spanish sentries in the Army and in the Navy. You will encounter them, many of them, in the courthouse and wherever else legal business is transacted. If you ever have dealings with the post office you will run into battalions of them patrolling the dark corridors of the postal laws and regulations. There is very likely more than one Spanish sentry guarding the routine of your family life.

In the inner fortress of our own minds these sentinels police our thoughts with the authority of yellowing orders from a long-dead past. Don't underestimate habit. And don't underestimate the power of directives handed down from long ago, however irrational or obsolete they may be today.

Let us say we have a method of evaluation based on a new look at current facts. Comes the opportunity to act, in the stock market or in some other area of life. What do we do? Do we follow the conclusions of our method? No! Too often, after having gone through all the intellectual labor of setting up a good method, we revert to something out of the long ago. Something we have always done, something father told us, something we learned in school, something . . . we don't know where it came from. When we are forced to make a fast decision under pressure, we are very likely to revert to our habitual responses, inculcated years ago.

Often our action will be diametrically opposite to what our considered reason would indicate we should do. This is what people mean when they say "you can't change human nature."

You can! You can change your own human nature, and to your great advantage, but you should know that after you have thoroughly absorbed all the arguments and feel that you now how to tackle a problem, those little devils start creeping back in again. Unless you watch yourself, you're back doing it the old way all over again. Hence the familiar wail, "How could I have been so stupid as to buy that stock?"

CHAPTER 74   CHAIN AND FLASH REACTIONS

"Never be in a hurry to do something stupid."
Lee Richartz

You may have known some anxious mother who seemed able to build a catastrophe out of the simplest, most ready-to-hand materials. If she went to the store and left the front door open, the children might wander into the house for a drink of water. Then they might want to explore the medicine cabinet above the washbasin. There might be some of those pills Uncle Henry took the time he had the spasms. If they took those pills, it might make them sick. If she didn't get home in time, they would be dead. The poor woman could have them all dead and buried before she'd walked a single block.

One thing associates with another. If I say "pen" you may think of "ink." If you say "cat" I think of "dog." Things and events we have seen or heard at the same time, or in the same place, or which have the same names, go together. Past experience and habit build up chains of association. You can go from one to another like chain lightning: The squeak of a door in a dark room in an unfamiliar house may suggest a sinister creeping figure. The intruder has a knife. He is coming across the room to where you lie. He is about to plunge the knife into your ribs! You break out in a cold sweat and get up quickly to turn on the lights—and of course there is no marauder there at all. Just a door that squeaked a little and started a chain of associations in your mind.

People can become panicked when a chain reaction leads to the possibility of a disastrous outcome. They can become overwhelmed with greed or lust or envy when such a chain races from some simple fact through a chain of associated abstractions to some very high order conclusion. The thing can all happen in a flash.

In fact, if it didn't happen in a flash it probably wouldn't happen at all, for very often the chain will break down under any close and leisurely examination. You can be panicked out of stocks you may have bought, and then a day or so later wonder just what go into you. People lose their nerve. People go to pieces. And when they look back at the awful Thing that threatened them, it wasn't really very awful at all.

The way to protect yourself from being stampeded by a chain or flash reaction is to delay your response. That is not an easy thing to do without training and practice, not when you so easily jump to a conclusion and feel confronted by an immediate and present danger. But the habit of delay can be learned. You are already familiar with the old formula for controlling your temper: You just count to ten. Sometimes it may not work—you may have good reason for your anger—but sometimes it can save you from an unjustified outbreak. Certainly the principle is good.

If you will just take a few moments to examine the territory before acting on the maps alone, you will often save yourself a good deal of trouble. It may be that the reaction is one that brings on fear. It may cause anger. It may lead in other directions. But the few seconds you may take to ask yourself, "Is this really what it seems to be, or is it largely a big build-up in my mind?" can pay you rich dividends.

The man who hesitates is not so often lost as the one who does not hesitate. When the salesman's voice on the telephone suggests that you act at once so as to get those fast, enormous profits, it will be worth your while to take a little time to look at the facts. Otherwise, the high-order hope of quick, easy money may stampede you into very heavy losses.

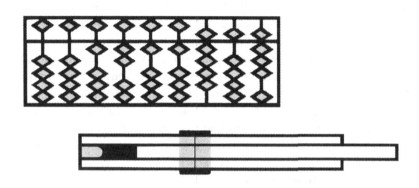

CHAPTER 75   NUMBERS CAN BE PITFALLS

Regard your education as a conspiracy to brainwash you into behaving like a sheep, or a lemming (depending on the quality of your school or the nature of your background). Somewhere, some time (perhaps right here), a teacher will shock you to the realization that the world is only partly arithmetic, that skepticism as to received knowledge, common opinion, and truth bear more intellectual truth than blind belief. In short, you will be led to an examined life. (Hopefully, these days you won't have to drink hemlock for it.) Consider carefully the differences between arithmetic and logarithmic thinking.

Take a paper napkin. Place it on the floor in the corner of the room. Tomorrow morning put another one on top of it. The next day two on top of those. The following day, four and so on, doubling the number each day for just 30 days. How high a pile? A foot? 100 feet? 50 miles? Figure it out. If you're not familiar with geometric progressions, you may be surprised.

Then try this. You have $3,500 in the bank. I also have $3,500 in the bank. You tell me you have drawn your money out of the bank and used it to buy a certain stock at $5, which you feel will be worth more soon. I do not take the tip at once, but several weeks later when the stock is selling at $7, I take my money out of the bank and invest it in the stock. Three months later, the stock having happily advanced to $12, we both sell out.

Since you bought yours first at $5 and I paid $7, you have more profit than I do. Would you say 20 percent more? 30 percent more? 50 percent more? 100 percent more? Would it surprise you to find that it was very close to 100 percent? That you had made practically twice the profit I had made? Figure it out. But don't feel too chagrined. The treasurer of one of our important corporations gave me 30 percent as the answer. Almost everyone will underestimate.

What happens in these cases? How can figures play such dirty tricks on us? Of course, like all other errors where our maps tell us one thing and the territory turns out to be something different, it is not the territory that is wrong. Somehow we have learned some things that aren't always true. Isn't it amazing, when you begin to look around, how much of what we have learned has to be revised, re-dated, or re-specified? In this case of the two stocks, what we are bucking is the logarithmic nature of the real world around us, as opposed to the arithmetic world we learned about in school. We still think, but for the most part with arithmetic maps.

The difficulty here probably comes from at least two sources. In the first place, here are, of course, many instances where things appear in arithmetic relations. If we count the houses along the street it is a matter of one, two, three, four. In fact, all the counting we do is arithmetic. We count money. We count days. We count the number of stocks that have made new highs for the year.

This leads to a second point: Because so many of the simple transactions we use in early childhood are arithmetic in nature and involve positive whole numbers, that is the kind of mathematics we are taught in school. We learn that John has seven apples and in an outburst of generosity gives Charlie two of them and Andrew one. Mary gets an allowance of 15 cents and earns 20 cents more delivering a package. And so on.

The result is that we become accustomed to regarding the world as being made up of things that can be expressed in positive whole numbers. The intervals between two consecutive whole numbers are equal. The difference between 6 and 7 is exactly the same as the difference between 16 and 17.

What we learn early, we learn well. Fortunately, before it is too late, we learn about negative whole numbers, and about fractions both as ratios and as decimals. But unfortunately, by the time we begin to study proportion and percentage and matters like that, we have become pretty well bored with the whole subject of math (which is not exactly taught along inspired lines in most schools), so we stop learning and go forth in life to seek our fortune, and we really haven't very much except the two-plus-two-equals-four type of figuring.

There is nothing wrong with this—in its place. It is valid in many situations, and in dealing with counting problems it permits of exact answers.

This is true in a way. He is making the not altogether unreasonable assumption that the declines from 20 to 15, 15 to 10, and 10 to 5 are equal, and that the decline from 5 to 0 is equal to all the others. He is wrong, however, when he tells you, as he will, that JFK has already had its down move, that it can't go down much more. Dick is so sure of this that he will give you quite a battle if you so much as question him. For it stands to reason that the stock, having dropped 15 points from 20 to 5, cannot go down another 15 points.

It is true, arithmetically speaking, that JFK is approaching the bottom area. But this is definitely not true in the world of ratios. If you were to tell Joe that the stock could go down just as much if he bought it at 5 as if he bought it at 20, he would think you were crazy. If you told him the stock could go right on down without any limit, he would know you were crazy.

But look! If I buy JFK or any other stock at 20 and it goes down to 10, the value of what I own has diminished by 50 percent. If I had bought 100 shares, it would have cost me $2,000 at 20 and would be worth $2,000 at 10.

Now if I should buy $2,000 worth of the stock at 10 and it goes down to 5, what is my stock worth? It is worth $1,000, and the value of my investment has diminished by 50 percent.

Suppose I buy $2,000 worth at 5. A decline to 2 1/2 slices 50 percent from the market value; my stock is worth only $1,000.

Name your own figure. Buy the stock at $1. It can go down to 50 cents. Buy it at a dime. It can go down to a nickel. At any price, no matter how low, the stock could slide another 50 percent and cut your capital by 50 percent.

Not only that. We have only used the figure 50 percent as a convenient example, but if a stock can decline 50 percent it can decline 90 percent, and it can make this decline from any point, no matter how low. Among the famous last words of the market, one of the most famous is, "They can't go much lower!"

CHAPTER 76   THE WONDERFUL CURVES

Einstein when he discovered compound interest is reported to have said something like, "Eureka! Compound interest is the true miracle of mathematics." When we break from the cage of arithmetic relationships we can discover the beauty of nature, the algorithm of growth—both in snail shells and compound interest.

What we have been talking about in the past chapter is the logarithmic relation. It is a matter of ratios rather than ordinary addition or subtraction. It is the basic pattern of growth for many things in nature, and for some things in finance. The logarithmic relation operates all around us every day in plain sight, but if we have been trained only in additive relations, we do not perceive it. We are like color-blind people, seeing only certain parts of the scene and missing the beauty of chromatic harmony. For the logarithmic aspect of nature is as beautiful as the bright colors of spring or the crystal etchings of frost in winter.

The principle of logarithmic growth is so simple that it is hard to understand why we so persistently overlook it. It is simply the very usual way in which capital at interest, many plants, and some animal increase: by adding a certain proportion of their present size during each successive interval of time. Placed at interest computed annually at 10 percent, $100 will grow to $110 in a year. At the end of the second year it will have added 10 percent of the new total of $110, and so will have grown by $11, bringing the total to $121. At the end of the third year the total will again increase by 10 percent of the base, $121, adding $12.10 in interest for a total of $133.10. The fourth year total will be $146.41, and so on.

You will notice that as the principal increases, the increment, figured as a constant percentage, will also increase in numerical value. This will be true whether the growth rate is 10 percent, 30 percent, or 90 percent. It will also be true whether the growth is compounded every year, semi-annually, weekly, daily, or whether it is computed as an infinite convergent series to show the continuous rate of growth (if we assume that growth is being added in every tiniest instant of time).

Because the size of the increment is proportional to the size of the principal at any particular time, we can say that the rate of growth is proportional to the state of growth (where "rate" is considered to mean the added quantity of dollars, pounds, inches, or whatever is the unit of growth). This is the primary law of growth for many things, not only money in the bank but many organisms in nature: pine cones, nautilus and snail shells, the twigs on trees, and sunflowers, to name just a few examples of the law in operation.

If you were to mark a snail shell into sections covering the same angular distance, you would see that each segment of the snail's house is the same shape, though the segments are much smaller near the center and become larger as you progress outward. Any one of the sections would look very much like any other section if you magnified or shrunk it.

If you assume that the snail will add one of these sections each month, you will see that with each successive month he is adding a larger extension to his house; but each new addition represents the same percentage increase. Because of this constant percentage change, the snail shell presents a curve that is the same shape in any stage of growth. A baby snail will resemble a grandfather snail, only in miniature. Leaving out practical matters of getting enough food and maintaining structural strength, there is no limit to the size the curve of the snail's house could be carried to.

Look at it as a mathematical curve. It could continue adding constant percentage increments indefinitely. It could be drawn as large as you wanted it. Conversely, there is no limit to how far back you could run it, going in toward the center. Theoretically, the segments go on getting smaller and smaller, but there is no end to the mathematical series, nor to the curve.

You may recognize at this point the similarity between the snail's house and Dick Milhous's stock as discussed in the previous chapter. There is no limit at either end. Here is a similarity between two abstractions—the behavior of a stock chart and the shape of the snail's house— is of tremendous practical importance. Both the stock price and the snail's house are essentially logarithmic functions.

A good many stock analysts now use a type of paper known as semilogarithmic, meaning that the price scale is logarithmic but the time scale is linear. Some years ago I designed such a paper especially for stock analysis. This TEKNIPLAT charting paper is laid out on a scale similar to the scale on a slide rule. The spaces on it are numbered, but they are not equal spaces. They are so ruled that two equal vertical distances on the paper always represent the same percentage change. When a stock advances 10 percent from 20 to 22, it moves up the same distance as another stock that has advanced 10 percent from 60 to 66, or from 100 to 110.

When a stock declines 10 from 100 to 90 or from 30 to 27 or from 10 to 9, it is possible to compare the actions of stocks at different prices more fairly than by the arithmetic scale. You can see how this explains Dick Milhous's problem: If a constant percentage decline is always represented by the same distance on the paper, then in a decline of 50 percent the distance from 200 to 100 is the same as from 50 to 25, from 4 to 2, from 1/2 to 1/4 or from 1/256 to 1/512. A 50 percent decline is always possible from any price, however low. A 50 percent decline will always have the same effect, that is, it will cut your capital in half. Therefore, there is no zero on the logarithmic scale. It extends from the infinitesimally small to the infinitely large.

The logarithmic spiral, which is the curve we saw in the snail's house, is of course the visible expression of the logarithmic relation we have discussed in connection with stocks. The slide rule and the snail shell express the same mathematical pattern. It is not only the property of the snail and of stock prices and bank interest and other business functions. It is also visibly expressed in many forms in nature, as we suggested earlier. If you examine the arrangement of the seeds in a sunflower head, you will see that there are two logarithmic spirals, one having a rather sharp pitch to the center, the other taking a more leisurely course at a more oblique angle. A pine cone also shows two intersecting series of logarithmic spirals running at different pitches. Although it is not quite so easy to see, the angular spacing of small twigs as they grow from the branch of a tree or shrub is also a logarithmic sequence.

From the purely practical point of view of understanding how stocks move, it will be important to observe and absorb these logarithmic relations until it is second nature to think of things in terms of percentage or ratio changes. But aside from the business of making money, the wonderful world of the logarithmic spirals contains so much beauty and so much of the sheer wonder of pattern and rhythm (I should add here, "as I see it," though I feel sure you will, too, when you look into it) that it seems a pity our children are not schooled from the very start to see the world in broader terms than the true but sometimes terribly misleading arithmetic relations.

There are logarithmic spirals that generate the most interesting designs. As Jay Hambridge pointed out in a study, "Dynamic Symmetry: The Grecian Vase," the harmonies that emerge from the properties of the logarithmic spiral were at the root of much of the greatest architecture, sculpture, and painting of the ancient Greeks. Some of the spirals are close relatives of other forms. There is, for example, a "root three" logarithmic spiral that is tied to the 30° - 60° triangle, the "root three" rectangle, and the hexagon; the spiral is a joy to experiment with. There are others, too, that have almost magical qualities in their various relations.

If this is a digression, it is a deliberate one. I would like to feel that you want to know more about the wonderful curves, for they are among the great beauties of nature.

CHAPTER 77   LOSSES CAN BE PITFALLS

If you take a loss personally, you would be better off not participating in areas where uncertainty reigns—either that or developing the perspective to see that losses are an inevitable part of life and investing. Losses are an unavoidable part of the process of investing. Viewed if not with equanimity at least, with acceptance, they are concomitants of profits. A hard lesson to learn.

This is a sad subject, and we will make this chapter a short one, but a few words on the subject of losses are in order.

Nobody really likes to take losses. Losses represent hurts. Much earlier in this book we showed how people will feel badly hurt by experiences that would not be so terribly painful if their outlook were just a bit different—for example, the hurt of being second in a competitive examination out of 135 students.

Since the worst hurt of all is an injury or humiliation to the self-esteem, it is not surprising that a good many investors will take some rather terrible monetary beatings before they will admit to their brokers, their friends, and most especially themselves that they have made a mistake. Of course, if they saw things a little differently, making a mistake might not loom so large or so shamefully in their perception.

Very often, too, it might not be really a matter of making a mistake at all. It could be that conditions had changed, and a new territory calls for a new map. But, as you know, some of our friends will defend the map as if it were a matter of sacred honor, regardless of whether it still represents the territory or not. A defense of obsolete maps can lead to terribly heavy losses, in the market and elsewhere.

What constitutes a loss depends largely on your value system. What may be a matter worse than death to one individual may be no more than a pain in the neck to someone else. It's a matter of degree. Furthermore, there is a matter of level involved here, that is, the level of abstraction.

Suppose I enter into a series of trades in commodities and the results of these trades are something like this: loss, $150; loss, $75; loss, $225; gain, $1,500; loss, $180, loss, $50. It is perfectly true, at the level of individual study of each transaction, that I have had five losses and only one gain. But at a slightly higher level of abstraction, where we combine the operations to get a net result, it becomes clear that I have profited considerably on the series as a whole.

It seems childish and silly to bring up such a simple and obvious point, yet so inflexible are some people's aversion to loss (any loss) that such a series of transactions is an abhorrent nightmare to them. They literally cannot stand it. I have personally known traders in both stocks and commodities who, although they were making profits on balance, were so upset, so badly hurt, by the incidental losses that they quit the market entirely. It would be hard to understand how people can ignore or jeopardize their own material interests as many do unless we understood how important it is to them to protect their self-esteem and their self-regard, the way they feel about themselves.

It is possible to learn to see things in a different light so that some of the terrifying losses and threats of loss do not seem so horrible. We can take a lot of losses if we know what we are doing, and if we can see and fully appreciate that the losses are not unbearable. In many cases we may find that the losses are an essential part of the means that is justified by the end.

One habit that tends to distort perception and to increase nervous tension about accrued losses is the practice of comparing every quotation with the price at which a stock was bought (or, in the case of short sales, sold). Harry will come in and tell you that MNO is now selling at 23 "but I paid 28 for it, and if it gets back there I'm going to sell and get my money back."

Why 28? The market doesn't know and doesn't care what you paid for a stock. There are times when the smart course would be to buy more stock at 23 and to hold when the stock advanced to 28, to 35, to 60. There are other times when the best action would be to sell the stock immediately at 23 or whatever you could get. Unless you have some very good technical or fundamental reason why the stock should be sold at 28, there is no reason to make that particular price a sacred cow. Wouldn't it be better to forget the price you paid and just take it from there on its own merits? If the stock is acting all right, hold it, regardless of what you paid for it. If it is not acting all right, sell it and be rid of it.

CHAPTER 78   PROFITS CAN BE PITFALLS

Is it greed or fear that moves markets? Perhaps it's personal psychic questions. It may not be greed that moves the investor to take his profit prematurely—it may be the fear of missing the top. That is, just as losses can present painful problems, so can profits, if they are not the right kind of profits—the kind that proves to ourselves our acumen, intelligence or our moral and financial superiority. The mature trader, on the contrary, does not focus so closely on semantic analysis. He lets the profits and losses fall where they may.

Almost everything we have said about losses can be applied, sometimes with a reverse twist, to profits. The same type of individual who is so badly hurt by a small loss will become very nervous when he has a profit. In fact, it is hard to say which is more painful to him: to be losing money or to be making accrued gains but dreading the possibility of a reversal that will wipe them out.

It hardly seems necessary to point out that there is a good deal of either/or in this. The implication is very strong that unless one makes profits all the time and has no losses, he is no good.

As usual, there is no in-between in the mind of such a man. Anxiety holds back the nervous trader from taking his losses early. He dreads them so much. He hopes to avoid them entirely by waiting. It is also anxiety that forces his hand when he has a profit. It is not exactly greed, it is really anxiety, something akin to fear. So, all atremble lest his two or three points of gain be swallowed up in a reaction, he takes his profit, prematurely. This ensures good commissions for his broker, but it also effectively cuts out the chances for him ever to make a substantial gain.

As we saw in the case of losses, part of the blame for this premature selling should be laid to the habit of comparing the price of a stock with "what I paid for it." It won't hurt to repeat here that the market is not interested in what you or anybody else paid for a stock. You can see this very clearly if you realize that investors and traders are buying stocks at every fraction of a point up and down the scale, and it does not make sense to say that your best policy is to sell at 10 points higher than your cost or on an advance of 15 percent, since then each buyer at a different price would have a different objective, and some indeed would have as their selling point the very price at which you might be buying. The continual reference to cost price, especially if it is coupled with an objective based in some way on that cost price, simply leads to a mechanical system, something like the systems that are hopefully tried out each season against the wheels at Monte Carlo. That kind of system does not lead to success.

We mentioned anxiety as a reason the nervous traders sell out prematurely to take a profit. But the major fear may not be fear of monetary loss. It may be something quite different. It may be, in fact you must know from your own experience that it often is, the fear of not catching the top. They want the top so badly. Superiority, being on the up-and-up—there is so much magic in these up-and-down words. The top is pretty absolute. Half way is not the top; 80 percent is not the top. It is either/or.

The unhappy part of this reaching for the top is that the nervous trader seldom gets it. He will almost invariably reach out too soon and pluck his budding profit before it has really blossomed at all. In a way he will be less hurt by taking the profit prematurely than he would if he allowed the gains to run and eventually sold out after the top, on the way down.

This should be underscored. He will buy a stock at 26 and sell it at 30 to take a four-point profit. If the stock then advances to 40 he will not feel too seriously injured, for he can comfort his tender ego with the soothing thought, "I realized a good profit; now I don't care where it goes." But one has the feeling that if he had continued to hold his stock, saw it go to 40, and then watched it break down to 34, he would not be nearly so happy. For it will be much easier for him to rationalize the taking of the four-point profit on the way up than to justify his action on selling on the way down, even though his profit might be twice as large.

Although profits and losses make up the story of market success and failure, it is probably a good thing not to concentrate on the detailed record of these profits and losses. It is not possible to fret oneself into opulence by torturing some sort of victory or make-believe victory out of every single trade. What will be far more productive in the end is to formulate a method of evaluation (which becomes, in effect, the method of prediction), test it, revise it continually as necessary, and then give it your full confidence, letting profits and losses fall where they may.

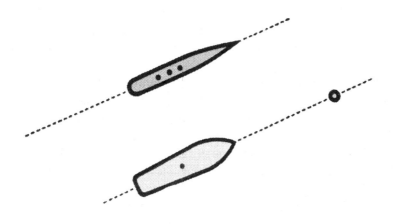

CHAPTER 79   COMMON SENSE CAN BE
                A PITFALL

Common sense, supplemented or created by our education in Euclidean geometry, leaves us quite certain that parallel lines at sea cannot intersect. Surprise. It is not a Euclidean problem, and the problem is misframed to begin with. Common sense has enough pragmatic truth in it to represent a danger to the unwary. None (or all) of it can be used as a guide without skeptical testing. "You can't go broke taking a profit." Is that so? How do you know that? In this case the exact opposite within the Magee method is probably more true. A better formulation is to take losses quickly and profits slowly.

Suppose that in some sort of naval maneuvers an oil tanker is ordered to take a course parallel to that of a destroyer, the course to pass through a specified buoy or marker. Common sense tells us that there can be one and only one course that fills these requirements, since one and only one parallel line can be drawn to a given line passing through a specified point not on the given line. We learned this in school.

We also learned that parallel lines are lines that never meet, however far extended, and that are in all parts equally distant. By "line" we mean "straight line." Since a straightest line is the shortest path between two points, we could define a straight line on a surface as the path of a tightly stretched string that lay entirely on that surface. Now if the captain of the oil tanker has put his ship on the course parallel to the destroyer and pointing in the direction of the buoy, we could check the accuracy of his navigation, if it were possible to stretch tightly a string along the line of the destroyer's course and along the tanker's course and then check whether these lines in fact were equally distant in all parts. We could do this, at least theoretically, by setting out lines supported by cork floats along each of the courses.

As a matter of fact this will probably not be necessary. For if you consider the matter, you will see that no matter what course the tanker sets, it will intersect the course of the destroyer if extended far enough. You can verify this by marking straight lines on an orange, and by straight lines we would mean, of course, lines that are the shortest distance between two points, in other words, great circles.

Any two great circles will intersect. Therefore, there is no such thing as lines being parallel on the surface of a sphere. Any two great circles, which are the closest things to straight lines here, will always intersect. So it is not possible for the tanker to take the course ordered. It cannot be done on the surface of the sea.

Common sense in a case like this would trick a landlubber because he would not realize that the surface of the sea is not a plane, and the laws of Euclidean plane geometry do not apply on any large area of the ocean. He must use a non-Euclidean geometry. So often people will vehemently, angrily, insist that what they have learned is "common sense." They will shout at you and snarl at you and tell you that what they believe "stands to reason."

So it does. It stands to reason in terms of the data they have abstracted and the methods they have been taught. But they should realize that there may be some conditions where a new way of looking at things is called for. Time was when it stood to reason that a flying machine couldn't get off the ground. Common sense, more recently, would show that man couldn't expect to fly faster than the speed of sound and live. Common sense provided and still does provide a good many remedies and health measures, from avoiding drafts and keeping our feet dry to taking daily sunbaths in ultraviolet light. Common sense tells us that the Republican point of view, or the Democratic point of view as the case may be, will save the country. Common sense tells us the way to solve our social and political problems are to turn to the wisdom of our forefathers.

Common sense warns us against selling stocks short, ever. And against buying stocks that are not earning and paying good dividends. And against trading on margin. Common sense tells us no man ever went broke taking a profit, and leads us to take our profits quickly. Common sense suggests that we buy stocks that have declined greatly and are now at their eight-year lows.

In short, common sense often seems to approve opinions and actions that do not stand up under scientific examination. What we call common sense appears to be a kind of intuition. It is derived, of course, from what we have previously learned, but it often perpetuates obsolete ideas, false theories, superstitions, prejudices, hopes, and desires, in short a hodgepodge of undigested and inadequate concepts.

This, of course, is not entirely fair. Not all of the opinions that we call common sense are faulty or inadequate or obsolete. In fact, it may be because so much of our common sense is very good sense and very useful in making valid predictions that a faulty common sense can be so very dangerous.

We might compare it to a system of coinage. Where there is only an occasional counterfeit, it is likely to sneak unnoticed into circulation. It is certainly not necessary to reject all that passes as common sense. But we can avoid losses by testing and checking wherever we can. As we have suggested before, we can start by asking the questions "Is that so?" and "How do you know that?"

CHAPTER 80   THE PIG WATCHERS

The truth is that we are all pig watchers whether we want to be or not. As any coffee-house metaphysician will tell you with great assurance (as Plato did), we are only watching shadows on the wall of the cave when we think we are observing reality—whether it's a real pig or a hand shadow puppet is not ours to know. We have to live with reality as its facts are handed to us. Pure technicians will work at the level of reality and facts they can observe and manipulate without speculating about the pig. They will observe and abstract symbols from events. Fundamentalists will study pigs till they are blue in the face (the fundamentalists, not the pigs). Time for a little fun!

This chapter is utterly mad and I hesitate to bring it into the orbit of this book at all. However, I can do so without too much loss of face by giving full credit to my brother, Beverly Magee, who first outlined this outlandish analogy to me several years ago.

You may be familiar with Wendell Johnson's discussion of reality as he presents it in his fine book *People in Quandaries*. He points out that, beyond the system of abstractions and symbols that constitute our perception, we have no knowledge of reality. We can explain the "how" of things from what we observe, as we might examine a sealed watch and then construct theories of what was inside it and what made it go, but we cannot get inside the watch case of reality and find out "why" and all about it.

Beverly suggested during a coffee-and-beer session after one of our school evenings that the reality in the market was largely unknown, like most realities. He reviewed the facts that we see only part of the end results of what is going on, and that while we may abstract some data and come to some valid conclusions that have predictive value, we are not ever going to know all the details, and we are never going to lay hands on the ultimate "why" of most market phenomena.

"It's like a pig in a barn," he said. "One of those big barns, all closed up on the ground floor but with a hayloft above, with a large open door. On the ground floor there may be various animals, with their food, bedding straw, and watering troughs. We have been given to understand that there is a pig in there. He has a wide leather belt or harness around his body, and on the top of it there is a ball-and-socket joint. A long pole is attached to this joint, and the pole extends up through a small hole in the center of the ceiling so that the top of the pole is visible through the hayloft door. The pole comes up through the floor and stands four or five feet high above the surface."

"Now, when the pig moves about, the pole will be moved also. It will move to the left as seen through the hayloft door when the pig moves to the right. It will move to the right when the pig moves to the left. It will rise higher from the floor when the pig is near the center of the barn and it will move lower when the pig goes off to the sides of the barn."

To us as pig watchers, the question of what kind of pig, or what size or color, or for that matter whether it is a pig at all, is not important. We are perched in a nearby tree watching the motion of the upper part of the pole, the only part we can see, and we are going to make observations and deductions and perhaps predictions concerning the situation below.

Watchers who are not comfortable with highly abstract symbols will assign meanings to the pole's movements. They will try to interpret these movements as corresponding to various assimilative, combative, or copulative actions of the pig. Those who consider themselves pure technicians will watch the pole and work entirely on the basis of what the pole has done, is doing, or might be expected to do according to trends, repetitive motions, and extrapolations.

This, as we said, is all utterly mad, especially if one adds, as my brother did, that the view into the hayloft is not complete and continuous, for we must assume that all this goes on during a dark and rainy night, so that the end of the pole is observable from time to time in the intermittent illumination of lightning. There was more. Quite a bit about the shouting crowd of us speculators in the tree, betting on each next move of the pole, even selling each other pole sheets and pig forms.

Mad it may be, but in observing whatever they can of the motions of the visible end of the pole, the pig watchers are abstracting at a low level from a directly visible external reality. They have established certain facts, and from these facts they may be able to come to some valid and useful conclusions. It could be questioned whether the attempts of others who may try to predict the motions of the pig—by reading up on pigs and by thinking about pigs and by asking their friends how they feel about pigs and by following the latest statistics on pig production and the visible supply of corn—will in the end lead to better predictions.

The technical method in the market is concerned with high-level abstractions. We are dealing with facts that are already some steps away from the ultimate underlying reality. But we are dealing with facts, and we are dealing with a simple, straightforward body of information, limited as it may be; what we lose in detail, we may gain in not being burdened by the crushing load of extraneous and irrelevant data.

CHAPTER 81   THE LIMITS OF PREDICTION

With a little reflection we would all play and wager even money that we would not draw a spade from a card deck. We would continue to play this game even if we drew a series of spades, because we know that the immutable laws of probability will eventually assert themselves and we will win in the long run. But there are those who will bet even money that they will draw a spade, and after a few successes feel confirmed in the rightness of their method. Right and wrong, either/or—these people cannot live with a method that embraces uncertainty rather than shunning it. They do not have sufficient awareness to examine their methodology and repair it.

So far as the stock market is concerned, the use we will make of all the study and observation we may do is largely to anticipate and predict the probable future course of market values. To a very large degree, the value of all study and experience in any of life's activities is a matter of predicting probable future events. Certainly all planning, anticipating, budgeting, organizing, and preparing relates to the future; it involves considerable prediction or expectation of things to come.

There is not space in this study to go into the detail of technical market analysis, which is one of the methods of market prediction and the one with which I am most familiar. This subject has been taken up in some detail in *Technical Analysis of Stock Trends,* which Robert D. Edwards and I wrote. However, in a few words, one could say that the technical method, like any other method of prediction, involves looking at the past, checking whether the present conditions are greatly different, making allowances for any differences, and then drawing certain conclusions based on these studies as to what seems most likely to happen in the future.

This is not a particularly mysterious process, although in its details it may involve a tremendous amount of sheer labor. The principles involved are simple enough. For example, if I have the past record of a series of numbers that runs 7, 7, 7, 7, 7, 7, 7, 7, and the present term of the series is 7, I would predict with some confidence that the next (future) term will be 7. If the past series runs 3, 4, 5, 6, 7, 8, 9, 10, and the present term of the series is 11, I would predict that the next term will be 12. If the past series runs 3, 6, 12, 24, 48, 96, and the present term is 192, I would predict that the next term will be 384.

Depending on the total picture one has, one may look for a continuation of a constant number, an arithmetic progression, a geometric progression, an exponential progression, a cyclic or wave-like rhythm, or any form that seems to fit the past and present facts, projected into the future as if we were continuing some sort of orderly pattern.

The trick, of course, is to find the orderly pattern, which may not be a simple function but may be a combination of several quite different functions. Also, one must be careful not to let one's enthusiasm run wild to the point where one sees patterns and rhythms where none actually exist. It is necessary, too, to be on guard all the time against the various pitfalls we have discussed, the prejudices and attitudes that are so ingrained in us that they may distort our vision and slant our evaluation. It is because these ingrained opinions are so deeply a part of our value systems that they can be so damaging if they are distorting our perception of the facts.

That may be why it is almost impossible to learn stock trading or commodity trading solely from reading a book or attending a class. It requires days, weeks, months, sometimes years of personal close observation and experience to implement the reading or the classroom study. It takes that time and that experience to revise the old and sometimes faulty concepts.

For they are not going to erase themselves or amend themselves just on the strength of your intellectual acceptance of a new viewpoint alone. The new ideas must be developed until they become the habitual responses.

One of the old tendencies that can be a dangerous pitfall is to predict stock price in terms of a change in the major trend. This probably comes out of a whole complicated evaluation in which we appraise a stock according to certain fundamental facts about the company it represents. Such an attitude can lead to a frame of mind where any considerable advance in the price of a stock leads to a certain habitual response, namely that the stock is over-valued. The conclusion, of course, is that eventually the stock will find its true value, and the prediction from all of this is that the stock should be sold.

The same situation in reverse occurs when a stock has declined sharply. The tendency is to "feel" that the stock is priced too low, is under-valued, and can't go much lower, etc. These reactions lead to a prediction that the stock will shortly advance in price, and therefore that it should be bought. Sometimes this type of prediction (that the trend will reverse itself) will be confirmed in the future action of the stock. However, before pinning too much confidence on this particular method, it would be well to check the record of past predictions made on this basis. You may find that it is much harder than you thought to predict even approximately when or where the turning point will come.

For myself, I would prefer to make exactly the opposite prediction. If I had only the choice of predicting a reversal of a major trend or a continuation of the major trend, I would have to choose the continuation. As Bob Edwards has put it, and I would agree, "A trend should be assumed to continue in effect until such time as its reversal has been definitely signaled."

However, what we are talking about here is not the detail of prediction, not the application of technical methods, but something much more basic: the limits of prediction.

If you consider the question of whether the trend or direction of a stock's price should be predicted in the expectation of a reversal of the major trend or in the expectation of a continuation, you will see that we are once again talking about an either/or situation. Wherever we can, we try to frame the problem so that we can change the either/or to a matter of degree. Then we will be able to answer the question in several, or many, ways, and not in just two ways.

Sometimes, as in this case, we cannot exactly change the either/or question to one of degree, but we can do something that serves much the same purpose: We can reduce it to a probability. If you say U.S. Rubber is going to go up and I say it's going to go down, then in month or whatever time we agree on, we can take a look at it and say, "You were right," or "I was right."

This, again, is the two-valued situation, the either/or, which is what we are trying to avoid. You see, in this view, if your predictive method is right it will give you the right result. If the stock goes up in price, then you are right, your prediction is right, and your predictive *method* is right. But if the stock goes down, you are wrong, your prediction is wrong, and your predictive method is wrong.

This leads to trouble. You might be quite right about U.S. Rubber this month, you might be right about Granite City Steel next month and about Northern Pacific the following month, but sooner or later you will be wrong on one. This, almost by definition, makes your method itself wrong, at least in that particular case. It either discredits your method entirely or it casts a shadow and a doubt on it. At the very least it destroys your confidence. (And let me interrupt here to suggest that you consider for a moment other kinds of prediction outside of the market. You will see how this same failure and demoralization can occur wherever you attempt to set up a perfect either/or predictive method.)

But we don't have to do it in a two-valued absolute way! We can recognize certain limits of predictive expectation in terms of probabilities, and then we will not continually be afraid to use our method because of our lack of confidence in it. We will not be expecting more from our method than we can reasonably hope for. And we will not be basing our method on a few accidental successes.

Is this clear? Do you see that a very stupid method of prediction (such as betting even money that you can draw a spade from an ordinary deck of cards) could at times produce a succession of wins. If you should see someone make such a bet over and over again, would you feel it was a right method of prediction, even if he won eight times in succession?

To put it another way, suppose you were to have the chance of betting even money you would not draw a spade from the deck. Every time you drew a heart, a diamond, or a club, you would win. Only when you drew a spade would you lose. Under these conditions, if you were to lose several times in a row, would you discard your method as wrong? Would you reverse your method and bet that you would draw a spade, merely because of a run of luck against you? Isn't it possible to say that, providing the deck of cards is an honest one containing the usual cards and properly shuffled, it makes no difference how many times you win or how many times you lose. This does not affect the rightness or wrongness of your method of evaluation. Your best policy is to continue to use your evaluative method so long as you are convinced that it is based on adequate data and valid reasoning.

Of course you know this. You know this from what you have previously abstracted from your experience in drawing cards from decks. It seems terribly redundant to have to go through this long discussion of something (perhaps an elephant stuck in your front entry) so obvious, so plain. You know that neither the roulette croupier nor the owners of the casinos care very much whether you or any other player wins or loses. If the casino's bank is well-heeled, the method of valuation will wear down the string of luck or the system of any roulette player, as every professional gambler knows.

The method of evaluation used by the professional gambler is not based on being absolutely right on any particular play or series of plays but on a prediction as to the most probable outcome of a long series of plays taken as a whole. Why is it, then, that so many people either have no real evaluation method at all or follow one that represents so little first-hand checking and verifying that it may be worse than useless? Could it be that, because they are so deeply trained in either/or and right and wrong, they cannot habituate themselves to a method based on uncertainty?

If we know that on the basis of past experience and in view of the present outlook we may expect to win seven times out of ten in an even-money series of bets, we can accept this seven-out-of-ten probability as something akin to what would be a measure or degree in some other types of problem. With certain reservations and precautions we can accept this as the measure of our expectation, and by continually re-checking and verifying we can adjust and refine this until it becomes a highly dependable tool, so long as the basic conditions of the contest do not change materially. We can operate on this basis with considerable confidence, and with this foundation for our confidence we will not need to be right all the time.

Think what this means. Consider the nights you have lain awake and worried about what the market would do tomorrow, or whether XYZ would go up or down before the end of the week. You will not be able to eliminate all anxiety about the market, but you will be able to reduce greatly the amount of your tension and worry, since you will not feel threatened with a total failure of your method every time a stock moves a point or so against you.

What we have done here is to set some limits on the predictive science. The average man seems to recognize no limits whatever. What he so often seeks, and demands, is an infallible method of reading the future. He is so sure that if he only keeps trying and searching he will come up with the right method, that charlatans milk him of millions of dollars every year by supplying spurious perfect systems. (This is true in many other streets besides Wall Street.)

We have set limits. We have stopped short of the 100 percent upper limit, representing infallibility, and we have set our goal considerably above the zero of the thoroughly discouraged cynic who feels it is all just luck. By observing the results of a method as applied in the past and noting the number of successes and failures, we can gauge the past success of the method. We can then project these results into the future as a probability and say, "I believe, on the basis of the past records, that this method will probably produce an average net return of between 20 percent and 30 percent per year."

That statement isn't nearly positive enough to satisfy the man trained to think in absolute terms. Neither is the expected return anywhere near as large as such a man would expect (on the basis that he will be always right). Neither is it definite enough, for the man we are speaking of does not think of somewhere "between"—he wants it right out, plain and sharp. Of course, the chances of our being totally defeated are much less than his, but for him it is necessary to reach the top, and that means shooting at nothing short of perfection.

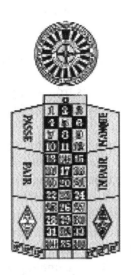

CHAPTER 82   IS THE MARKET A GAME?

The market is a game and is not a game. The market is an economic device for determining the exchange value of goods and money. People who participate in the market are gaming in that, like many other life situations, such as military campaigns, it may be gamed.

Using this metaphor we may analyze the market looking at the essential factors of games: (1) the odds; (2) the strategy of the opponent; and (3) the payoffs of the available choices.

We have spoken of flipping coins and drawing cards in connection with predictive methods. We have mentioned bets on the outcome of these operations. Since what we are interested in is the development of predictive methods that can be applied to market situations, the question arises, Is the market, then, simply a gambling game?

If by a gambling game we mean a contest in which the sole purpose is the gaming itself, and in which the result is determined largely by luck, then the market is not simply a gambling game. Under the conditions of the fairly free competition that is an essential part of the democratic way of life as we know it, we must have some means of determining the exchange value of goods and money. The market is the means of this evaluation. It does, however, have some of the features we associate with gambling. It involves winning and losing, although it is certainly not merely the transfer of gains and losses from one participant to another as in a poker game since it is tied up with many basic economic and monetary factors.

If one regarded the market as a poker game one of several factors he would have to consider is that in the market the value of the chips is continually changing. Viewed as a game it is more like poker than like shooting craps or tossing coins, since it involves not only pure luck, but a considerable degree of strategy. But where a crap game, a poker game, or a horse race serves no real purpose other than to provide a means for gambling (leaving out the somewhat thin claim that horse racing contributes to the improvement of the breed), the gambling aspect of the market is incidental to its evaluative function, just as the gambling element in insurance is incidental to its protective purpose.

There is another sense in which the market can be considered a game. The word has been used to designate any situation in which a stake is put at risk on the outcome of a future event. This would include not only all pure gambling games but also any speculative business enterprises, such as opening a store, buying a stock of materials, or the agreement to perform certain work according to the terms of a contract and within a definite time limit. The term game, in this sense, would also involve other questions where future events may decide the outcome of a present decision. For example, the decision to buy personal liability insurance or to take one's chances without it could be considered a game. Or whether to go into business after gaining a B.A. degree or continue one's studies toward an M.A.

We could even consider some situations as games where the stake was not expressed in money or goods, though we are not going to go into these fields in detail here.

The game-like problems of evaluating the probable future are present in almost every decision of life. We sometimes speak of the game of love, and certainly the weighing of values between solitary independence and the mingled joys and burdens of a shared life has something of the nature of a game. Even in questions of ethics and morals, there is a game-like element of prediction and of evaluation, as in analyzing what might be the advantages and disadvantages of attempting to cut down a rival for an important job: one's possible monetary gain or increase of importance in the company versus contempt for one's self and feelings of guilt on the other. It would be interesting to frame a number of such situations in terms of game problems, but that is beyond the scope of this book. In the sense in which games are studied there is a stake, not necessarily monetary, that is risked against certain known or unknown odds pursuant to certain known or unknown or partially known strategies. Such games would include various forms of gambling; they would include markets, insurance operations, military and naval campaigns, and a great many problems that come up in engineering, sociology, medicine, and many other fields. In going into such a game there are three principal factors to be studied: (1) the purely mathematical odds; (2) the strategy of your opponent, who may be a person, a group, or nature; and (3) the payoff on each of the available choices.

CHAPTER 83   THE PURELY
MATHEMATICAL ODDS

Lessons from the dice, or the die: You can spend a few days rolling a die and recording the results (perhaps a good exercise for some unbelievers) or you can accept this elegant and simple explanation of mathematical odds, but that is what happens when the game is not fair because the die is loaded. For the process we follow in such a case is like the method we follow for living life skillfully and investing to obtain acceptable results.

If someone produces a pair of dice and sets one of them on the table in front of you, what predictions can you make about the result of a toss?

If you assume that the die is honest and that all faces are as nearly alike as they can be made you would not be able to favor the chances of one side coming up over any other, so by a sort of negative reasoning you would be forced to give each of the six sides an equal chance. You would probably say, "The chance of throwing any particular number from one to six is one out of six," so the correct odds for a bet on any selected number should be five-to-one. This would mean your best prediction would be that if repeated bets were made on a single number at 5:1 odds, the result would tend to be fairly even; neither you nor your opponent would have an expectation of advantage.

If you chose two numbers, the chances of throwing one of the two in a single throw of the die would be predicted at one out of three and the correct odds to make the game even would be 2:1. If you chose three numbers, the expectation would be one win out of two throws, and the odds for an even game would be 1:1, even money.

Any of these three situations is what has been called a fair game, that is to say, neither you nor your opponent has any predictable advantage. In such a game, the result on any throw must be pure luck. No positive or absolute prediction as to the outcome of the next throw will be valid. The expectations are even, meaning that since it is not possible to give one number a specific higher expectation than any other, we must assume the chances are equal for each.

This does not mean, however, that the results will actually be fair, for although it is not possible to predict which player in a even, fair game of pure luck will come out ahead, the chances are very high that one will win and one will lose, and it may be definitely predicted that there will be runs of luck of various degrees. The more throws that are made, the smaller will be the expected difference between the winner's hoard and the loser's in terms of the percentage of the total money wagered, but the difference in terms of number of dollars may be expected to increase. With a greater number of throws we may expect a greater number of runs of four wins in a row, or five wins in a row. Also, with more throws we may expect to encounter a longer maximum run, say of fifteen wins or twenty wins in a row. The distribution of these differences and these runs can be plotted in terms of expectancy and distribution.

It is not our intention to go very deeply into probability studies here, but there are one or two important points that can apply to dealings in markets, as in other problems of life. One is that it is not good tactics to enter a game situation in which pure chance is the major factor, and in which the expectation of winning is less than even.

Thus, with the single die we would make a single number bet if we were given odds of 6:1; we would be indifferent to such a bet with odds of 5:1, and we would not make any bet if we were offered odds of 4:1 or less.

Furthermore, we would have a clear understanding that even with the favorable odds of 6:1, we might experience a run of bad luck in which we could lose many times in succession; while this would not affect the validity of our decision to play, it could deplete our capital or wipe us out entirely unless we took steps to protect ourselves.

It is this particular trap that has caused the downfall of so many players in games like red dog, where a player holding, say, the ace of spades, ace of hearts, king of diamonds, and king of clubs could be beaten only if the next card turned happened to be the ace of diamonds or ace of clubs. Any other card would give him a win. If, as sometimes happens in red dog, the pot was enormously swollen, the player might be tempted to bet the entire pot, perhaps hundreds or even thousands of dollars on the nearly sure thing. This would be a case where the mathematical odds of winning were overwhelmingly in the player's favor; yet it might be bad tactics for him to risk perhaps a year's pay on the outcome of what is still an unknown future event. Many a red dog player has rushed in to such a play to his sorrow, not realizing that in spite of extraordinarily good odds, the 1:23 chance of ruin is too large to justify risking everything.

We would safely make a bet of any amount, we could stake everything we owned and life itself, that two of the Navy's rocket satellites will not collide in outer space. That is of a degree of improbability that approaches the infinite. But we cannot, without proper safeguards that we will discuss a few chapters further along, risk your entire fortune on just a little better than even odds—or even a good deal better than even odds.

There is one point we did not even consider in connection with the die: Before it is thrown we can look it over as it lies on the table, but we have no way of telling whether it is actually an honest die. It might be weighted inside so as to favor one number and make that number come up more often than the others.

Suppose we were told by a trustworthy informant that the die was loaded, but we were not told which number would be favored by the loading. In this case we would know before the die was thrown that the expectation for each of the sides was not equal. We could no longer make the prediction that the chances were the same for each number, for we would know that they were definitely not the same and that in a long series of throws one of the numbers would tend to pile up a much larger number of hits than the others. However, in this case (not knowing the favored number), we would not be any better off than in the first case where presumably the die was fair and all numbers had an equal expectation, for we could not assign the higher expectation, which we know will apply for one of the numbers, to any particular one. Therefore, if we are required to lay out our tactics and place our bets in advance we would have to proceed as if each of the numbers had an equal expectation. It would be a perfectly justifiable assumption under these conditions, and would give us the chance to make the best plan possible with the data we had.

As soon as the die is actually thrown, however, we can begin to collect statistical information to supplement the theoretical predictions we had made. If the die is a fair one, we will find that after a number of throws have been made, the distribution pattern will begin to show the tendency for numbers to come up in approximately equal ratios, and the deviations from equal distribution will show normal variations. Given a large number of throws, a trained statistician could detect the effect of any loading, not only as to the favored number but to which degree the number was favored.

Thus we can take our theoretical guess (this is a high abstraction) and use it as a prediction. As the play progresses we can take the actual observed results (abstractions of much lower order), and feed them back in order to check and if necessary correct our original guess. In this way we have a continually self-adjusting predictive method; this is the process we outlined some chapters previously as the basic method of evaluation.

Even in matters of pure luck, such as the drawing of cards, the turn of a roulette wheel, or the toss of a die, we do not need to depend wholly on what we have concluded by logical deduction, nor on what we have been told or what we have read. By using our experience as it unfolds to give us a statistical check, we can correct our appraisals to take care of any error or omission in the original theory, or to allow for new or changed conditions.

CHAPTER 84   THE STRATEGY OF YOUR OPPONENT

There are games of chance and games of strategy. Flipping a coin is a game of chance. The market is a game of strategy, a game in which mathematical probabilities do not rule. There the player plays against an opponent who is the market, the market being the high order abstraction representing the sum total of all the other players participating.

By strategy we do not mean doctoring the dice or marking the cards. We mean a considered plan of action within the rules of a game or contest by which one opponent pits his intelligence against another's. In the case of flipping coins, tossing dice, drawing cards, etc., there is no strategy in this sense. The game is decided in terms of the odds, and of course, on the outcome of the flip, toss, or draw, which would be a matter of pure chance.

There has been a vast amount of study of systems of winning in games of pure chance, usually games in which the odds or payoff are loaded against the player to start with. It is true that even in a loaded game, such as the commercial games in any gambling casino where the house takes a constant percentage, the outsider sometimes wins quite heavily and for an extended period of time, but except for these fortuitous runs of luck, the system player in such games usually comes out poorer than when he went in. No one has yet devised a system that will ensure an expectation of winning against such games.

In the games of pure chance, whether or not they are loaded against the outside player, it is possible to make a reasonable estimate of the mathematical probabilities as well as the normal random deviations to be expected from the ideal distributions. And once you have made these estimates there isn't anything you can do by planning to increase the mathematical expectation of winning.

The situation is quite different when we come to games of strategy. These games may or may not involve pure chance as a factor, but they do involve, as a rule, the intelligent planning of an opponent. This complicates things enormously. The game of paper, scissors, and stone is a case where pure chance doesn't enter at all. Scissors can cut paper, stone can break scissors, and paper can wrap up stone. Therefore, scissors win over paper, stone over scissors, and paper over stone. If your opponent chooses paper and you choose scissors, you win. If he chooses scissors and you choose paper, he wins. If he chooses paper and you choose stone, he wins. Since each choice is made simultaneously, it becomes a contest in which each tries to read the other's mind.

Poker, on the other hand, is a game that combines pure chance as represented by the deal and the draw of the cards, with the planning of a campaign in which the opponent tries to read your mind and if possible to mislead you into misreading his mind.

Poker is a game that can be used as a sort of simplified map (an abstraction) of certain other types of contest, or rather, certain aspects of the game of poker are similar to some aspects of other kinds of contest. For this reason poker provides a good analogy for clinical study where the game we may be interested in might be something far more complex, such as the market. You may not recognize the stock market or the commodity market as very close counterparts of the game of poker. And in truth they are not. Neither is a guinea pig a close counterpart to a man, but the guinea pig can be used to study certain physical conditions that may have similarities to those in men. For that matter a water pipe is not very much like an electric wire, but it sometimes helps in teaching elementary science classes to understand how electricity on a wire acts in some ways like water in a pipe.

You may not recognize the market as your opponent in the contest or game. Keeping in mind what we said about this analogy being a generality it may not surprise you to know that the opponent is not ordinarily to be considered the person from whom you buy stock or to whom you sell it, nor even the class of those who buy and sell stocks. Your opponent in this case is the market itself. It is not specific and certainly not personalized. You are playing in this contest against a high abstraction rather than a person or people. It's like playing a game of tennis against a high cement wall.

While many games of strategy do involve human opponents in situations very much like a poker game (as in an auction, a directors' meeting, an election campaign, etc.), there are many other games, especially in scientific and economic work, where the opponent is so vaguely defined that he appears mainly as the other side of your transaction. In such a game your wins or losses would not be transferred from the opponent's tank into yours (assuming the unit of value in the game was measured as a liquid), but you might consider that your winnings were pumped into your measuring tank from a large lake, and your losses drained from your tank back into the lake. You would be measuring the degree of your success or failure not in terms of the gains or losses of a particular other person, but as affecting you only, the opponent being considered to be an infinite bank.

In such cases, we could speak of our opponent as nature. This is not a very good choice of word, but since we have explained what is meant, you will understand. Thus, if I were to buy 5,000 shares of Central Violeta Sugar, I could consider not only the effect of the acquisition on me and my affairs, but also the effect of my purchase on the floating supply of the stock. If I were to buy 5,000 shares of General Motors, while this might have a large effect on my own affairs, the reduction of the floating supply in GM would not have any visible effect. This is because, unlike a thin stock such as Central Violeta Sugar, there is a tremendous floating supply or lake of shares in GM. Similarly, when you are buying a very thin commodity you must consider not only your own side of the transaction, but its effect on the supply side: if you should be buying one of the big commodities like wheat, you would be dealing with a supply so vast that your purchases could have no substantial effect on it. Since in general we avoid the thin situations where even a moderate amount of trading tends to create severe strains in the supply-demand balance, we will normally be dealing with stocks and commodities that do not have the specific human quality of a personal contest.

There are traders today, and there have been many in the past, who enjoy the matching of wits in what amounts to a man-to-man contest. Very often market commentators, market advisers, or investment brokers will promote some situation where a very small number of shares of a stock may be available; a small issue, an issue in which many shares are tied up or closely held, a situation in which the key to the problem is a policy of inter-personal strategy.

This is quite different from the cases where the supply is so large as to be virtually unlimited. The whole strategic problem becomes quite different when it is possible to buy or sell in any amount at any time without visibly affecting the market.

Actually, of course, any purchase or any sale, however small, is going to have some effect on the supply, just as taking a teaspoonful of water from the ocean will to some degree lower the level of the ocean. It is also true that under certain conditions of panic or boom the status of even large stocks can be affected. For instance, if a popular radio commentator were to tout a particular stock, even a large issue, he could temporarily distort the normal supply by creating an artificial demand. But in the main, where we are dealing with the important stocks listed on the big exchanges, we can assume that our transactions will not materially affect the supply. We can assume that for all practical purposes it is unlimited, and we can assume a certain continuity and stability to that supply. We can consider it, collectively as a unit, as if it were an opponent in the game of our market operation; and we can assign certain habits and characteristics to It and deal with it as if it were, in a sense, a person.

This does not eliminate the need for strategy on our part. The supply of the stock, or the open interest of a commodity is not really a personality, but it can be considered to represent the collective personalities of all of those who are concerned with it. We have set up an imaginary person who combines the hopes and fears and expectations of all the individuals who are involved in the stock or the commodity. It is, in a way, as though the stockholders or commodity traders had elected in a democratic way a representative or champion to handle their interests. It is this imaginary person who faces us across the table as our opponent.

Recently a great deal of research has been done on game theory. This subject has tremendous implications in military and scientific work. Much of the theory involves new and difficult mathematics. Fortunately, some of the basic principles are not too hard to understand, and have practical applications in stock and commodity market study.

Pure probability mechanics are not enough when you are dealing with strategy situations, which these are, where beneath all the vast complexities of the seething markets there lie the intelligent plans and tactics of individual human beings. In collectivizing them all as an abstraction, we must not lose track of the fact that the problem still involves matters of human intelligence competitively engaged in a contest of evaluation. There is a great deal more to this than pure chance.

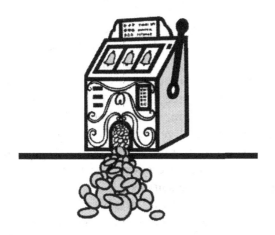

CHAPTER 85   THE PAYOFF

Have you ever contemplated why people (not just Russians) play Russian roulette? Of course they win the money when their opponents lose (and blow their brains out). More important than the money, though, is the thrill of danger and of having won the biggest gamble of all—life itself. So too, do speculators and gamblers—and the naïve and ignorant—attempt to make a killing in the market. By contrast, the aware strategic player considers his expected losses and his worst possible losses rather than being blinded by the big payoff.

When radio giveaways started. First it was a box of soap flakes. Then it was a fur coat. Pretty soon the sponsors were offering trips to Bermuda or Hawaii, then cash prizes and bigger cash prizes, and then, as the TV age came into its own, great bundles of big money, with Cadillac convertibles to the losers for consolation prizes. What more could anyone ask? Big, showy prizes, lots of money, and no work. Something for nothing in a big way.

Lotteries have always been popular. In some countries a few pennies will get you a chance to win a huge fortune. Not much of a chance, but something to pin one's dreamiest hopes to, especially if one needs so badly to dream and has so very little in reality. We have lotteries in the United States, too. At least I suppose you can still go into a cigar store or lunch room and buy a ticket on the treasury balance or the day's take at Pimlico and on the remote chance that your number, in full, might come up. Your fifty cents stands to win you five thousand dollars. We have the numbers for the very poor and very stupid. No! Stupid is too strong a word. Uninformed, yes. Ignorant of the true odds against them, yes. But when you are low enough in the economic peck-order you need something to buck up your frustrated spirits.

It's the old story; a man's self-esteem is his most valuable possession. While he may be on half-time at the shop and have a sick wife at home, if he carries in his pocket the magic number that might produce the big payoff this very afternoon, who can say that he's not getting full value for his money? What price self-esteem?

Whether a game is a matter of pure chance or involves strategy angles, you will find that most people will look for the big payoff. After all, the big prize is not the money; it's the winning of it. It's blowing it in and feeling of being on top of things. It is telling the neighbors about winning the Chevrolet grand prize at the bingo game. It is that feeling that I do amount to something after all that counts. If it were not for that it would be hard to explain why people do play gambling games. More often they cannot afford to play them, in terms of ordinary common-sense economics. The odds in all commercial gambling schemes are shamelessly loaded against the customers. They don't seem to care much about the odds.

This may not be entirely because they don't understand or can't figure the odds. It's more that they don't seem interested, as if the odds were not really the most important angle. And psychologically, from their own point of view, perhaps the odds are not so important. What does seem important is to maximize one's gains. It's not much fun to play the odds-on favorite, not much of a victory to take a small niggling profit on what is almost a sure thing. This is not going to soothe anybody's aching ego. What will make the skies light up and the bells ring is to walk up to the window with a $50 win on a $2 ticket. It's the long shots that pay off in thrills and satisfaction. It's the big payoff that you can talk up at the bar. Not because you need the money! But because it shows how right you were. A very smart Joe! Picks 'em right! Not just lucky: cagey, too!

This all involves—well, it involves a good many of the faulty or absolute evaluations we have analyzed before. The need to be right is evidence of the either—or dichotomy in action. A money prize, whether earned or merely the result of pure chance, as a sign of importance and success. The general attitude of inferiority. The inability to evaluate the real chances of winning, and, of course, the extreme view that the biggest prize is the only one worth going for.

People like big payoffs. One of the most typical human traits in market operations, or for that matter in any game operation, is the desire to make a killing.

Unfortunately, it's too often the player himself who gets killed. Just how far people can go in pursuing the payoff regardless of consequences appears in the almost daily headlines reporting the passing of some poor devil who tried his hand at the good old game of Russian roulette. We don't know the details of the wagers involved in these games, but whether the nominal prize was measured in hundreds or in thousands of dollars, it seems clear that the real prize was something else. For a man does not bet his life against a $100 or against $10,0000, not even at 5:1 odds. The real prize must appear to be vastly more valuable. The only prize that could warrant the risking of life itself in a deliberate wager would be the preservation or enhancement of self-esteem. So the real expected payoff in a game of Russian roulette is not the stake that lies on the table, but the intangible payoff of glorifying the ego. And a man with an adequate feeling of security and self-esteem would not need to take such desperate measures to win such a prize.

This is the psychopathology of the gambler in which money, property, even life itself is wagered against an intangible abstraction. The whole viewpoint of the habitual gambler (and in this sense we must now include a good many market traders) is defensive. He is trying to bolster up his finances and his self-esteem. Too often he succeeds in doing neither. Worse than that, the very methods by which he tries to help himself contribute to his further demoralization. If he were able to stand back and look at himself from a distance as if he were someone else, he might see that he would have a lot more to talk about and feel good about if he could protect and build up a solid backlog than he can by plunging for the big payoff—even if he should win.

For one thing, if he could somewhat reduce his demands to be top dog, he might be able to settle for something less than the top payoff without feeling humiliated. But as things are he is not willing, in fact he is not able, to make any compromises. You cannot talk with him about safety of principal because his whole idea of the game (whatever game it may be) is to plunge, and plunge, and plunge, and hope that he doesn't get wiped out, and hope that he will make the big killing.

Since we cannot reach him in his present frame of mind, let us talk over the problem a bit.

Suppose we forget the big payoff for a moment and consider the other side of the picture entirely: not how much you are going to win if you win, but how much you stand to lose if you lose. You will certainly agree that you expect sometimes to lose, and, of course, you hope sometimes to win. If the game is one of pure chance and if the probabilities are heavily loaded against you, wouldn't it be a good idea not to get into it at all? Not unless (without kidding yourself) you can go into the game just for the fun of it, playing pennies or nickels or dimes, and not caring whether you win or lose. Certainly you are not going to buck a percentage game that is unbeatable on the long term with any sizable amount of money, regardless of how big the top payoff may be.

If the game is one where strategy enters into it materially, you may feel that you can cope with your opponent on his own terms. You may feel that you can out-smart him. Assuming the mathematical odds are not so heavily against you that your strategy would not have much chance, figure out what strategies you might use. Then consider the various courses you might take, and put yourself in your opponent's shoes to see what he could do to you in each case. You may find that his best reply to certain of your available plays could be extremely damaging to you. In certain other plays you might make, the very worst he could do would not cause you too serious a loss. True, in these latter cases you might not stand to win the biggest payoff. But if you plan out and carry through a strategy that will make sure that your losses are held to a minimum regardless of how intelligently your opponent attacks you, your winnings may ultimately amount to more than you could expect by shooting continually for the big payoff.

In theory and in actual application this process of evaluating a game situation is rather complicated. It is not possible here to go into the details of it. As a matter of fact it is not necessary to go into great detail, for if you can simply grasp the big fact that the big payoff is not always the most profitable goal in the long run, and the fact that before counting unhatched profits one should allow for the possibility of the most serious loss that may be incurred. Then you will have the rough outline of a most practical method of dealing with strategy problems.

CHAPTER 86   FRACTIONIZING VS. MAXIMIZING

In place of rolling the dice of our lives and our portfolios on right/wrong, either/or, big killing/total loss, we adopt a scientific method of fractionizing our gains. This is accomplished by adopting methods that give us some probability of success and diversifying our bets, taking our manageable losses with discipline, allowing our profits to accumulate with patience, knowing our method is rock solid for the long run.

When we spoke about predictions and the degrees of predictability, ranging from the nearly certain to the almost impossible, we outlined the problem of everyone who has to make decisions on a hundred and one matters concerning the unknown future every day of his life. To the man who is dedicated to absolute rightness, any method of making these decisions on a maybe basis leaves a great deal to be desired. As long as he is so dedicated, he is going to batter his brains against the unattainable, in the hope that if only he can know enough or all about it, he can come up with the right answers all the time.

403

His intellect may tell him that this is not a reasonable hope, and in actual experience he knows that not all of his predictions come out as he anticipates. But since he has no other method of dealing with the situation he goes right on looking for perfection; being continually frustrated, he becomes discouraged.

He will tell you with a good deal of bitterness that, "It's all right to talk about 'probabilities,' but what about the market right now? What about U.S. Steel right now? Is it a buy or is it a sell? Is it going to go up or going to go down? The wrong answer is going to mean a loss. What do I do about it?" He knows, part of him knows, that even if U. S. Steel looks like a buy according to the very best and most complete information he can get today, tomorrow there may be a shake-up in the company's directorate, or an adverse court decision, or a general smash in the market as a whole due to some scare or national disaster that nobody could foresee. Yet if he is going to deal in stocks he has to make decisions and face these unpredictable future events.

What steps can he take to protect himself against the unpredictable? He could take one big step if he would use the method that any insurance company uses to protect itself. He could diversify his holdings. Travelers doesn't know whether Aunt Matilda will break her arm tomorrow or not, and certainly the company is not going to study Aunt Matilda's personal life in every detail and follow her around all day to guard against a claim on her accident policy.

The insurance company doesn't worry much about Aunt Matilda, for it has hundreds of thousands of policies covering many other aunts and uncles and cousins in every part of the country. It hasn't even tried to make any precise and absolute predictions about what will happen to any one of them, but the company does have a method of evaluation, based on a good deal of past experience. Its own records will show about how many policyholders will probably break an arm in the next six weeks, give or take a reasonable margin of error. While this doesn't help very much in telling Aunt Matilda's particular fortune, it does make possible extremely precise predictions as to the whole group.

You and I cannot do exactly what the insurance company does. We do not have the capital to invest in thousands of different stock situations. It would not be a practical way to invest in any case. However, we can study the record of hundreds or thousands of stocks in their past actions; we can note certain sequences of events, and we can establish certain correlations. We can't tell what any particular stock will do or when, but we can learn to foresee the probable action of any stock with a good deal of success. Our prediction, if carried forward in the record of several hundred stocks, will be valid within the reasonable limits of expected error, as long as the general patterns of stock behavior do not change radically and suddenly.

Over the entire period in which records of market action have been kept, the basic behavior of stocks has changed very little. Such minor changes in the typical habits of stocks as have occurred can be allowed for, in that if we have formed certain opinions as to how stocks will probably act, we can from time to time revise and bring up to date this overall map to meet any new conditions. This is the method of evaluation and prediction for stocks—not necessarily the only method, but typical of evaluative methods in many lines of study: We look at the past, extract the generalized patterns, similarities, correlations, and project these into the future as a basis for prediction.

Being an abstraction this method deliberately ignores much detail. (It doesn't care to know too much about Aunt Matilda's affairs.) Being a high abstraction with the conclusions expressed only as probabilities, it assumes from the start that some of the decisions made on this method will turn out wrong. But there is also the big assumption that if the method is valid and the probabilities assigned are reasonably correct, the results, applied to a number of decisions, will be correct within the expected limits.

Notice *within the expected limits*. When the insurance company writes an accident policy for Aunt Matilda, the expected limits of its prediction, for all the accident policies they may have, are very narrow. It can tell you down to several decimal places what the annual total of claims will come to. With the man who buys a single stock or makes any single decision on a matter involving uncertainty, the expected limits of success or failure are much wider; in fact, he may be little better off than if he flipped a coin so far as the expected outcome of his single prediction. But you and I can take a point somewhere between the fine precision of a big insurance operation and the out-and-out gamble of the plunger. Assuming that we have some idea what to expect in the long run, based on careful study and observation, we can avoid the extreme risk of bad luck by making several commitments.

We will not make any commitments unless we feel the probabilities favor our success. That is, we won't take a chance on something in which the probabilities are loaded against us.

How would this work? Let us assume that we have developed certain evaluative methods. We have spent some weeks or months or years observing past history. We have made our tables and charts and break-downs, and we feel that we have abstracted certain factors, that, if they occur together, point to a probability of, say, 55 percent that certain consequences will follow. For instance, we may find that a particular type of breakout from a long-term formation in a stock, accompanied by a certain volume of activity, seems to lead to a substantial up-trend in 55 percent of the cases over a period of years and in many different types of stock. If we entered twenty situations having this probability, using $1,000 in each, we could assume that as long as this probability held true, our expectation of the result would be eleven wins and nine losses.

Let us for the moment assume also that the wins would each give us $1,000 profit, and the losses would each involve the total loss of the $1,000 put up. The theoretical result of eleven wins in which we would make $11,000 profit and nine losses in which we would lose $9,000 would be a net profit of $2,000, or 10 percent of our capital.

It would be a little easier to study the effect of diversification if we change the terms of the problem slightly. Instead of winning even money eleven times out of twenty, we might expect to win exactly half the time, but each win would give us $1,200 instead of $1,000. Thus, in twenty commitments, totaling $20,00 invested, we could expect to win ten at $1,200 each, or $12,000, and to lose ten at $1,000 each, or $10,000. This would give us a net profit of $2,000 for the twenty trials, as above, or 10 percent of the total capital, the same as before. This is, in effect, a percentage game, in the same sense that the business of an insurance company is a percentage game. You (the insurance company) is counting on the relatively small expectation of a percentage gain in each transaction to give protection to capital over the long run, and to compensate for the taking of risk (which is the business of both speculators and insurance companies).

In order to gain any real protection, however, you must diversify your holdings in such a way that you do not stand to lose everything on one single disaster. You may have an expectancy of gain amounting to 10 percent on each transaction. At these odds, your mathematical expectancy would be a gain of $2 000 on an investment of $20,000.

But if you were to wager your $20,000 in one plunge on the even-money chance of recovering either $22,000 or being wiped out, you would still be risking your entire fortune on a 50 percent chance of total loss. On the other hand, if you were to make twenty successive wagers of $1,000 each on the same terms (in each individual transaction you would stand to recover either $1,200 or nothing), your chances of total loss in the entire series would be less than one in a million.

You could and would have some losses, but they would not take everything you had and wipe you out. The chances of losing even half your capital would be something less than one out of eight, and this would leave you still with a stake for a comeback.

One could say that the probabilities of fulfilling the mathematical expectation of ultimate profit in a game such as we have described, where only a small portion of the capital was used in any one commitment and where there was a constant favorable percentage, are astronomical. At any rate the chances of ultimate success are tremendously greater than those in, say, the opening of a new store or establishment of a law firm. It is not necessary, of course, that the twenty partial commitments be made in sequence, one at a time. All of the capital can be used at the same time if desired, with the same results.

The great difference between this method and the usual way of shooting the works is that you will not have all the eggs in one basket, for each separate unit will be invested on its own merits and in various types of situation. Some of these may be in railroads, some in aircraft, others in motors or utilities or building materials or bio-tech or tech. Some may be long, some short. It is variety that gives strength to the method, just as a fagot of small sticks may be much stronger than a single log of wood.

This method we have outlined in very general terms can be applied in many ways to almost any market operation. It will not appeal to the out-and-out gambler, since it is not spectacular. The nervous and insecure gambler does not have either the patience or the confidence to wait out a method that is almost sure to produce a moderate gain over the long pull while giving him an enormous degree of protection. He wants to dash in quickly and grab a fat profit, then stand back and wait for another opportunity to grab and run. However, by fractionizing instead of maximizing profits the investor who can follow through on a balanced and diversified program will stand to gain not only greater profits in the long run but peace of mind as well.

An essential part of this whole thing is the acceptance of the probability of some losses, which we mentioned briefly in passing. Since the losses are expected in advance and have been already considered and discounted, they cannot hurt too badly. Whereas the plunger is out on a limb, completely at the mercy of whatever unpredictable reversal may strike, the balanced and diversified investor cannot be hurt badly by an adverse move—he has already taken it into account as a possibility—and part of his holdings are so placed that they will act as insurance against any collapse or runaway inflation in the market.

The method of designing a balanced and diversified program is taken up in some detail in Chapter 37 of *Technical Analysis of Stock Trends*. Essentially it is a matter of study in individual trends of particular stocks and, instead of plunging all out on the long side or the short side, taking a position which the strongest-appearing securities are held long and the weakest short in a ratio corresponding approximately to the ratio of the number of strong-looking stocks to the number of weak-looking stocks in the whole market (or at least in the group of stocks one has under study).

What we are talking about here is not a single or a magic way of dealing with the market.

The point of this book does not lie in some formula or system at all. The big point is the acceptance of a new outlook, one that provides the tools for coping with the unpredictable future. The devices we use for handling this problem in stocks are much the same as those we can use in other problems: We give up the attempt to be perfect. We stop trying to maximize our gains. We settle for a great number of small satisfactions and victories instead of the big showy killing. We plan to take small losses in stride. We follow a carefully worked-out method of evaluation and prediction, and we stand ready to change it as new conditions require.

Change the terms slightly and this formula will apply to business problems generally, to family problems, and to personal conflicts and tensions. It is simply the scientific process applied to every-day life.

CHAPTER 87   ACCENTUATE THE NEGATIVE

Positive (absolute) thinking has its drawbacks. If we measure our expectations (including the absolutist positive words we use to think about them), we can plan for reality. We can expect setbacks and failed predictions and view them as a part of the universe we operate in. A part of that is limiting our profits by hedging. Less profit, yes, but sounder sleep.

One of the ways we are educated for failure and despair is the training we get to think positively.

The man who uses the word perhaps very often is not considered a dynamic thinker. We have been given the idea that it is better to come right out with a strong opinion than to be, as they say, wishy-washy.

Read the editorials in your paper. Listen to the political speeches and sermons. Go over the letters to the editor. You will find a great deal of absolutely loyal, utterly depraved, 100 percent American, completely ruined, supreme happiness, etc. These are not measured words. They are absolute, hard, unyielding words. They are words likely to be colored with emotion, in fact they seem more like rallying cries to a cause than considered statements of thinking men and women.

In developing methods of evaluation, in prediction, and in any analytical work you will find it more useful to use a less dynamic, one might even say negative, approach. There are times when "I don't know" is the best answer to a question. Perhaps, maybe, sometimes, to a degree, up to a point, for some people, under these conditions, as I see it, so far as I know, probably, unless the conditions have changed . . . all these are good honest phrases expressing doubt or limiting the area covered by accompanying statements. Use them! Learn to think in negative terms! You will not be disappointed so often because you will not have claimed so much. You will not be crowding yourself to believe more than you know.

Coupled with statements as to the probability of predictions coming true, these negative and doubt-expressing phrases can give you a realistic idea of just how far the limits of your knowledge of a situation really go.

The questioning phrases also underscore the possibility that a change in your expectations can occur, either due to the strategic operations of a personal opponent or due to some basic change in the market, commodity, economy, or whatever you are evaluating.

Very often the best protection against defeat is to make your plans on the assumption that one's opponent has found out one's strategy; similarly, the best protection against total ruin can be to assume that some part of one's predictions are going to be wrong. Since if we take the extreme point of view on every part of our program we will be exposed to crippling losses on even a moderate set-back (for instance, if we went 100 percent bullish to the extreme limit of our resources), it will be safer to expect some degree of set-back, and to assume the possibility of a serious reversal. We can protect ourselves against these eventualities by deliberately damping our enthusiasm. Instead of going 100 percent bullish, we can take a predominantly bullish position but cushion it with a few short sales in weak-looking stocks. In this case we do not really expect to take a profit on these short sales. We may expect, in advance, to have some moderate loss on them if all turns out as we hope it will. The small losses will be the premium we have paid for protection, in case of a real collapse, our insurance short sales will soften the blow and greatly reduce our losses.

What we have outlined is a deliberate policy of expecting certain losses, of planning to take them as part of the cost of protection. It is a studied policy of avoiding the attempt to make a perfect score. It is an example of hedging that could be extended in principle to other market problems, and to problems not connected with the market including some of those in our personal lives. By accentuating the negative we can avoid the pain of complete disappointment when a completely optimistic plan falls flat.

In effect what we are doing is trading some part of the shining opportunity for a considerable portion of solid security. We can take the job we are sure of instead of gambling for the big opening. We can settle for Jane next door, instead of seeking the princess. We can buy insurance and pay premiums for protection we hope we will never have to cash in on. We can, by hedging and compromising, reduce our demands, step up our accomplishments, and in this way narrow the frustrating gap between our aspirations and our performance.

CHAPTER 88   NET LONG-TERM GAINS

**Take it easy. This may be the only place you'll hear this advice this
lifetime—except from Sheraton Hotels, when you will rush to vacation taking with you, your laptop, e-mail, voice mail, cell phone, and
type A cholesterol. The Greeks would have said "measure in all
things-excess in nothing." Ancient advice perhaps even more important today, a couple of thousand years later. Practicing general
semantics by keeping perspective and staying attached to the realities
of life and the market will help you take it easy.**

Perhaps you, like so many of us, were trained in the hard tradition that if
you want to amount to anything you have to strive for perfection. Parents
and teachers have held up before us the ideal of making every moment
count, hitching one's wagon to a star, getting to the top. Congressmen
have sounded off about the indomitable spirit of enterprise. We have been
exposed to directives and precepts about how to do something called succeed.

Since we never had it quite straight just what was meant by success,
and since the details of how the indicated power drives were supposed to

get us into orbit have not been precisely delineated, it's no great wonder that a good many of us try to play it safe by going all-out all the time. We don't exactly know where we're headed or what the prize is, but we feel we can't afford to lose it, whatever it is. We want all the money we can lay our hands on, we want all the power we can grab, we want everybody to love and admire us, we want to be good and pure and generous. We want all there is of whatever has the seal of approval of our culture, anything that has a good label, regardless of whether it's what we really need or want, and regardless of whether it is compatible with some of the other things with good labels.

Since for so many of us it must be either this or that, nothing inbetween, we have to go all-out in a blind and desperate competitive race with no one to tell us when we have crossed the finish line, and no idea whether we are really on the course. We just go like hell until we drop in our tracks. If the race looks hopeless, if we feel we cannot expect to come in first, then all is lost, for second is no better than last in an either/or world. We drop out of the race and don't even try any more. Perhaps we turn to liquor in a serious way to cover up the hurt of losing. Or shut ourselves up tight in a little world of small routines and time-consuming rituals, so that we can justify our feeling that we are above the grab for status, or wealth, or fame.

This is the other side of the either/or: the demoralization, when nothing matters any more. But, to live a happy life you don't have to own U.S. Steel*, or be president of the United States, or marry the richest girl in the world. If you can get away from the symbols of power, wealth, and approval and take a hard look at the particular facts in your particular life, you may find that what you really need and want isn't nearly so hard to get as the concept of success that has been subliminally impressed on your value system. If you haven't been so blinded and so conditioned to conformity that you can't feel any desires outside of the standard symbols, you can make your own deal with the world on your terms, and not its terms. You can set your sights on a goal that meets your necessary and sufficient specifications of a full and adequately successful life.

What does this mean? In material matters, it means that for a ring, husband, family and house in the country, she might want to be a CEO much more. Not every man would need a Cadillac to set the hallmark of

* U.S. Steel 1956 = Microsoft 2000 = "X" 2050.

success on his career. He might actually get a lot more fun out of a small sailboat, or a new sound system. Not every male would respond to the sexual appeal of the voluptuous woman so insistently advertised as a fashion necessity. There are other fetishes that can be quite as interesting. Most of us know, even though we don't act accordingly, that piling up money is not the first and last end of a business or professional career. It's possible to get a lot of satisfaction and a lot of prestige along with a moderate salary.

Perhaps the slogan, "take it easy" would come nearest to explaining the different viewpoint we are suggesting in this book. All the discussion of measuring and of infinite-valued orientation amounts to an argument for moderation. All the study of hedging and partial commitments in the market comes to much the same. In line with this new (and perhaps radical) thought, we try to find the easiest not the hardest, way to do things. We don't necessarily shoot for the top, we just try to make a passing grade. We don't necessarily go for millions; perhaps tens of thousands or hundreds of thousands will buy us all we can ever want. We don't grit our teeth and decide always to be right in our judgments and never to take a loss. It's amazing how many losses a man can take, if he knows what he is doing, and still come up with a net profit.

By deliberately putting aside the mantle of the saint, the robe of the dictator, or the silk hat of the tycoon, we can go about the business of getting ourselves enough virtue, enough power, enough wealth, and enough love with a great deal better expectation of reaching our goal, and a lot less anxiety. It's possible under these conditions to take it easy to a degree most people would hardly believe. By cutting down one's over-high aspirations they become much, much easier to achieve. This leads to self-confidence, to a feeling of accomplishment, to security, and very likely to more effective efforts since there is not the continual worry and tension that goes with trying to earn more or achieve more than is humanly possible. Thus, a man who is willing to settle for the girl next door instead of the story-book princess will increase his chances of success in the field of romance and save himself a great deal of heartache.

In the market it's very much the same story. You have watched the nervous, jittery men who pace around the back of the brokers' board rooms, suffering with every tick of the ticker, uncertain, irritable, and anxious. With their absolute standards they cannot afford to be wrong, and to be right they must make a profit on every trade, must buy near the bottom, sell near the top. In order not to feel they have failed, they must do the impossible.

It isn't necessary. If a small part of the energy that goes into the fruitless, unplanned drive for absolute success could be used to observe the market as it really is and to develop a basic method of evaluation, these poor harried souls could rest so much easier. They could go a day, or a week if need be, without ever looking at the tape. They could afford to be wrong quite often; they could take quite a lot of small losses and still do very well in their market operations, possibly better than they are now. They could, if they were willing to give up the all-out drive to win all, operate in bull markets and bear markets, in stocks or in commodities, without ever having the feeling that a slight mistake on their part or some event entirely beyond their control could wipe them out. It's just a matter of being willing to open one's eyes and see not just one side, but many sides of a question: To be willing to diversify. To be willing to hedge. To be willing to sell short. To be willing at times to take three small losses in order to get one substantial gain.

The prize? They would not look for the top. Would not pile up a colossal fortune for one's heirs and the tax authorities to wrangle over. Would not ever become a wizard of Wall Street. Would not be the master of the market or the universe.

What would it be worth to feel secure, and reasonably protected because one had a moderate position? What would it be worth to avoid the headaches, the threat of ulcers or of heart failure? What would it be worth to be able to think serenely and enjoyably about the market, instead of fighting it like a cornered animal? What would it be worth to have peace of mind and a better chance for steady, reasonable profits? What would it be worth to have time to read, to fish, to take pictures, to be with one's family, to sit on the bank of a quiet pond and watch the clouds float by in a blue, blue sky? What would it be worth to have the time to do the experiments and carry out the projects one has been planning to do all these years and never got around to? These are the kinds of values we are thinking of. By eliminating the unnecessary worries and tensions of life, general semantics can make it possible for us to realize our potentialities in our own right and in our own way to a much greater degree than most of us can do under the distorted and unrealistic value concepts we have acquired from the culture in which we live.

As you may have gathered, all of this is a non-social point of view. It calls for a sharp and drastic break with much of the tradition and custom of our environment. It calls for a new point of view, not only in the market but in matters of politics, the law, religion, family life, social ambitions, and most especially in the aims and goals we set for ourselves and how we regard ourselves in relation to the world around us. It's non-social in that sense. It is not, however, un-social, and certainly not antisocial. It is not a move against one's fellow man to want to take a hard look at one's own real needs and aspirations. It is not against society to repudiate folkways, creeds, superstitions, pre-scientific theories, and obsolete directives that no longer fit the facts. It's not against people to chuck out all the nonsense and insanity that have kept man ignorant, hostile and worried.

The purpose of general semantics is to keep up to date the maps by which man lives. We have today the physical machinery to make a world where more people can be healthy, and well fed, more free from hostility and more free for the pursuit of happiness than at any time in the history of the world. We are not doing a very good job of putting this machinery to work.

There is not too much time left.

It is time to put away childish things and become mature human beings.

INDEX